VOLUME 33 • NO 4 • OCTOBER 2004 • ISSUE 213

Henri Cartier-Bresson 1908–3 August 2004, co-founder of Magnum Photos: Spain 1933.
Credit: Henri Cartier-Bresson / Magnum

WE'RE PLEASED TO ANNOUNCE THAT FROM JANUARY 2005
INDEX ON CENSORSHIP WILL BE PRODUCED AND DISTRIBUTED BY
THE DISTINGUISHED INTERNATIONAL PUBLISHER **TAYLOR & FRANCIS**

IN GOD WE TRUST

URSULA OWEN

When John F Kennedy ran for president of the United States in 1960, he had to convince Protestant voters that his policies would not be dictated by the Vatican. Nearly half a century later, John Kerry faces the opposite problem; he finds himself confronted by conservative leaders of his own Church who want him to promise that his Catholicism will have everything to do with his presidency (p17). We may expect modern secular states to establish a separation between church and state, but the fact is that religion is becoming increasingly mainstream in politics (p8), not just in the USA but across the world.

So what are the consequences of this increased intimacy between religion and the state? *Index* reports on the power of faith and its paradoxes in the political arena: Ruchir Joshi looks at the long history of the exploitation of religion by successive 'secular' governments in India (p164); Isabel Hilton examines the state's attempts to control the ever increasing number of religious groups in China (p200); while Nilüfer Göle imagines an enlightened multi-faith identity for Europe (p110).

The responses of governments to extremist manifestations of Islam are now setting the agenda for political action. Since 9/11 barely a day passes without stories about Islam in the media, and subjects once confined to rarefied academic debates have entered the mainstream of public consciousness and political debate. We report on the fierce arguments over women wearing the *hijab* (pp72, 117), and profile the Grand Ayatollah Ali al-Sistani (p78), *marga* (guide) of 150 million Shia worldwide, who has consistently called for democracy in Iraq, and is deeply opposed to the theocracy of neighbouring Iran. From Iran itself, Mohsen Kadivar (p64), often referred to as the 'Luther of Islam', shares this view. Looking at the Arab/Israeli conflict, Zeev Sternhell controversially claims that at the heart of democratic Israel lies a fundamental religious nationalism that believes the land was given to the Jews by God (p178).

Meanwhile, Andrew Graham-Yooll tells us that liberation theology is back in the barrios of Argentina (p37); Irena Maryniak surveys post-Soviet religion (p43) and Philip Pullman reminds us that secularism, too, has its tendency towards irrational absolutism (p156).

Wrapping religion in the flag has become a strong feature of faith – and intolerance – in our time; patriotism becomes available only to a particular group and God is turned into a partisan for its political objectives. *Index*, for the first time in its history, devotes its country-by-country monitoring to the scale and nature of religious intolerance today. ❑

IN THIS ISSUE

Wearing
the veil >>

CONTENTS

Locust Fork, Alabama USA 2003: 'Elect JESUS your Savior and Lord'.
Credit: Abbas / Magnum

THE CHRISTIAN CHURCHES

THROUGHOUT THE CHRISTIAN WORLD, THE ARMIES OF GOD ARE ON THE MARCH. FUNDAMENTALISTS BATTLE TRADITIONALISTS; LIBERATION THEOLOGY AND THE CHURCH OF THE POOR ONCE AGAIN FACE OFF AGAINST THE VATICAN. IN THE USA, THE 'BIBLE BELT' IS PRESIDENT BUSH'S MOST LOYAL SUPPORTER IN HIS ELECTION BATTLE; IN RUSSIA AND MUCH OF THE FORMER COMMUNIST WORLD, GOD IS STRIKING BACK AFTER YEARS IN THE SHADOW OF MARX. AND EVERYWHERE IN THE WESTERN WORLD BELIEVERS ARE LEAVING THE INSTITUTIONAL CHURCHES TO FORM THEIR OWN SECTS. NEVER SINCE THE MIDDLE AGES HAS THE CHURCH BEEN SO ENGAGED IN POLITICS. WHERE DOES GOD STAND IN ALL THIS?

IN PLACE OF ENLIGHTENMENT

SARA MAITLAND

GOD HAS ENTERED THE MAINSTREAM OF POLITICAL DISCOURSE AND A VARIETY OF FUNDAMENTALISMS ABOUNDS

The re-emergence of religious discourse in public life seems to have caught many of us on the hop: baffled, irritated and uncomprehending. For over 250 years, Western democratic thinking has argued, and even fought for, the secularisation of the public domain and the political arena. There has been a steady erosion of the influence of religion in education, an increasing sepa-ration of Church and State, and – in a curious manoeuvre – a steady move towards the general privatisation of 'morality' and particularly sexuality. By the second half of the last century, indeed, one might have thought the battle was won.

And now, apparently from nowhere, we are seeing a religious reflex strike back. 'Fundamentalists' of diverse kinds are suddenly dictating the agenda, certainly in the USA and the Middle East, increasingly in the Indian subcontinent and, in a very different form, in parts of Africa; even in Europe. 'Extremists,' we mutter. But an extreme expression of anything requires a non-extreme version. I cannot quite believe that there is a solid, enlightened, secular centre fringed around by, but totally disconnected from, some clumps of religious extremists.

What I see instead is a faltering, a loss of faith, in the whole Enlighten-ment project. If 'the best lack all conviction' then 'the worst' will be 'full of passionate intensity'. Should we choose to bolster the liberal position, renew the secularist commitment of the Enlightenment – actually work on it, rather than take it for granted – or begin the exhausting and risky task of trying to establish some new philosophical model?

Here are some of the key questions:

- Has the Enlightenment project delivered all the goods that it is going to deliver?
- Is the language of 'unalienable human rights' capable of delivering equity and justice more broadly than it has, to date, accomplished?

- What might religious faith, or similar forms of commitment, be offering people and communities at this specific cultural moment?
- Does individualism, as we have come to interpret it, inevitably favour the strong over the weak? If so, is this acceptable?

What I want to do here is mount an argument that the Enlightenment has now run out of steam. In the re-emergence of theocratic politics we are seeing one possible response to this: the Next Big Thing. If progressive liberals don't like this, they had better think of some alternatives fast. I am not sure that I am entirely convinced by this argument, but I believe it deserves serious consideration.

By Enlightenment, I mean that shift that surfaced in the eighteenth century and by which individualism, freedom and change replaced community, authority and tradition as the core European values. It was optimistic and rationalist, and developed a language of natural law, inherent freedoms and self-determination. It was an excellent philosophical underpinning for the upwardly mobile bourgeoisie who patented it. Communism attempted to take those core values beyond their entrepreneurial base and seems to have failed.

Enlightenment ideology is secularist. It need not have been. Even Thomas Jefferson, probably the least religiously inclined of the signatories of the US Declaration of Independence, believed that a nation could not be governed without God – even if this took the form of slightly misty Rousseauian deism. None the less, for historical reasons, the Enlightenment movement became first anti-clerical and quickly anti-religious. At the personal level, religious sentiment was replaced by romantic love and psychoanalytic self-exploration. At the political level, it was replaced by nationalism. That is to say the body and the body politic are mirror images of each other: the idea that an individual should be self-contained, self-managed and have clear and well-protected boundaries was mirrored in a political model of the nation, which, through romantic notions of freedom, was given a highly emotive value; and was imposed, artificially, on colonised territory, where it too often has no emotive meaning.

Post-Romantic liberal culture has focused on the emotional and subjective experience of *the individual*. Over the past two centuries it has given a new meaning to the word 'individual' – an illuminating development. Etymologically, it is fairly obvious that 'in-divid-ual' means 'that which cannot be divided', distinct parts that cannot be separated.

*William Blake
(1757–1827),
'The Ancient of Days'
from* Europe:
a prophecy, *1821.
Credit: Fitzwilliam
Museum Cambridge /
Bridgeman*

Before 1650, the common usage was theological – a way of describing the Holy Trinity: 'To the glorie . . . of the hie and indyvyduall Trinitie' (1425). But it had also had a wider frame of reference and particularly referred to married, or conspicuously loving, couples. In *Paradise Lost,* Adam addresses Eve

> . . . to have thee by my side
> Henceforth an individual solace dear,
> Part of my soul I seek thee, and thee claim
> My other half.

It was only later that human beings' individuality was deemed not to extend beyond their own skin and that the impress or penetration of the other became perilous to the integrity of the person.

Curiously, my edition of the *OED* has not caught up with modern 'individualism' and still sees it as a moral failure: 'self-centred conduct; egoism'. But it is on an atomised and very new understanding of the individual that our interpretation of 'rights' is based. Inevitably there are hairline fractures.

For example, one necessary myth of liberalism is that all rights and freedoms are compatible. The liberal tradition insists that I cannot (not 'may not') gain my proper rights at the expense of yours. Or, put another way, we cannot and do not need to rank 'oppressions'. All struggles for 'rights' enhance the rights of others. This was axiomatic to many of the campaigns and liberation movements of the twentieth century but increasingly is turning out not be true. Part of the underlying importance of *The Satanic Verses* episode was the way it exposed the fact that Articles 18 and 19 in the UN Charter of Human Rights were incompatible: it proved impossible to defend both freedom of speech and the right to have one's religious belief and practice respected. The (almost certainly improper in classical Muslim terms) application of the fatwa against the book and its author Salman Rushdie unfortunately blurred the issue, but in fact there were a surprising number of 'free-speech fundamentalists' as well as religious fundamentalists vigorously contesting which right should be given priority.

It has become clear that there is also an inherent conflict in Article 26 between parts 1 and 2, and part 3:

Article 26 states:

1 Everyone has the right to education . . .
2 Education shall be directed to the full development of the human personality and to the strengthening of respect for human rights and fundamental freedoms. It shall promote understanding, tolerance and friendship among all nations, racial or religious groups, and shall further the activities of the United Nations for the maintenance of peace.

But:

3 Parents have a prior right to choose the kind of education that shall be given to their children.

What are the rights of parents who do not wish their children to be educated in understanding and tolerance? Those parents who do believe that God made the world in seven days? That their girl children's interests are best served by arranged marriages? That their sons' and the community's interests will be best served by polygamy (or even clitoridectomy)?

In Article 29 (2) the nature of the problem becomes explicit:

> In the exercise of his rights and freedoms, everyone shall be subject only to such limitations as are determined by law solely for the purpose of securing due recognition and respect for the rights and freedoms of others and of meeting the just requirements of morality, public order and the general welfare in a democratic society.

Whose morals?

I sense that none of this would matter too much if it was clear that the political and social framework was in fact delivering (even if slowly) the 'goods' that it has promised. Let me be very clear: Enlightenment rationalism has delivered quite remarkably well for 200 years. As the woman who is writing this I cannot be other than aware of it. Of course I'd put my money on liberal democracy: I'm a natural for it. I do very well out of it. I am a divorced female person who has chosen to have two children both of whom have survived into adulthood. I am educated, earning, autonomous and free to make (tax-assisted) provision for my old age. I can set up home, enter into contracts as an equal party and express my sexuality as I choose. I can worship (or not) in the religious tradition of my preference without anything more oppressive than the mockery of my friends.

But this cannot blind me to the fact that there are a great many people for whom things are not working out so well and who have very good cause to feel they have drawn the short straw.

There are some blatant facts that suggest the exhaustion of the liberal individualist ideology in the face of post-modernity. Individualism favours the strong. The entrepreneurial mercantile bias of the Enlightenment is becoming very clear in a global economy in which the richer areas of the world endorse (indeed, through the IMF, compel) free trade in commodities, but not in labour. Immigration law prevents the free movement of labour.

The pending ecological debacle has thrust a new issue on to the global agenda. Can a non-human species, a specific environment or a planet (or parts of a planet) have 'rights'? Can future human beings have rights? How might we assess these rights in relation to our own rights? Can the individualist tenor of Enlightenment ideology even frame the questions, let alone offer useful answers?

Above all, quite simply, liberal representational democracy with universal adult suffrage – the natural political expression of Enlightenment philosophy – has not delivered equality or even prosperity. The gap between rich and poor individuals within all liberal democratic nations is growing. So is the gap between rich and poor nations.

In the light of all this it is not entirely surprising that the project is seen by some to be faltering. In the West the signs of this faltering are tentative, dispersed and hesitant but they are undeniably there. On the one hand, there is an exponential growth of a new expression of Christianity, which is simultaneously biblically fundamentalist and charismatic. (Charismatic theology stresses freedom in the spirit beyond and outside the law, and the continuing revelation through the Holy Spirit to the individual. Biblical fundamentalism stresses the inerrancy of scripture and the fixed, unchangeable nature of authority. They ought to be incompatible.)

On the other hand, there is an equally fast growth in 'scientism' (by which I mean a fundamentalist understanding of science, and scientific methodology as the 'only true way' to interpret any data). This is of course not liberal, and it is not scientific. When a leading scientist can say: 'When we have devised and done the experiments we *will* prove xxx,' the whole enterprise starts to look a bit silly. Scientism remains oddly and unscientifically optimistic, despite the scientific caveats entered, for example, by Gödel and Heisenberg, that science can deliver all knowledge and that 'one-level explanations' can explain all levels of experience. This, together with the continuing denial that there is subjectivity in scientific research, the mockery and abuse with which some members of the 'scientific community' greet any dispute with their authority, and the passion of internal dispute within that community are all paralleled very precisely by the worst aspects of religious fundamentalism.

At the same time, we are seeing a profound mistrust and cynicism about science and its methods. Scientific evidence is treated with scepticism. Quasi-religious beliefs and attitudes – usually called 'spirituality' – are flourishing among precisely those people who see themselves as autonomous and independent individuals. The 'dietary laws' of a great many of my friends make cooking for strict Muslims a doddle; their devotion to their therapists makes the authority of priests, gurus or imams look flimsy. The most surprising people have a 'faith' – in exercise regimes, astrology, fortune telling and rituals in eclectic and syncretic varieties. The '12 steps' of Alcoholics Anonymous, which are now applied to endless lists of life problems, is in effect a religious programme. AA begins where both Christianity and Islam begin: you admit that you cannot manage your own life and hand it over to a 'higher power'. Thereafter, you become a member of a born-again community to whom you have particular obligations and in exchange for which you can look for absolute succour. Shops are full of 'mind, body and spirit' books, tools and ornaments all offering/preaching versions of the Happy Life. Following the canonisation of the late Princess of Wales, there are wayside shrines for every deceased car driver, and candles lit and silences kept for more and more public events. Every practitioner of these and similar cultic activities believes in the efficacy of their chosen 'religion' and disbelieves in everyone else's. Essentially, you have religious conviction and practice without either anchoring tradition or moderating cohesive ground rules – individualist religion has to be the worst of both worlds!

Elsewhere, the religious dimension is being absorbed into history, geography, literary criticism and the social sciences. The 'turn to ethics' in contemporary Continental philosophy seems to have readopted a whole range of religious categories and concepts (and not simply for right-wing ends). The notion that religious conviction, culture and practice forms identity, in ways we more traditionally understand class, race or gender as doing, is growing. Religion is increasingly being seen as worthy of attention, as interesting in itself, across a wide range of both popular and academic discourses.

If this re-emergence of religious sensibility is apparent at the centre we should not be at all surprised that it is also appearing in more extreme and active forms within populist and anti-liberal movements. Quite simply, a religious paradigm, political and personal inasmuch as they can be separated, offers – at least at first glance – a real antidote to the problematic failures of liberal Enlightenment individualism.

Religion reinscribes community and mutual obligation, but in a framework of choice rather than of destiny. Religious affiliation is genuinely transnational; this is why in the West, still dogged by nationalism, we have great difficulty in coping with the international dimension of Islamic-based terrorism. The number of newspapers that rushed to tell us, in shocked tones, that the Beslan terrorists 'weren't Chechen', as though somehow it would have been better if they had been, is interesting. In many of Bush's statements about 'the axis of evil' I hear a strange sub-textual suggestion that part of their evil is that they aren't 'patriotic' in the old nationalist sense, which might be addressed with the old rules of play – diplomacy, bribery, threat and ultimately war. It is somehow more acceptable to bomb people in the name of 'national interest' than in the name of any other group interest.

For the price of acknowledging that 'higher power' and surrendering your individuality to its rules you can genuinely meet your fellow human beings on equal terms and, moreover, with a mutual interest, not as competitors with equal rights. The prostrations of Islamic prayer reflect this visually: the word 'Islam' means submission; the obeisance was a posture of surrender and self-humiliation that no one in the original desert culture was entitled to ask even of a conquered enemy. This equality, moreover, is guaranteed by an authority (God), which has no need to defend its own rights against yours.

Religion claims, though on rather different grounds, a similar explanatory and predictive role as modern science, but it is more egalitarian: its power does not lie in criteria beyond the capacity of most people to understand, let alone critique. The histories of Islam, Christianity, Buddhism and Hinduism suggest that they are not intrinsically inimical to arts, pure sciences or technological progress. All the global religions have at least a strong strand within their traditions that favours tolerance and reconciliation. They also have appalling records in all these areas, but so, if we are honest, do liberal democracy and the political tradition of the Enlightenment. Fundamentalism of all flavours (philosophical, religious or political) leads to violence.

Most religions can also provide an intellectual framework for looking at questions of ecology, the sharing of resources and the management of reconciliation. There are obligations beyond rights, precisely because the created order is created – and not by us.

There are, of course, problematic aspects of any religion in a global context. All expressions of faith (even post-Enlightment scientific faith) are culturally determined and shaped; if not nationalist they are certainly tribal in origin. Faith is inevitably a 'truth claim': a variety of truth claims is going to generate tension. It is genuinely hard to negotiate a dialogue between, say, a person or group who 'believe in one God . . . maker of heaven and earth' and another person or group who believe that different species are mechanisms for the directionless replication of genes. I would hope that the two have different ideas about how to deal with various human situations. The serious believers in the major world religions simply cannot configure themselves around the dominant model of atomised individualism. Some faiths (Christianity, Buddhism) have developed authentic traditions of separation, withdrawal or quietism, which allow adherents a non-social, apolitical expression of incorporation. Some (Judaism, Islam) have little or no such interpretative tradition. They are indelibly communal – 'political' in the original sense. This is nearly incomprehensible to the European mindset.

The point is that globalisation and 'total communication' oblige such differing world views to negotiate daily, hourly and by the minute. Being trapped in a lift with people you didn't much like to start with can raise tensions and generate 'extremism' in half an hour. In this sense, the first thing we need to do urgently is stop being surprised that there is a serious problem – and that, as always, it will express itself in extreme forms.

I have no particular optimism that religious politics will be more effective in solving global problems than the present post-Enlightenment model, but I can entirely see why it is re-emerging as a possible direction; and the only possible response to it in the short term must be to recognise how faith-driven the liberal post-Enlightenment individual rights paradigm is too. In the longer run, we need to work on evolving both a language and a social model that create a space for dialogue.

Of course this is less painful for me than for many, because I do actually believe in God – and in the disciplined communal expression of that belief in religious practice. I am, therefore, already convinced by the idea that less individualism, more dependency, more permeability of the boundaries of the self and more responsibility to a shared and mutually developed 'common mind' might not be an entirely bad thing. It is certainly one worth exploring. ❑

Sara Maitland is a writer of both fiction and non-fiction. Her most recent book is On Becoming a Fairy Godmother, *a collection of short stories (Maia Press, 2003). She is presently writing a cultural history of silence*

THE GOD GULF

FRANCES CAIRNCROSS

IN NO OTHER COUNTRY OUTSIDE THE ISLAMIC
WORLD IS RELIGION SUCH A CENTRAL
ASPECT OF POLITICS AS IT IS IN THE UNITED
STATES. FOR MANY AMERICANS, IT WILL BE
THE KEY ISSUE IN THE ELECTIONS

'John Kerry doesn't seem to get this,' wrote David Brooks, a columnist on the *New York Times* earlier this year. 'Many of the people running the Democratic Party don't get it either.' Mr Brooks's concern: a mere 7 per cent of Americans told opinion polls that Mr Kerry was a man of strong religious faith. 'That's a catastrophic number,' complained Mr Brooks. 'Unless more Americans get a sense of Kerry's faith . . . they will be loath to trust him with their vote.'

Religion will be one of the key issues – for many Americans, *the* key issue – in deciding how they vote. In the religious attitudes of Americans, therefore, may well lie the best predictor of their voting intentions in the coming presidential election. In no other country outside the Islamic world is religion such a central aspect of politics as it is in the United States. Under President George W Bush, who credits Christ with rescuing him from the demon drink, religion is an integral part of White House life. David Frum, a former White House speech-writer, recalls that the first thing he heard Mr Bush say in the White House was, 'Missed you at Bible study.' Mr Bush may run the most religious White House since Jimmy Carter (who described himself as 'born again', baffling the Washington press corps), but that great sinner Bill Clinton was also publicly enthusiastic about his faith. His autobiography recounts how, as an eight-year-old, he began taking himself to church, and as a 10-year-old he publicly committed himself to Jesus. An American president doesn't have to be a saint, argues Mr Brooks, 'but he does have to be a pilgrim'.

Religion and politics have always been closely intertwined in the country. Alexis de Tocqueville, visiting in 1831, remarked: 'On my arrival in the United States, it was the religious aspect of the country that first struck my eye. As I prolonged my stay, I perceived the great political consequences that flowed from these new facts.' From the country's earliest days, 'religion and democracy reigned together', in de Tocqueville's phrase. Thomas Jefferson, the most secular signatory of the Declaration of Independence, understood as well as anyone the public importance of religion: 'No nation has ever been governed without religion,' he insisted. 'Nor can ever be.'

For many Europeans, the public role of religion in the US is both bizarre and sinister. They are confused by the absence of an established Church or national religion that characteristic of so much of Europe – and by the constitutional separation of church and state (p88). How can a country where the Supreme Court debates whether the Pledge of Allegiance should refer to 'one nation under God' also be keen that its politicians make a public show of religious observance? But, because religion matters at the ballot box, a far more serious question is whether religion is now exerting a distorting influence on America's foreign policy. The deepening tensions with Islamic countries in the aftermath of 9/11 and the deteriorating relations between Israel and the Palestinians have put the spotlight on the impact of evangelical Christianity in Washington.

The contrasts between America and Europe are nowhere stronger than in attitudes to religion. In Europe, the religious beliefs of political leaders play virtually no part in politics and, when they do, they are a handicap, not an asset. 'Does the fact that George Bush and you are both Christians make it easier for you to view these conflicts in terms of good and evil?' Jeremy Paxman, a British television interviewer, memorably asked Tony Blair when the British prime minister returned from talks with George Bush on the eve of the invasion of Iraq. 'You don't pray together?' From Mr Blair's uncomfortable response, many British people assumed that the answer was yes. Both the tone of the question and Mr Blair's embarrassment say much about the squeamish way European voters look on public displays of religion.

In Western Europe, modernity has turned out to be the foe of religion. 'My American friends' eyes stand out on stalks when I say that I don't have a single friend seriously interested in religion,' says Karen Armstrong, a British ex-nun and writer on religious topics. Observance has declined at astonishing speed, even in Catholic countries, to the point where Europe is hardly a Christian continent. In a recent special issue of *The Public Interest* on religion in America, Brian Anderson, a US journalist, argues: 'Almost everything about Western Europe's religious life conveys a sense of exhaustion and defeat.'

Waco Texas 1998: Compass employee (see p24).
Credit: Jonathon Hexner

Thus, in Western Europe, a mere 20 per cent of people go regularly to church; in the US, 47 per cent. In Europe, only 21 per cent say that religion is 'very important'; in the US, 60 per cent – three times as many. More bewildering for Europeans is the fact that 39 per cent of Americans share their president's conviction that they are 'born again', and that 58 per cent think that the only moral people are those who believe in God. Mr Anderson quotes Michael Novak, a Catholic theologian: 'More people in the US attend religious services on any given weekend than watch football – in all the stadiums, on high school football fields, college campuses and all the television sets of the nation put together.'

There are, moreover, some indications that religious fervour is on the increase. An article in *The Economist* last November by John Parker pointed out that the proportion of Protestants who regard themselves as born again has risen from around 40 per cent in the late 1980s to over 50 per cent today. A snapshot of US congregations in *Faith Communities Today*, published last year, found that congregational growth went hand in hand with 'clarity of mission and purpose', with the use of electronic music and with an emphasis on abstention from pre-marital sex and a strict sense of morality among worshippers. Traditional, liberal Churches such as Episcopalians and Methodists have been losing ground inexorably to evangelicals, the most fervent Christians.

Why is religion so successful in the US, compared with Europe? One answer is that Europe is the exceptional society, not America: Christian congregations have been growing in many parts of the world, including Asia and South America. The growth has been more often in evangelical Churches, including Pentecostalists, the fastest growing Christian movement on earth, than in the traditional denominations. Even in east London, there are now twice as many Pentecostal congregations as Anglican ones. Another answer is that the US has benefited for three centuries from a free market in religion. Determined to avoid Europe's tradition of state-supported religion, the early colonists created a free-for-all. There never was a one-size-fits-all monopoly religion. Instead, churches have always had to vie for congregants. The monopoly churches of Europe, by contrast, have never learned this skill and so, in a world that prizes consumer choice, are threatened with extinction.

Religion and voting patterns are closely correlated. Evangelical Protestants are now the largest single religious denomination in the US; its membership encompasses almost one-third of US adults. White evangelical voters have correspondingly increased their political clout: they now account for almost one-third of registered voters, compared with just under a quarter in 1987. Not only have their numbers grown in that time; they have shifted their support from Democrat to Republican. Studies by John Green of the Ray Bliss Institute at the University of Akron find that 40 per cent of the votes won by Mr Bush in the 2000 election came from white evangelical Protestants, and another 21 per cent came from other white Protestants. By contrast, only 26 per cent of Al Gore's vote came from white Protestants. In the coming election too, Mr Bush's most reliable supporters will be evangelical Protestants.

But two things qualify this apparently straightforward picture of the intertwining of evangelical and right-wing politics. They are, first, the parallel emergence of a secular lobby that is as forceful, in its way, in the Democratic Party as the religious right is in the Republican and, second, the impact of intensity of religious belief on political stance.

The growing size and cohesion of the secular left has been the most ignored but important story in politics in the past decade, in the eyes of Louis Bolce and Gerald De Maio, two political scientists at Baruch College. In an article earlier this year in *First Things*, they argued that the 'secularist' tag now discomfited Democratic presidential political candidates as much as the 'liberal' label has long done. 'Underlying Democratic unease with secularism is their recognition that an overt and public embrace of secularism is politically damaging in the United States,' they added. Secular voters are now the bedrock of Democratic support, accounting for about 15 per cent of their base, or only a slightly smaller share than white Protestants account for in the base of the Republic Party. This is dangerous. Although Americans have lost most traces of religious intolerance, 41 per cent now say that they would never vote for an atheist, far more than would refuse to vote for a Jew or Catholic. Mr Kerry's voting record, say Messrs Bolce and De Maio, puts him dangerously in the secularist camp.

The Democrats cannot afford to become the party of secularism. That would doom them to eternal obscurity. To have a chance of power, they have to woo religious moderates of all denominations. For the second complication of the God Gulf in the US is that it is not a straight split between the secular left and the religious right. On the contrary, the voters most likely to support Mr Bush are not necessarily evangelicals but are members of all churches who are most committed to their belief. It is those who go to church most frequently and who take their doctrine most seriously who are most likely to express support for Mr Bush, whether they are Catholics or Protestants. Those of the faithful who are most lukewarm, in both church attendance and doctrinal belief, are more likely to support Mr Kerry.

Moreover, Mr Bush, too, needs the support of these moderates. In an article in *Washington Monthly* last year, Amy Sullivan pointed out that 'Bush has maxed-out his support with conservative evangelicals: 84 per cent voted for him in the 2000 election.' To win the coming election, she argued, Mr Bush will need the support of religious moderates, 'one of the least appreciated swing constituencies in the country'. These 'swing faithful' feel uncomfortable about Mr Bush's ties with the religious right and might therefore settle for Mr Kerry, raised a Catholic, if he has got the rhetoric right.

What impact does the struggle for the soul of the US have on its politics? The battles that have roused most passion have been over domestic issues: abortion, stem-cell research, state support for faith-based charities, school vouchers, homosexual marriage. All these issues pitch the secularists against those with strong religious views. For example, more than three-quarters of secular voters oppose laws restricting abortion, two-thirds back gay marriage, and over half are against school vouchers. By at least equal margins, religious traditionalists take opposite views on these issues.

But what of Islam? The events of 9/11 produced some expressions of crude hostility from the religious right. Jerry Vines, a leading Southern Baptist, called the Prophet Mohamed 'a demon-obsessed paedophile'. Franklin Graham, son of Billy Graham, one of the most successful evangelists in the US, described Islam as a 'very wicked religion'. When, in the summer of 2003, the University of North Carolina asked its freshmen to read a serious and analytical book on the Quran, there was uproar. A number of students took the university to court. Joe Glover of the Family Policy Network, a fundamentalist lobbying group that supported the students, denounced the Quran as inflammatory stuff to put before the young. 'It says, "Fight and slay the pagan wherever you find them,"' he complained.

This, it should be said, is not an attitude that President Bush has encouraged. Instead, he has gone out of his way to emphasise his high regard for Muslims. Asked by a British journalist whether he thought that the God of Islam was the same as the God of Christianity, he replied, 'Yes.' But Islam is one strand of religion that is little represented in US politics. This is not surprising. America's Muslim community is both extremely new and extremely small. It is also – unlike most of Europe's Muslims – well educated and relatively wealthy. Thirty years ago, almost the only Muslims in the US were black converts; today, reckons Hillel Fradkin of the US Ethics and Public Policy Center, there are probably 2–3 million US Muslims, of whom 35–40 per cent come from South Asia and only 25 per cent from the Arab world. Unlike Europe's Muslim communities, those in the US are widely dispersed geographically, and more than half have incomes of over US$50,000 a year. They are predominantly engineers, academics and doctors: nearly 60 per cent hold college degrees. Even before the events of 9/11 unnerved them, they were a small and relatively unimportant lobby, certainly if compared with the well-organised and lavishly financed Jewish lobby.

Where the Middle East is concerned, the religious right is extremely vocal. Because many evangelicals believe that the complete restoration of the nation of Israel is a prerequisite for the Second Coming of Christ, they have been an even more powerful lobby for taking a tough line on Palestinians. Jerry Falwell, pastor of the Thomas Road Church in Lynchburg, Virginia, is one of many evangelical divines who is uncompromising in his support for Israel. 'God has blessed America because of our support for the state of Israel,' he asserts.

But does this shape US policy? Undoubtedly, religious extremists do not call the shots in many of the areas of domestic policy where they campaign. Abortion remains legal and so does homosexuality. The religious right alone, important though it is as a source of votes for Mr Bush, is never likely to vote for Mr Kerry in large numbers. Politically, it has nowhere else to go.

However, as the battle for America's soul grows more polarised, the danger is that religion and religious issues will increasingly colour political debate. That may shape some policy responses in both domestic and foreign issues. Certainly, that will deepen the misunderstanding between religious America and secular Europe. Unless, of course, Europe has a Damascene conversion. Unimaginable? Most of the attitudes that shape America eventually acquire counterparts in Europe. Faced with Muslim religious enthusiasm, Europe might – just might – develop a Christian fundamentalism of its own. ❑

Frances Cairncross *has recently left the staff of the* Economist *and is Rector of Exeter College Oxford*

WACO TEXAS

JONATHON HEXNER

Birthplace of Dr Pepper and pop star Jessica Simpson, the town of Waco (pop 113,000) is located in Central Texas approximately halfway between Dallas and Austin. As in so many other towns of its kind, religion reaches into the fibre of daily life and determines its character. Waco burst into the US consciousness on 28 February 1993 when the Bureau of Alcohol, Tobacco and Firearms (ATF) raided the Branch Davidian 'compound' in search of illegal weapons. The Branch Davidians, a Seventh Day Adventist sect, were prepared for the attack and retaliated vigorously, killing four federal agents and wounding 16 others. The next day, the FBI took over the operation and a stand-off ensued. For 51 days, the gaze of the popular media was locked on a plot of desert the Branch Davidians called 'Mount Carmel'. Stationed three miles away, the networks all broadcast the same shot of the compound for 51 days. On 19 April 1993, the government initiated a tear-gas attack intended to drive the Branch Davidians from their church home. The compound burned to the ground. More than 80 people perished.

A few weeks after the tragic Branch Davidian fire, I drove to Waco to see the wreckage for myself. I arrived on 4 July 1993, just in time for the Independence Day fireworks. I returned for the Independence Day festivities for seven of the next eight years. These photographs were created in Waco between 4 July 1993 and 4 July 2001. ❑

Jonathon Hexner is a photographer and visual artist based in Cambridge, Massachusetts. He recently left his job at Harvard University to open KRUX Projects, an art gallery in New York

Fourth of July celebration, 1998: pointed squirt gun.
Identical twins with their mother at the Brazos River

Cycle Sunday, Heart of Texas Fairgrounds, 5 July 1998

Opposite, top: Bubba Blackwell (finger raised), seen with his brother-in-law, claims to be 'a sold-out believer in Jesus Christ'. Bubba broke Evel Knievel's record of jumping over cars on a Harley-Davidson earlier in 1998

Opposite, below: front entrance of the Waco Christian Fellowship Church. Biker members ride to church on Cycle Sunday, many wearing leathers; for some it is their only church visit all year

Above: a customised Harley-Davidson parked outside the church during the service: 'For God so loved the world that he gave his only begotten Son, that whosoever believeth in him should not perish, but have everlasting life' (John 3:16). The sermon involved a fog machine, a Christian country rock band, a motorcycle stuntman and Pastor Robert descending from the rafters on a zip-wire to deliver his message, 'Wings of a Dove', which was inspired by an episode on the Oprah Winfrey show

Above: children's books at the Compass Christian Lifestyle Superstore, 6 July 2000

Left: guitarist of Cross Country, 'The Christian Country Music Association's 2003 Music Evangelists of the Year', at the finale of the Cycle Sunday celebration, 1998

Opposite: life-size Bibleman display at the Family Christian Stores, July 2000. 'Armed with the Sword of the Spirit, the Breastplate of Righteousness and the Helmet of Salvation, this caped Christian stands ready to battle evil'

Official Cape & Mask Set

THE
BIBLEMAN
ADVENTURE

LIVE

BIBLEMAN

CONQUERING
THE WRATH OF RAGE

NEW RELEASE
ALSO AVAILABLE ON DVD

*Top: the new Branch Davidian church, 1998, constructed
on the site of the church that burned down in 1993, seen
though the wreckage of a burned bus left behind by
David Koresh and those who perished with him*

*Above: Independence Day, 4 July 1998:
fireworks on the Brazos River*

I SAT IN LEONARDO'S SEAT
LEONARDO BOFF

THE FATHER OF LIBERATION
THEOLOGY REMEMBERS THE DAY
THE INQUISITION TOOK OVER

Twenty years ago, on 7 September 1984, I sat on the very same seat as Galileo Galilei [condemned to imprisonment for heresy in 1633] and Giordano Bruno [burned at the stake for heresy in 1600] in the Palace of the Holy Office in Rome – formerly the Inquisition – to defend the opinions expressed in my book *Church: charisma and power.*

To be summoned to appear before the Catholic Church's highest doctrinal tribunal is not a commonplace event in the life of any theologian. What effect did the events of my judicial proceedings within the former Inquisition in 1984 have on me?

My immediate feeling was that I was being kidnapped by the 'Red Brigades'. At 9am, the Vatican officials came to fetch me and before I could say goodbye to my Superior they grabbed me and pushed me inside a car, which sped to the nearby Vatican. Swiss Guards escorted me from the car to the lift. On the floor above, two other guards were waiting for me together with the Cardinal Inquisitor, Joseph Ratzinger, attired in his formal cardinal's robes.

I was wearing my simple friar's habit. To ease the tension I greeted him in his native Bavarian. But I was taken straight through a carpeted hall, some 100 metres long, lined with Renaissance paintings. At the very end was a tiny door, so small that I had difficulty going through it into the tiny, book-lined room with its small podium, on which sit both the Inquisitor and the object of his inquisition. A notary by our side would be taking everything down.

Proceedings began without further ado. I interrupted the Cardinal, however, and said to him, 'My Lord Cardinal, in our country we are still Christians; before we start any serious business we ask for God's protection.' Surprised by this, the Cardinal immediately started the ritual recitation of the *Veni Sancte Spiritus.* Within a juridical concept of the Church there really is no place for God.

Aparecida do Norte, Brazil 1996: posing with the Pope and Our Lady.
Credit: Abbas / Magnum

I started reading what I had prepared. The Cardinal interrupted me only twice. First, he wanted to know what an Ecclesial Base Community was; he thought it was a communist cell where militants were trained, because in these communities we are always talking about struggle. The second interruption led to a debate that has continued to the present day.

He stated: 'The Church of Christ is only to be found within the [Roman] Catholic Church. There are only elements of Christ's Church within other institutions: it is rather like having doors and walls, but not enough to make a complete house. These institutions are not churches and therefore cannot by rights be called churches.' If we take any account of tradition, I consider this offensive, arrogant and simply wrong.

There was a break for coffee in the large hall. Officials appeared from everywhere, each one with his copy of the condemned book asking for autographs. This greatly irritated the Cardinal. I wrote the same thing in every copy: 'Conserve Jesus' inheritance: freedom won not with words but with his own blood.'

Alone with the Cardinal once more, we went on looking at the paintings until we stopped before a huge picture representing St Francis, in old, torn clothes, but transfigured in the sky above. On the ground below was the kneeling Pope with his triple crown. I said to the Cardinal, 'Here is the symbol of the Church we defend, the Church of the poor, represented by St Francis and the Pope kneeling in its service.'

The Cardinal said: 'You politicise everything. Here we simply see this as a work of art, not a theological statement.'

I then drew his attention to the great square iron windows. 'You have no eyes for Liberation Theology because you see the world of the poor through those square windows and so everything appears square to you.'

We worked for another hour. At the end we had a meeting with the two Brazilian cardinals, Arns and Lorscheider, who had come to Rome to support me. Cardinal Arns came straight to the point. 'My Lord Cardinal, we do not like the document on Liberation Theology that has just been published. We are asking for another document that will do justice to the churches that take the option for the poor and their liberation seriously. You have tried to build a bridge by using a grammarian and not an engineer. Allow our builders in and they will help you to construct a good Liberation Theology that will be of service to the whole Church.'

The judicial proceedings did not end with the 'dialogue' with the Cardinal Inquisitor. The last word had to come from the [Congregation for the Doctrine of the Faith's] body of cardinals [20] and Bishops [5] and from the Pope. It arrived in May 1985, when a representative of the Apostolic Nuncio in Brasília suddenly turned up at the entrance hall of the convent in Petrópolis where I was teaching. He handed me a booklet, printed by the Vatican Polyglot Press [now Vatican Press], bearing the title *Notification on the book 'Church: charisma and power, essays on militant ecclesiology'*. He said to me: 'While I pray in the church alongside you, you read this text: afterwards we shall talk.'

I read it slowly. It seemed to be a concatenation of random phrases totally at odds with my thinking. The representative came back and asked me: 'Do you accept or reject the text?'

I said to him: 'I accept it because it does not represent what I said. There are statements in it which even I condemn.'

'But do you accept it?' he insisted.

'Of course I do,' I replied.

'Thanks be to God, thanks be to God,' he sighed.

'Why so many thanks be to God?' I asked.

'Because,' he confessed, 'if you were not to accept this text we would have a serious ecclesial problem on our hands, and I would have to impose on you the canonical penalties contained in this envelope.'

After all this, I expected the whole business to die down. Imagine my surprise a few days later when a high-ranking Vatican official read out my penalties over the telephone:

- removal from the chair of theology
- removal from the editorship of *Vozes* and the *Brazilian Ecclesiastical Review*
- the imposition of an 'obsequious silence' for an indeterminate period during which I would not be allowed to speak in public or publish anything I wrote.

Basing my reply on Canon Law, I merely said: 'Only when the document is in my hands shall I submit to these penalties.'

It took 20 days for the document to reach me. Important bishops made it clear to me that the problem was more political than doctrinal. What was really at stake was keeping a tight rein on the National Conference of Brazil's Bishops' liberating drive. I was no more than a pretext. So weighing my words carefully I stated: 'I prefer to walk with the Church rather than alone with my own theology.' Thus the NCBB was safeguarded, the Ecclesial Base Communities were spared and so was Liberation Theology.

Eleven months on, under considerable pressure, on Easter night 1986, the Pope released me from the obsequious silence and the other restrictions. However, during Eco-92 in Rio de Janeiro I was informed by Cardinal Baggio and by the Minister General of the Franciscan Order that once again I had to submit myself to the obsequious silence and give up teaching theology. I also had to leave the country and, indeed, the continent. I was told I would have to retreat to one of our convents in the Philippines or Korea. Even there I would have to submit to all the penalties. I thought it over and made my decision: human rights are for theologians too; and a theologian also has the inalienable right to express himself. With great pain I said, 'I am going to change trenches while carrying on the same fight. I will not leave the Church, but will give up one of my functions within it. I shall carry on as a theologian and a writer, with one foot in teaching and another among the poor.'

Twenty years on, I see that there was something providential in what happened to me. The world's media picked up the story and ran with it. People discovered another type of Church, denuded of power, simple and prophetic; one that identifies with the poor and shares the denigration and persecution of which they are victims. People learned about a theology that places life at its centre, a theology that aims at the historico-social liberation of the oppressed and is not formulated exclusively for the internal edification of an ecclesiastical galaxy. Liberation Theology became the subject of conversation in the streets, in pubs and in intellectual circles.

People grasped the ethical dimension of a liberation that concerns itself with the vast majority of suffering humanity. They understood the basic argument: Christians, by virtue of the very fact that they are followers of the Nazarene, who was tortured and killed on a cross, are urged to be agents of this liberation. Moreover, it is possible to have a theology born as it were from this liberating commitment, faithful to the great tradition of the Church, against social injustice and in favour of structural changes. The image of God that follows from this theology is understood by everybody: God is more interested in justice than in ritual; is more attuned to the cry of the oppressed than to the laudatory praises of the pious. What really matters is what is done and not what is preached.

Finally, no matter how much the Church authorities consider themselves 'Most Reverend Eminences', they still continue to have the limitations inherent in the human condition. The great French theologian Yves Congar who defended me in the pages of *La Croix* (8 September 1984) put it well: 'The charisma of the Vatican's central power consists in having no doubt whatsoever. Well, to have no doubt whatsoever is at the same time magnificent and terrible. It is magnificent in that the charisma of the centre consists precisely in remaining firm when everything else around is in a state of flux. It is terrible in that, in Rome, we have men who have all kinds of limitations, in their intelligence, in their vocabulary, in their frame of reference and in their angle of vision. These men have brought all their weight to bear upon Boff.'

But far be it from me even now to see them as would the Grand

Inquisitor. In their way, they, too, claim to serve the truth. And in the end, truth and not they will have the last word.

I went to Rome a Catholic theologian and came back from Rome a Catholic theologian. No doctrine of mine was condemned, only 'some options that put the Christian faith in danger'. But options belong to ethics, not to doctrine. I am quite aware that in all this I was a mere servant. I simply did what I had to do, as a servant should do. ❏

Leonardo Boff *occupies the chair of ethics, philosophy, religion and contemporary issues at the state university of Rio de Janeiro. He has been a visiting professor at a number of universities and will shortly be teaching in Munich*

Translated by F and CA Pimentel-Pinto

SPEAKING FOR THE PEOPLE: ARGENTINA'S CHURCH NOW

ANDREW GRAHAM-YOOLL

THE CATHOLIC HIERARCHY LOOKS BACK WITH SOME EMBARRASSMENT AT ITS ROLE UNDER THE MILITARY, AND YOUNGER PRIESTS BECOME CURIOUS ABOUT THEIR REBEL PREDECESSORS

The Roman Catholic Church in Argentina was once the most conservative in Latin America. Backed by the patrician and landowning families and the military, the Church was strict, strong and undemocratic; along with the Church in Colombia, the Argentine hierarchy was reactionary in the extreme. Ironically, the Church in both countries also became the cradle, in the 1960s and 1970s, of the most revolutionary priests in the southern hemisphere. Today, Argentina's bishops have moved on, leading the path back to an essentially Christian role, working with the poor and speaking for them. This has been forced largely by the political openings offered by Latin America's secular democracy.

The change, in Buenos Aires at least, has been caused by the failure of the old-fashioned authoritarian regimes, by misapplied market economy policies and by a steady decline into poverty of a country of cattle barons who once felt rich on a world scale. They saw themselves as a nation of Europeans among indigenous neighbours. With defeat in the Malvinas/Falklands war in 1982, Argentina discovered that it had few European friends and no real allies in Latin America; it was forced to abandon the fantasy of being a rich, developed society. That is when the Church began to realise that Argentina's middle class was shrinking – from 60 per cent of the population in the 1960s to 20 per cent of 37 million inhabitants now; that military dictators were unreliable allies; and that the established religion had to stop messing about with virgin weddings and such nonsense and get on with speaking seriously for the have-nots.

In May 2002, officially acknowledged unemployment reached 21.5 per cent, and in some suburban belts it reached 50 per cent.

For thousands of people in Argentina today, the main source of income is scavenging for metal, paper and plastic that can be resold. Most cities in

Father José Di Paola, aka 'Padre Pepe'. Credit: Andrew Graham-Yooll

the country are witness every day to the protests of belligerent *piqueteros* (from the English 'pickets'), small armies of unemployed men and women hired by political fat cats to disrupt traffic in pursuit of pressure against the government. President Néstor Kirchner, who reached government with 22 per cent of the vote in May 2003, has antagonised many by refusing to crack down on the demonstrators, fearing that a single death or even one severe injury could bring about chaos. Kirchner, sometimes in the footsteps of the late General Juan Perón (1895–1974), claims he is looking to bring about a popular democracy.

'Democracy has to work for the people to be taken as a system that can be supported. Democracy is valued by the Church as a form of participation and freedom, but what I see is a Church that wants to take participation well beyond the ballot box,' said 'Padre Pepe', Father José Di Paola, the 42-year-old priest of Our Lady of Caacupé, in the Villa 21 Barracas, a 60-hectare slum on the south side of Buenos Aires, which gathers the poor from north-western provinces and immigrants from Paraguay (hence the Virgin of Caacupé, patron of Paraguay, *Index* 2/04).

'The Church today sees democracy as its own path. With democracy the Church has examined its own conscience, it has experienced its own self-criticism. Many realise that they should have spoken out at the time.'

'The time' Padre Pepe refers to was the 1960s, a decade now under revision by the young students for the priesthood, looking back on the priests who tried to be revolutionary. Events in the Church and politics moved rapidly and with surprising congruence over the decade. Vatican II, in 1962, marked a changing era. Its ideologue, Pope John XXIII, died aged 81 in June 1963. The legacy of the reformist Pope was reinforced by the Vatican document 'The Church in our Time', issued in October 1964. In what the capitalist world wanted to see as unrelated, but which activists saw as akin, the Tricontinental Conference in Havana, in January 1966, made a call for revolution in all developing countries.

Historically, it is probably Camilo Torres, the 'guerrilla priest' of Colombia, who sparked the idea of armed revolution as a possibility within the Church. On 15 February 1966, Torres was cut down in a battle and, as elsewhere in Latin America, the myth was born. Then came a remarkable document: in the message of the 18 bishops of the Third World who gathered at a conference in Medellín, Colombia, in August 1967, capitalism in Latin America was described as 'institutionalised violence', a concept that would later be seen as validating revolutionary violence. 'Liberation Theology' was born, the phrase coined by Gustavo Gutierrez, a Peruvian academic who had helped to draft the Medellín message. Two months later, Ernesto 'Che' Guevara de la Serna, aged 39, was killed in Bolivia. Another myth was born.

The ideologues of those years were few, and the names that stand out today are the Brazilians: Dom Helder Camara (1909–99), Father Leonardo Boff and Frei Betto, the priest best known for his *Fidel and Religion: Castro talks on revolution and religion* (Simon & Schuster, New York, 1987). There were others, of course; and there were many martyrs.

By 31 December 1967, 270 priests in Argentina had signed their support for the message of the bishops of Medellín. In August 1968, Pope Paul VI travelled to Medellín. One reason was to further the Vatican's work among the poor; the other and more urgent mission was to admonish the rebel priests.

The general then running Argentina had the Roman Catholic leadership in his pocket. He saw the rebels as the vanguard of a revolution and felt justified in having them arrested on suspicion of aiding the budding guerrilla movement. One priest, Father Alberto Carbone, was tried for conspiracy in 1970 in the trial of several guerrillas charged with the abduction and murder of a former president, General Pedro Aramburu. Carbone was acquitted. He has been a priest for 50 years and is admired by the younger lot today.

Argentina in the 1970s saw an amazing slaughter. A popular Third World priest, Father Carlos Mujica, was murdered by a government-employed triggerman in May 1974. That was two months before the death of the ageing President Juan Perón plunged the country into a bloodbath. After the military coup of March 1976, the regime declared open season on rebel priests. Four members of the Irish Passionist order were murdered on 4 July 1976 in Buenos Aires, almost certainly by police. The only person ever charged was a journalist who accused the judge of dereliction of duty. Two more priests were murdered in the north-western La Rioja province in the same month. And a few days later, in August, the bishop of La Rioja, Monsignor Enrique Angelelli, died in a mysterious car accident hours after a Mass for the two murdered men.

The Church, to its shame, never had much to say about any of its casualties. And throughout the dictatorship, its hierarchy did very little to rescue the thousands of 'disappeared'.

This dark and distant period has to be seen in the context of regional power and wealth at the time, but it also helps to explain the political change the Church has undergone. Just a few years later, when Monsignor Oscar Arnulfo Romero (1917–80) was murdered at the altar in El Salvador, the outcry was worldwide. Argentina had to wait for adjustments further into the 1980s when divorce was accepted by the bishops and contraception as well. With that out of the way, the hierarchy began to pay attention to the collapsing social fabric.

After watching the decline throughout the 1990s – a decade of privatisations of state-owned utilities now mostly owned by Spanish and French corporations – the Church entered the social scene in 2002, the year Argentina defaulted on US$1 billion of its foreign debt. It has inserted itself

Buenos Aires cathedral 2004: in Latin, 'May your people be saved' and graffiti in Spanish on a column, 'IMF out of Argentina'. Credit: Andrew Graham-Yooll

as a mediator between government and people and negotiates on behalf of the poor as a quasi-corporation. Most recently, for instance, the Church charity Caritas has taken over the management of a housing development for 200 families on an old airfield north of Buenos Aires. The Church's stated political aim is respect for democracy – but would the politicians show some respect as well, please.

'What we are lacking at present is a review of the ideas that made Vatican II valid in the developing world in the 1960s. It was the message that led many priests to challenge the existing order at the time. Of course we are concerned about traditional issues such as abortion and contraception, but we must rethink the Church on all issues that matter to society. These concern urban safety and the environment, and we have to look at what feeds the growth of the local mafia and its subsidiary, the drug traffic, as well as at the desperate poverty that has caused child deaths from malnutrition in a country that exports food,' Padre Pepe says. He speaks in a tiny office behind his church, sitting under a portrait of Christ and another of the murdered Father Carlos Mujica. 'We cannot wait for others to do things.' Padre Pepe should know: a large white cross at the entrance to his slum records the names of parishioners who have died by knife or gun in the violent nights of Villa 21.

Padre Pepe speaks of a nostalgia in some of the younger priests for the activism of the rebel priests, a memory, he says, that is fed by debate and by discussion of what it was they wanted to build. The new breed is involved in politics through its social work: missionary commitment is strong among the indigenous and the poor, which can involve violent confrontation with police bosses in the slums. Nobody wants to talk of political change. The language is too controversial now and the past deaths are a continuing presence. The political profile may grow, but it is too early to guess.

'What the Church needs to do now is further its commitment to the people, to the poor. There is far more respect for national and popular culture than there ever was. This has been made possible with democracy. There was a time when anything "popular" was subversive. Now the Church sees it as an objective of its own. But we must have more commitment, from everyone.' ❏

Andrew Graham-Yooll is editor of the Buenos Aires Herald

AMONG THE OLD BELIEVERS
IRENA MARYNIAK

TWO POWERFUL INSTITUTIONS GUARD THE
FAITH BEHIND THE OLD IRON CURTAIN:
PATRIARCH AND PAPACY KEEP THE FAITH BUT
WITH RATHER DIFFERENT CONSEQUENCES

A procession in the enclosed grounds of the Jasna Gora Monastery is a step into a world where rationality has been left behind and enchantment holds sway. Jasna Gora, the Mountain of Light, is home to the Black Madonna of Czestochowa, Poland's most venerated holy image. Its fortifications are charged with the promise that anything is possible: a miraculous healing, a political transformation, an apparition, the intervention by saint or deity into the causal flow of things. History, chronicle and folklore tell us it has all happened. A medieval queen's shoe, imprinted in solid stone after an act of charity; a Swedish army of 3,000 repelled by 160 soldiers and 70 friars in the seventeenth century; a victory over the Soviet army on the banks of the Vistula in 1920, arranged and overseen by Mary, Mother of God and Queen of Poland.

In places like Jasna Gora people walk on their knees. Approaching the altar where the icon is displayed amid gleaming votive offerings, I was impatiently shoved and elbowed out of the way by a group of women in headscarves scrabbling for communion. With so many communicants to serve the priest sometimes runs short; and, in the presence of the sacred, rules of civility don't hold. The girl beside me might have been a linguistics student, the florid-looking man behind a banker, but many of the women who come are farmers' wives and they know where their priorities lie. They are hungry for redemption and the support of providence and, amid the disorientation and excitement, they demand to be touched brutally, definitively by the divine.

Times of religious effervescence like these, Emile Durkheim said, are the galvanising moments when social identities are formed. In Czestochowa, Vilnius or Medjugorje they occur daily: at any Mass or liturgical service; at high feasts commemorating victories or disasters; as people intone the rosary; at the point of transubstantiation when divinity becomes a communion wafer and vice versa. If God stepped into history and became man a little over 2,000 years ago, then why not a wafer, a bit of bread, a goblet of wine? Why not, the Russian Orthodox Christian tradition dares suggest, potentially anything?

Such happenings exist outside the spectrum of secular hours, they touch a sacred eternity when time is gathered together and memory, present and future are rolled into a chaotic bundle from which anything at all might emerge. And afterwards people go back to the job or out for a doughnut and, except for that glowing sense of belonging, forget (because to remember would be to exceed the bounds of profane consciousness) until the next time.

In Central, East and Southern Europe, the aggregation of Christian experience merged in memories, languages, histories and identities is framed and protected by two immensely powerful institutions: the Roman Catholic and Orthodox Churches. In these parts of the Continent, nations and states still remember that they serve a more elevated meaning and intention. The Russian Federation is the seat of 'Holy Russia', destined to save the world; Poland is 'Christ crucified among the Nations' with a vocation to redeem humanity; the Serbian nation has been called 'to defend Christian values and culture' in the south.

Albanian and Bosnian Muslims may disagree; they may feel baffled and enraged when the Russian Orthodox Patriarch Aleksi declares Kosovo 'a holy place for Orthodoxy'. But parts of Europe never much touched by the Reformation or the Enlightenment set little store by relativist discourse or doubt. They are mapped by polarities of belief, suspicious of questions and they can be rough. In the south and east of Europe there is intense anxiety, still, about perdition and longing for deliverance from poverty, ill health, fear, memories of prison camps, slaughter and war. Railway sidings throughout the region still display the kind of carriages used in the 1940s to transport Jews to Auschwitz or Poles to Siberia; and less than a decade ago tourists pony-trekking in the southern Hungarian hills near Pécs – now part of the European Union – could hear the shooting over the border in Croatia. The anguish that prompts a religious response, the sense of an uncanny world's cruelty and uncontrollability lives on, especially in rural areas or urban complexes where people in search of work have settled with neither friends nor support systems. When community collapses, religious faith or belonging can seem to help. It suggests the possibility of another order and intention, visible only in controlled settings but immanently present nevertheless.

Jasna Gora/ Czestochowa 1967: procession with Poland's most sacred icon, the Black Madonna (see also p205). Credit: Keston Institute

In the worn, grimy cities of communist Poland, with crushing shortages of housing and community care, an alternative shape of things seems visibly at work in the network of Catholic churches and convents throughout the country, open, accessible, airy and impeccably maintained. The altars covered in white cloths and decorated daily with flowers communicate the sense of a compassionate presence which contrasts sharply with the sense that no one outside cared. That, as well as the mythology, the evenings of drama, poetry and music, the social welfare assistance and – on the whole – the civic trust, was what drew people. In a nominally atheist state more than 90 per cent of people said they were Catholics.

How far this belief went and how far it goes now is hard to say. Attending Mass was a political gesture under communism; today it is a way of demonstrating patriotism for the benefit of Brussels, Moscow, Berlin, Paris, or anyone else who may be watching. Before 1989, the Church's astonishing institutional power offered a base and a forum where such displays could be made with relative impunity. It protected Poland's generic culture and spoke a language that, people agreed, coded their personal and political sensibilities. It was traditionalist (Rome's more liberal modernising gestures after the Second Vatican Council in the 1960s seemed to pass it by), eclectic in its capacity to absorb superstition and folk culture, insistent on the effectiveness of faith as fact not as system, and a keeper of the imprints of historical memory. It pulled time together, so that no Polish Catholic could ever forget that she was the bearer of a traditional resistance to outside domination and oppression, or that this was morally and sometimes materially underwritten by that tiny but spectacularly influential state in the Italian capital: the Vatican.

Between 1945 and 1989, the Church nurtured the Polish ambition to be an agent in history and an acknowledged presence in Europe – as it had since Poland adopted Christianity in 966. It preserved the yearning for an independent national and political identity, frustrated since the end of the eighteenth century by partition, occupation and Soviet communism. There were also hints of a controversial apostolic mission in the East, which the outside world, and Russia in particular, could never quite ignore, and everything was packaged and purveyed to congregations in overflowing churches on Sundays. Perhaps Catholicism, with its fierce resistance to the Hegelian interpretation of history, was, as Mikhail Gorbachev said in an interview with the BBC, 'the core of resistance to communism'. If so the election of a Polish pope in 1978 proved to be its catalyst.

Karol Wojtyla is known to have felt bitter and betrayed by the Yalta agreement that brought Central Europe under Stalinist rule. He had also had first-hand experience of life in Nazi-occupied Poland and was secretly studying for the priesthood in Krakow while more than 200,000 people, mostly his peers, were being killed in the 1944 Warsaw Uprising. Czeslaw Milosz once suggested that Pope John Paul II was motivated by his sense of the link between the living and the dead, a doctrine built deep into Catholic

Kursk region, Russia 1991: Procession of the Cross. Credit: A Kolybalov

mysticism and labelled the 'communion of saints'. As a Krakow intellectual he was also doubtless affected by the messianic ideas that steep the work of nineteenth-century poets such as Adam Mickiewicz and Juliusz Slowacki. But most of all he had to live up to expectations raised by a daunting and potentially embarrassing prophecy. In 1848, Slowacki had penned a poem familiar to most educated Poles about the coming of a Slavic pope who would transform the world and not 'take fright / At sabre-thrust / But brave as God himself advance to fight'.

The Pope's visit home in 1979 has been compared, in terms of historical importance, to the assassination of Archduke Ferdinand in Sajarevo, which led to World War I. It introduced a feeling that repression and lack of choice were not inevitable in Poland, and that the existing state of things could be transitory. As the Church took charge of security and crowd control for the duration of the visit, public behaviour seemed to change and it looked as though, in a framework like this, people could organise themselves from the grass roots up. With an infallible pope calling them to take courage, what cause was there to be afraid? The upshot was the formation of the Solidarity Trade Union in August 1980. Over the next decade it spurred the non-violent opposition that broke the back of communist regimes throughout the region.

Historically, but also theologically, Central European Catholicism has demanded belonging as much as believing. Active participation in the communion of the Church, the communion of saints, the communion as sacrament, is all part of the call to salvation. Polish faith is about a communal experience. It is untouched still by the Western Protestant perception that religion is a private matter. Lech Walesa, a devout Catholic who believes in Hell and the power of faith to move mountains, remembered the papal visit as a watershed, when people understood what a great force they were, if only they mobilised their convictions in the way their faith demanded.

All this is a hard act to follow. The Polish Church now has to compete with political pluralism, better communications, the possibility (if not yet the fact) of a new prosperity, and the public pursuit of secular happiness. The kind of decline in religiosity visible recently in Ireland, or in Quebec in the 1960s, has been widely predicted and might be expected to take on a momentum unprecedented in Poland's history. But there has been no sign of it yet. There may be considerable selectivity in moral attitudes over issues such as contraception or pre-marital sex, but the Church has seen no falling-off in Sunday attendance since 1989, even among the young. In Poland, even more than in other parts of Middle and East Europe, the perception of religious belonging still seems to be most of all about a visceral participation in a collective spirit expressed in ritual.

Two early Soviet revolutionaries, Anatolii Lunacharskii and Maxim Gorkii (both firm atheists) once suggested that tapping collective creative powers, the energies that crowds release, could form the gods that made social bonds. 'The people . . . are seeking the means of fusing all the forces on earth into one, and creating out of it a splendid and beautiful god who shall embrace the universe,' Gorkii wrote in his 1907 novel *Confession*. The collective aspect of religious faith, which Gorkii saw as a practical way of consolidating social and political change, puts Polish Catholicism firmly and paradoxically into the tradition of Eastern rather than Western Christianity.

According to Russian Orthodox teaching, redemption itself is something that happens in community, within the Church, through the connection established with the transcendent during the liturgy and carried out into the profane world. God's energies form an interface between matter and divinity. They are accessible and can be touched through the discipline that creates the hotline between the sacred and the profane: prayer. Humanity is called to participate in the transfiguration of creation, *theosis,* the divinisation of matter, and the mission of the Church is as far as possible to incorporate everyone in this process. The emphasis is on ritual over theology; experience over ideas; faith over intellect; and liturgy over labour. Above all, integration is preferable to isolation.

This kind of faith has implications not just in terms of world view but in politics. Even when the treatment of the Orthodox Church in Russia was at its worst in the 1920s and 1930s, or in the early 1960s, the Church's policy was not to resist but to accommodate and absorb, to save the Church institutionally as a unit, rather than let it abandon its heritage and go underground. The Russian Orthodox Church never created the kind of surrogate civil society that grew up in Poland even though its hierarchy and clergy were repressed, its believers persecuted and its rights disregarded. Historically, it had accepted the authority of the state and its right to legislate in temporal matters, and under Soviet rule it continued to do so. In addition, an Orthodox Church is bound by its structure to be the spiritual agency and expression of the state. There is no single focus of supreme authority like the Pope: Orthodox Christianity is composed of several self-governing 'autocephalous' Churches that run their own affairs and are identified with their respective nation state: Russia, Greece, Romania, Serbia or Bulgaria.

The tendency in Orthodox states has been, therefore, for the Church to lose its independent voice. In eighteenth-century Russia, under the reforming Tsar Peter the Great, the Church became in effect a department of state dealing with education and social welfare. That tradition, and its role in the Soviet system – when it was infiltrated and repressed on the one hand, and wheeled out to represent the USSR at international peace conferences on the other – makes it, by default, a state actor with a national and international policy agenda. The Russian Church falls more naturally into an autocratic order than a democratic one. Pluralism, tolerance, diversity and a global perspective do not form part of its frame of reference. Its focus is national but underpinned by a theological brief to incorporate the peoples of the world under its mantle and redeem them. Division of any kind is a metaphysical anxiety; the prospect of any kind of union supports the ecclesiastical principle of conciliarity – 'sobornost', coming together – and spells success.

When in 1999 the Belarusan President Alaksandar Lukashenka proposed a Slavic Union between Belarus, Russia and Yugoslavia, Patriarch Aleksi called it a symbol of 'the great miracle, the return of the people to the Mother Church . . . the guarantee of our common spiritual triumph'. The Russian Church's support of Serbia during the Yugoslav war is another case in point. More recently, there have been signs of concern over Fidel Castro's flirtation with the Patriarchate of Constantinople. When Patriarch Bartholomaios consecrated the first Orthodox church in Havana in January 2004, the Moscow newspaper *Radonezh* suggested this was a challenge to Russia and Cuba had 'officially swung round to Washington'.

For those worried by the implications of belonging to a Church theologically entangled with state interests and political expansionisms, the solution tends to be withdrawal into a more interior religious mode, or into fringe sects. To some extent, communism in any case forced the development of a privatised form of religiosity. This was true even in Poland until the late 1970s. People gathered quietly in churches, flats or cellars, shared their religious high and separated without comment. Not much else was possible.

In the immediate aftermath of the 'velvet' revolutions of 1989, those drawn by the swell and success communicated by established churches returned to the fold. Anyone who wanted to touch the spontaneous religious spirit – free of dogma, second-hand spiritual experience and institution – could also look around in the expanding religious market.

By the mid-1990s, the carnivalesque aspect that accompanied the arrival of new religions in Central and Eastern Europe was beginning to pall. People had seen mass assemblies of Jehovah's Witnesses, US-style evangelical TV programmes by Pentecostal preachers, billboards advertising Transcendental Meditation and Scientology. They had met Hare Krishnas, Mormons and Moonies. They had been introduced to New Age ideas about the infinite powers everyone has within their reach from the mysterious but basically benevolent universal force that exists in all things. They had been offered financial incentives and trips to the West. Some had been blackmailed or drugged. In 1994, over 2,000 state schools in Russia were using 'moral textbooks' furnished gratis by the Reverend Moon's Unification Church; within two years, Patriarch Aleksi was protesting at incursions from Catholic and Protestant groups into Orthodox canonical territory, and sectarian interlopers. The Church, he said, had an obligation to 'battle for people's souls by all legal means available, rather than allowing them to perish'. Laws were duly adopted against proselytism, and the rights of foreign religious organisations and minorities shrank. Recent polls suggest that 75 per cent of Russians say they are Orthodox, but only up to 3 per cent attend Orthodox liturgy every week. President Putin is reported to have a private 'confessor', and Russia's political and social elite like to meet up for Sunday liturgy at the Cathedral of the Mother of God of Vladimir in Moscow. Equally, 70 per cent of Russians believe in UFOs; 60 per cent in astrology; and spiritual healing, shamanism, neo-pagan cults and the abominable snowman have firm followings.

The urge to take control of one's own spiritual path, visit spaces beyond conventional consciousness and look for meaningful religious expression has spawned therapies, self-awareness groups and neo-religious trends in Western Europe since the 1960s. Personal fulfilment and self-realisation are expectations that have accompanied unprecedented affluence and economic development. They generated interest among communist elites in the 1970s, and travelled east in force along with the market. Evidently there has been no disenchantment with the domain of spirits and higher forces, no drive to secularisation in that sense. But in the West, as Charles Taylor has said, 'secularity' has been interwoven for decades with a drive towards a personal spirituality and an ethic that forces far more commitment on those who say they are religious than ever before. For the moment, in Middle, East and Southern Europe that burden of reflection and choice is increasingly absent. National Churches mediate and carry it and, for the present, people continue – in solidarity – to follow. ❏

IM

*Ayatollah Khomeini's funeral, Tehran 1989:
end of an era, not of a regime. Credit: Anon*

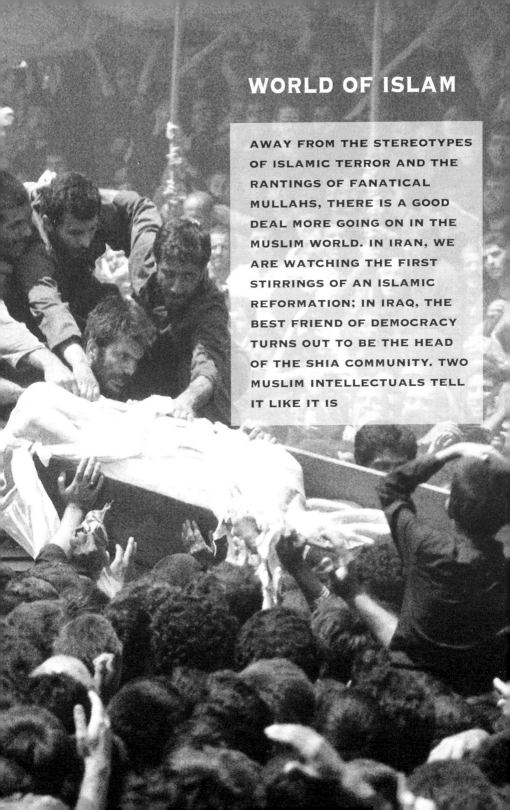

WORLD OF ISLAM

AWAY FROM THE STEREOTYPES
OF ISLAMIC TERROR AND THE
RANTINGS OF FANATICAL
MULLAHS, THERE IS A GOOD
DEAL MORE GOING ON IN THE
MUSLIM WORLD. IN IRAN, WE
ARE WATCHING THE FIRST
STIRRINGS OF AN ISLAMIC
REFORMATION; IN IRAQ, THE
BEST FRIEND OF DEMOCRACY
TURNS OUT TO BE THE HEAD
OF THE SHIA COMMUNITY. TWO
MUSLIM INTELLECTUALS TELL
IT LIKE IT IS

A WAR OF UNINTENDED CONSEQUENCES
THOMAS DE WAAL

HAS CHECHNYA REALLY BECOME A 'FRONT IN THE
WAR IN TERROR' AS PUTIN REPEATEDLY CLAIMS,
OR HAVE 10 YEARS OF RUSSIAN BRUTALITY AND
INTRANSIGENCE DRIVEN THIS TINY REPUBLIC INTO
THE ARMS OF ITS OWN RADICAL ISLAMISTS?

On the afternoon of 3 September, when the worst of the shooting had stopped, and the terrible aftermath of the Beslan school siege was only just beginning, I was sitting in a BBC World television studio talking live with a Russian analyst. A newsflash came up on the wire agencies: the Russian security services said that among the dead hostage-takers they had found nine Arabs and one 'black' (the Russian word, still used without embarrassment, is *negr*). My fellow analyst and I both agreed that, if this was true, this had a significant bearing on the nature of this horrible event: it meant Beslan had been attacked by a group with a clear link to the Middle East and the wider front of 'international terror'.

The next day, President Vladimir Putin delivered his address to the Russian people about Beslan. In a pained speech Putin told his nation that it was at war. He put his words in a strongly historical and international framework, appealing to nostalgia for the strong Soviet state and warning that Russia's enemies wanted to break up the country. The language was often obscure but the message was unmistakable: the threat emanated from outside Russia's borders. 'This is an attack on our country,' Putin said. The word 'Chechnya' was not mentioned once.

Slowly, however, a more inevitable truth began to emerge from Beslan: almost all the hostage-takers were from the North Caucasus. First, Russian officials admitted that the so-called *negr* was mistaken for such because his face had been coated in ash from the fire in the school. Then they started to draw back from their claims about the so-called dead Arabs. Later, the notorious Chechen warlord Shamil Basayev, who claimed to have planned the raid, said there were 31 hostage-takers, of whom only two had been Arabs.

The obvious truth was also, in its way, more terrible. It meant that the group of men and women who rigged up explosives in the gym of School

Grozny, March 1995: a woman weeps in front of her house as she returns to find it destroyed by the Russian bombardment of the town. Credit: Heidi Bradner

No 1 in Beslan and then presided over up to 331 deaths, 172 of them children, were almost all locals, who had a common language and culture with their hostages. Despite what Putin might say, despite some links with international *jihadis*, this conflict remains very much Russia's home-grown problem: its horrors have been bred locally.

How has it come about that a generation of village boys and girls, born in the atheist Soviet Union, have turned into Islamist suicide bombers and child-killers? What has gone so badly wrong? The answer of course, or most of it, lies in what has happened in Chechnya over the past 10 years, since the Russian military first went into Chechnya in December 1994.

Grozny, February 1997: an election poster supporting General Jokhar Dudayev – formerly of the Soviet military – is carried through the town during the presidential election campaign at the end of the first Chechen war. Dudayev became Chechnya's first independent president.
Credit: Heidi Bradner

The Chechen conflict is a classic case of the law of unintended consequences. Most obviously and disgracefully, a purported campaign by Boris Yeltsin in 1994 to reintegrate Chechnya into the Russian Federation and to 'restore constitutional order' ended up with the alienation of the entire Chechen population and a wanton outbreak of lawlessness by the Russian army.

On the Chechen side, perhaps the strangest unintended consequence was the way a whole segment of Chechen society discovered militant religion. Nowadays, the Islamist Chechens call Grozny, Chechnya's main city, Jokhar after the first president of their would-be independent state, Jokhar Dudayev. But Dudayev himself was a former Soviet strategic forces general, a product of the communist system with a Russian wife and a known fondness for cognac. His first Chechen constitution was modelled on that of

Estonia and in a 1992 interview with *Literaturnaya gazeta* he glossed it as follows:

> I would like the Chechen Republic to be a constitutional secular state. This is what we are striving for, this is the ideal we are pursuing . . . If religion takes precedence over the secular constitutional order, the Spanish Inquisition and Islamic fundamentalism in a strongly expressed form will appear.

Dudayev, like many other Chechens, tried to rediscover his Muslim heritage as a way of forging a new Chechen identity. But I heard people joke that he was so ignorant of Islam that he had apparently exhorted Chechens on television to pray three times a day.

The mountain villages of Chechnya give a better clue to the actual nature of Chechen traditional identity. They are dotted with tall stone defensive towers, built with amazing engineering skill. Exactly the same towers can be found on the Georgian side of the mountains, testament to a time in the later Middle Ages when the Chechens were mostly pagan. Islam began to arrive only in the eighteenth century, and it was of a very specific kind in the form of the two Sufi *tariqats* (brotherhoods), the Naqshbandia and the Qadiria. Dozens of shrines to Sufi saints and ancestors, traditional places of veneration as much for mountain forefathers as for religious figures, are dotted around Chechnya. These mountain village communities hold together with fierce traditions of collective decision-making, self-sufficiency and respect for tradition and the ancestors.

Then there is – or was – the other Chechnya, the more recent russified one. It was centred on the city of Grozny and its oil institute, university, museum, archive, schools. Slowly a new generation of Chechens was benefiting from Soviet education and a new professional class was forming. In the long run, it made little difference to this group of russified Chechens what kind of state they lived in so long as their basic rights and freedoms were growing.

Boris Yeltsin changed all that. By launching his brutal war in 1994 on Dudayev's strange, quasi-autonomous fiefdom, he basically destroyed Chechen society and left behind a gaping hole that is still unfilled.

It is hard to overstate the awfulness of the bombing of Grozny by the Russian air force in December 1994 and January 1995. The estimated casualty figure of 27,000 civilians killed is probably too high, but many thousands did die and mostly the weakest, oldest and most helpless, many of

Chechen village, July 2001: men try to salvage carpets from their home after Russian artillery have destroyed their street. Credit: Heidi Bradner

them ethnic Russians – all in the name of affirming that this city was part of the Russian state. Anyone who saw this apocalypse was moved to say, 'If this is the solution, then I would prefer the problem.' For me, the tragic absurdity of it was summed up by a household I visited in February 1995 in which the grandfather, a lame veteran of World War II, had just been knocked down and killed by a group of drunken Russian soldiers in an armoured car. The dead man was far more a patriot of Russian statehood than his killers were.

The Russian bombers not only killed thousands, they also destroyed urban and professional Chechnya. The oil institute, university and archive were all destroyed. By the spring of 1995, Chechnya was being run from the hills. This new Chechnya then began to experience another smaller incursion from the other direction. The first Islamic volunteers began to arrive, mostly from the east, via Azerbaijan and Dagestan.

The memoirs of the US Muslim volunteer Aukai Collins, entitled *My Jihad*, suggest how divorced these incoming Islamists were from the realities of Chechnya. Collins said he felt at home at the camp of the Saudi-born warrior Khattab because 'the Arabs were more religious'. The savage behaviour he meted out – the shooting of Russian prisoners for example – point to how the conflict was beginning to mutate into something even more dangerous.

The Chechen fighters slowly diverged into two streams. The main group of fighters in 1994–6 held arms out of a mixture of nationalism, anger, revenge and sheer desire for survival. The leader of this pragmatic nationalist cause, Aslan Maskhadov, another Soviet-educated army officer, became Chechnya's only ever legitimately elected president in 1997.

By the time the rebels had driven out the Russians and Maskhadov was the nominal leader, however, the Islamists who were beginning to run the show and getting a big influx of funds from Saudi Arabia and the Gulf

Outside Grozny, January 1995: the charred corpse of a Russian soldier who failed to escape from his tank during the disastrous Russian invasion of Grozny on New Year's Eve 1994. Credit: Heidi Bradner

Grozny, January 1995: Russian soldiers in gas masks search mass graves for missing comrades killed during the New Year's Eve invasion. Many who died were listed as missing in action and were accounted for only years later as a result of their mothers' searches for their bodies. Credit: Heidi Bradner

States. Hundreds of *jihadis* mistakenly identified Chechnya as a new bridge-head in their world struggle. One of them was Osama bin Laden's right-hand man, Ayman al-Zawahiri, who was detained in Dagestan and spent six months there on a false passport before being deported. Chechnya's second constitution, the political analyst Alexander Iskandarian likes to point out, was based not on that of Estonia but on that of Sudan.

Maskhadov's inability to stand up to the Islamists caused further splits and led eventually to the breakaway of Akhmad Kadyrov, a Sufi mufti and fighter, who switched sides to the Russians in 1999. He then became Chechnya's

Village cemetery, Chechen-Aul, October 2003: men gather silently around the bodies of fellow villagers found dumped in fields and on a nearby rubbish tip. They had been missing for over five days since being dragged from their homes shortly after the end of the Moscow Nord-Ost theatre siege. Credit: Heidi Bradner

version of Najibullah, ruling by corruption and intimidation, fighting his former comrade-in-arms Maskhadov and being made Russia's own president in Chechnya in 2003 – before he was assassinated in May this year.

In 2004, the Maskhadov fighters have been squeezed almost into non-existence and the chief conflict now going on in Chechnya is a civil war between Moscow's proxy army, led by the heirs of Kadyrov, and the Islamists, chiefly led by Shamil Basayev.

Does this mean that Chechnya has indeed become a front in the war on terror, as Putin likes to say?

Samaski village, 1998: in the lull between the first and second Chechen wars, children play in the only school to have survived, almost, Russian shells and bombs.
Credit: Heidi Bradner

Only up to a point. Certainly there was a *jihadi* element in Chechnya by the autumn of 1999, when Moscow invaded again. Yet there is no evidence that it has significantly increased since then: the high mountains of the Caucasus keep almost everyone out. War has depleted their numbers and Chechnya is far from being Afghanistan: it is a small place where most of the fighters actually live in villages most of the time and cannot afford to maintain large groups of foreigners.

What has happened is scarier than that. A radical fringe of the Chechens has become Islamicised without much foreign help at all. They have grafted what they have learned from Hamas and the Middle East – the paraphernalia of the suicide bomber, the videos, the belts strapped with explosives, the headbands and hoods – on to an older revenge culture and made themselves into very frightening creatures indeed.

Most disturbing are the 'Black Widows', the women who have now caused around a dozen suicide bombings associated with Chechnya. Information about them is very murky. It seems they have lost family members to Russian atrocities. Possibly some of them have been raped – one of them captured in Chechnya last year was certainly pregnant. And almost certainly they have been actively brainwashed by the militants.

To anyone who saw, as I did, Chechnya a mere 10 years ago, when it was still recognisably part of the post-Soviet space, all this is depressing beyond words. No society on earth perhaps has suffered such a precipitate decline. And in the wider Russia, a parallel corruption of views and attitudes has proceeded apace. The sense of 'otherness' between Chechens and Russians, who once shared so much, is now so great that bigotry that would have been shocking 10 years ago has now become mainstream.

Left in the middle between the two extremes is a silent majority of ordinary Chechens. It is hard to think of a more unlucky group of people. They have suffered 10 years of bombing, torture, looting and extortion from the Russian army and the depredations of the Islamist fringe. They have also – though they may be only dimly aware of it – been demonised by association by an outside world that all too often uses the epithet 'the Chechens' as a synonym for savagery and terrorism.

Most Chechens I speak to now say independence has disappeared from the agenda. The issues are survival, rights, security and reconstruction. It is clear to me that, given how Russia's security forces have caused Chechnya's problems, not solved them, the only way to break the cycle of violence is to internationalise it with monitors from abroad. But Moscow and the outside world are still a long way from acknowledging this. How much more pain will it take – how many more Beslans, dare I say, though I dearly hope I am wrong – before Russia and the rest of the world own up to their responsibilities to this unhappy place? ❑

Thomas de Waal is co-author with Carlotta Gall of Chechnya: A Small Victorious War (1997) and Caucasus editor at the Institute for War and Peace Reporting, www.iwpr.net

GOD AND HIS GUARDIANS

MOHSEN KADIVAR

CONTRARY TO THE MAJORITY VIEW, THERE IS
NO REASON ON EARTH — OR IN THE QURAN —
WHY DEMOCRACY SHOULD NOT BE COMPATIBLE
WITH ISLAM, PARTICULARLY IN IRAN

The concept of *velayat-e faqih* — the guardianship or vice-regency of an Islamic jurist — a Shia form of Islamic government, gained currency after its introduction by the Ayatollah Khomeini following Iran's Islamic revolution in 1979. After a quarter of a century, its compatibility with democracy has become one of the most hotly debated subjects in contemporary Iranian politics. Broadly speaking, there are three dominant strands in the debate: the official view of the Islamic Republic; that of the traditional Iranian reformists; and that of Iranian Muslim intellectuals.

The first holds that the 'absolute, appointed *velayat-e faqih*' is the only legitimate form of Islamic government during the occultation or the absence of the 12 Shia imams. Obedience to this government is a religious obligation on the population; the legitimacy of all decisions in the public domain depends on the approval of the supreme jurist, the *vali-ye amr*. In this interpretation, *velayat-e faqih* is not compatible with democracy; indeed, the latter is neither desirable nor beneficial.

The second opinion finds neither system entirely acceptable, but argues that by judicious adjustments to both, they might be combined to create a form of Islamic democracy that it labels 'elective, conditional *velayat-e faqih*'. According to this interpretation, the people or their representatives elect a jurist as the *vali-ye amr* for a limited period only. He would take over the government with the approval of the jurists and the people and would be accountable to the people.

The third and last voice in the debate is unequivocal: there is no valid religious authority for the implementation of *velayat-e faqih* in any form in the public–political sphere. Islam does not propose one specific model of government even though there are political systems with which it is not compatible. Democracy, which is based on popular sovereignty and participation, the rule of law and human rights, is totally incompatible with *velayat-e faqih* and clerical rule, which is a form of religious dictatorship. The view that the two can be brought into harmony by tinkering round the edges is based on a misconception of democracy and Islamic jurisprudence alike. However, this fundamental incompatibility presents no obstacle to the democratic government of modern Islamic societies.

It is this final position I wish to focus on here, but before doing so, there are a couple of points that need some clarification.

Although the term *velayat-e faqih* has become identified with the Islamic Republic and its founder, the incompatibility of *velayat-e faqih* and democracy should not be confused by equating *velayat-e faqih* and republicanism. The latter is certainly not synonymous with *velayat-e faqih*. Proponents of government by *velayat-e faqih* believe it would arise naturally and inevitably out of Islamic republicanism. Its opponents, on the other hand, believe an Islamic republic is perfectly capable of existing without *velayat-e faqih*; indeed, there are many among them who maintain that this is precisely what was offered the Iranian people in the preamble to the 1979 constitution, which had gained widespread popular support through a referendum earlier in the year. What they have actually ended up with over the past quarter-century is an uncomfortable and unsuccessful amalgam of the two: a *velayat*-based republicanism – *jomhouri-ye velayi* – in which government performs its duties under the supervision of the supreme leader.

Similar confusion arises when *velayat-e faqih* is equated with Islam and the assumption made that Islam is incapable of coexisting with democracy: that there can never be democratic Islamic governance. For those who have come to this conclusion and are unwilling to entertain any alternative, there is little point in the following discussion. Much the same applies to those who believe religion is an entirely private matter between God and the individual and refuse it any public role. For these fundamental secularists, any form of religious governance would inevitably be undemocratic and this discussion pointless. The relationship between *velayat-e faqih* and democracy is only of concern to those who believe Islamic government capable of democracy – more specifically, to those who would allow democracy to flourish in a religious society.

The questions being discussed here are less than 25 years old. They became relevant in or about 1979, when the *velayat-e faqih* concept was applied to the public sphere. Debate around these issues first took place exclusively among elites and prior to practical experience of the concept. The analysis and explanations they offered were mostly general and often ambiguous. At this early stage, the proponents of *velayat-e faqih* tried to

Tehran Saturday 31 July 2004: Mohsen Kadivar (R) with Hashem Aghajari, twice condemned for blasphemy and imprisoned for two years on the night of his release

portray this principle in a popular and democratic way. A decade later, having experienced *velayat-e faqih* in practice for 10 years, the general public joined in the debate and responses to the questions raised became more specific, more exact and much better clarified.

One might assume that democracy is a familiar concept around the world. However, in Iran, the arguments of its defenders, let alone its detractors, demonstrate many misconceptions, among them the idea that it is a 'Western notion' of a populist nature. If, for the sake of argument, we outline the essentials of democracy, its incompatibility with *velayat-e faqih* will become immediately obvious.

Democracy is the political system favoured in the modern world. In a democracy, those exercising authority in the public sphere are the people's elected representatives; their charter is to serve the public interest. Government is responsible to the public, comes to power through the will of the people and, after a specified time, peacefully transfers its power to its democratically elected successors. The equal right to choose and be chosen is among the most basic characteristics of democracy. In a democracy, decisions that affect society must win consensus. To summarise: the fundamental tenets of a democratic society are free and all-inclusive elections; transparent and accountable government; respect for civil and political rights; and the enabling of civil society.

An undemocratic regime is characterised by special privileges in the public sphere for an individual or class of elites; the permanent nature of office and the lack of a peaceful means of transfer of power; those in authority are above the law; the leadership is not accountable to the public; power vested in an individual or a group is unchecked and absolute; public demand for changes in the law are ignored. *Velayat-e faqih* provides for a religious autocracy, or at best a clerical aristocracy. Since the *vali-ye faqih* is the representative of the divine on earth, he is akin to God – 'He [God] cannot be questioned for his acts, but they will be questioned for theirs' (Quran Surah Anbiaa Verse 23) – with permanent, irresponsible, sacred and absolute authority in the temporal world.

None of the four principles of *velayat-e faqih* stands up to democratic scrutiny.

* *Velayat* **(Guardianship)**

Under religious guardianship, the general public is not equal to the jurists in their ability to make pious decisions or influence public affairs. In a democracy, everyone has equal rights and the right to influence public affairs.

Rather than being rendered incompetent or incapable of making proper decisions by the imposition of paternal oversight, citizens in a democracy are empowered to elect a representative government.

Only the views and opinions of the *vali-ye faqih* have any authority in the public sphere and the public is forced to obey his directives. In a democracy, public officials must have regard for the will and sentiment of the public they represent.

Under *velayat-e faqih*, everyone must seek the permission of the *vali-e faqih* for any decision or action in the public sphere. The situation is completely reversed in a democracy where all public officials must seek the people's consent if they wish to function in the public sphere.

- *Entesab* (Appointment)

Democracy is a bottom-up approach to government. The appointed *velayat*-based state is a top-down regime: election is the opposite of appointment.

Where a ruler is appointed, members of the public have no say in his selection or removal. In democracies, people elect and dismiss governments.

Under appointed *velayat-e faqih* the leader is appointed more or less for life; he determines the duration of all other public appointments. All political posts in a democracy are for a fixed term.

In the appointed *velayat*, the ruler is responsible only to God, not to any human agency. The elected representatives of the people are charged with holding a democratic government to account; government is accountable to the people.

- *Etlagh* (Absolutism)

Under appointed *velayat* the leader has absolute and unchecked power. In a democracy, all government officials have limited powers: there are checks and balances.

Under appointed *velayat*, the leader is not only above the law, he sanctions the law and can suspend the constitution. In a democracy, no one is above the law.

In a *velayat*-based state, the judicial, executive and legislative branches of government, together with the armed forces and media, are the instruments of the leader and operate under his orders. The separation of powers is fundamental to democracy.

- *Feghahat* (Qualification as a jurist)

Governance under *velayat-e faqih* is the exclusive right of Islamic jurists. Under democracy, the rights of one group are not favoured over those of another.

Under *velayat-e faqih*, Islamic jurisprudence provides the entire theory of government in all fields, from cradle to grave. In a democracy, society is managed on scientific principles; judges are not expected to plan the entire spectrum of political, economic, social and cultural life.

In short: to short-circuit any opposition, citizens must be trained in blind obedience to their leaders. No further proof of the incompatibility between the two systems seems necessary. However, attempts have been made to strike a balance between the two. These culminated in the theory of elected, conditional *velayat-e faqih,* propounded by the jurists of Qom and given expression in Ayatollah Hossein-Ali Montazeri Najaf-Abadi's *A Study of Velayat-e Faqih and Islamic Government.* He modifies three of the principles in the appointed, absolute *velayat-e faqih* theory and makes a significant advance on traditional Shia doctrine in the direction of democracy: all public officials, including the supreme leader, are to be elected from a list of jurists/clerics by the public, thus establishing an element of public participation; having established the public right to take part in the law-making process, the grounds for further development of constitutional democracy are laid.

Montazeri's analysis of the past twenty-odd years of *velayat-e faqih* in action led him to downplay the operational side of the doctrine in favour of its advisory and supervisory roles. Nevertheless, for a variety of reasons, this remains *velayat* by any other name, particularly in its restriction of the highest office to the clerics. It is extremely unlikely that Islamic jurisprudence is capable of producing effective solutions for the challenges of political and social management today. This exclusion also diminishes the public's role in the electoral process. Nor, finally, is there any provision for resolving major disagreement between the edicts of the supreme leader and majority public opinion. On the evidence of past events, the leadership is more likely to resort to force than bow to the public will.

So far, we have looked at all three possible systems without coming to any qualitative judgement as to which, in the end, is the best system of governance for a religious society. This is not so much a matter of deciding between the relative merits of the two formulations of *velayat-e faqih,* but of looking beyond them for an alternative.

Given that not even all Ayatollah Khomeini students subscribe to his theory of the absolute *velayat*; and that the revised version as expressed by Ayatollah Montazeri is still new, under-debated and has not, so far, been met with much enthusiasm among traditional Shia jurists, and that neither has any credible religious basis in Islamic jurisprudence for their introduction into the political sphere, we must pose the question rather differently. Have the expectations of religion, more particularly of Islamic jurisprudence, been unreasonable? Should one expect Islam to provide the complete blueprint for modern government? Does Islamic jurisprudence provide jurists with the necessary basis or insight to manage the political, social and economic complexities of today's world? And if not, what does?

From the core documents of Islam – the Quran, the life of the Prophet and the Shia imams – we learn the following:

- Islam is not limited to the individual's relation with God, it covers the range of daily life. Nor are its social edicts limited to ethical guidance and prohibitions; they also direct believers to action.

- Not all political systems are compatible with Islamic society and some are specifically forbidden. [For instance, communism or systems that are too intrusively secular and ban public displays of religious beliefs, as do France and Turkey now. Ed]

- Islam does not offer a specific and exclusive political blueprint for all societies, let alone for all time.

Religion itself is a constant, beyond place and time; if it were to take on temporal matters, it would risk damage to its essential nature. Furthermore, Islam acknowledges that human intellect and reason are capable of finding appropriate solutions to the problems of the temporal world. A pious individual must satisfy the requirements of his religion in all spheres, but religion does not negate the fact that politics is a human endeavour requiring political wisdom.

Velayat-e faqih has given rise to unreal expectations of Islamic jurisprudence. Islamic jurisprudence provides a legal framework in such branches of law as constitutional law, commercial law, civil and criminal law and the like; one should not expect it to provide detailed information on political and economic planning and management. Entrusting these and other specialised matters to lawyers would not work out for the best.

There is a difference between civil law and religious obligation. If a religious decree is to carry the force of law and punishment in the here and now, it must put on a legal suit by going through the civil law-making process.

Far from being a religious obligation, *velayat-e faqih* reflects Iranian Shia jurists' experience of monarchy and Eastern despotism. There is abundant evidence that its absolutism in the public sphere is wholly incompatible with traditional Islamic jurisprudence.

Velayat has no credible foundation in Islamic jurisprudence and its rejection does not in any way undermine any Islamic teachings, requirements or obligations. The choice between *velayat* and democracy is devoid of any religious connotation and should be made solely on the basis of reason: which system will be of greatest benefit to society? I believe democracy is the least flawed political system in the world today. Note I say 'least flawed': it is a far from perfect system but it is a product of reason. The fact that it was first practised in the West does not preclude its adoption in other cultures: reason extends beyond geographical boundaries. As Imam Ali says: 'Look into what is said, not at who says it.'

Democracy as a political system is as valid in a religious society as in a secular, or even one with a variety of religious faiths and ideological persuasions. The claim that democracy can only flourish in absolute secularism is unproved. However, the relationship between Islam and democracy, or the feasibility of a religious democracy, are outside my scope. I have assumed the advantages of democracy to be self-evident and am firmly convinced that it is possible to organise Islamic society on democratic lines. If a Muslim majority society decides to observe Islamic values and behaviour, it can incorporate these democratically: Islam as a religion can coexist alongside democracy as a modern approach to government. ❏

Mohsen Kadivar *is an Iranian cleric who was imprisoned in 1999 and spent 18 months in Tehran's Evin Prison because of statements critical of the Islamic Republic. He is currently president of the Iranian Association in Support of Freedom of the Press*

This paper was delivered at the Middle East Association of North America, Washington DC

'TELL THEM TO USE THEIR HEADS'

SHIRIN EBADI

FOR 15 YEARS, SHE HAS STOOD UP TO EVERYTHING
THE IRANIAN REGIME HAS THROWN AT HER AND
LAST YEAR, WHEN SHE WAS AWARDED THE 2003
NOBEL PEACE PRIZE AND BROUGHT IRAN ITS FIRST
EVER NOBEL, THERE WAS LITTLE REJOICING
AMONG THE HIERARCHY

JENANE KAREH TAGER *You've made a bit of a habit of 'firsts': Iran's first female judge in 1975; the first victim of the 1979 Iranian Revolution when you were dismissed from that job on the grounds of being a woman and therefore too emotional, too irrational; the first Muslim to receive a Nobel. Where do you find the strength?*

SHIRIN EBADI It's simple: I believe in God and in the path I have chosen. I was lucky to have a family that allowed my personality to blossom: I was surrounded by people who always stood up for their ideas without ever giving in or compromising. Take my father, for instance: he was close to the former prime minister Mohammed Mossadegh. In 1953, Mossadegh was overthrown in a coup instigated by the Americans and British after he had nationalised Iranian oil. For several years, my father was in a black hole. He could easily have risen again had he compromised with the CIA, which, as a result of the weakness of the young shah, held the reins of power. He always refused. I try to follow his example, to grit my teeth when pressures on me mount, to clench my fists, too, until my fingers are blue. But sometimes I hate myself and discover I am still weak.

Yet it is poignant that you always put your faith first. Even when you received the Nobel, you presented yourself as first and foremost a 'Muslim woman'. Haven't the ayatollahs succeeded in turning you off religion?

Why should they? When I talk of Islam, I mean the true Islam, not the Islam riddled with lies that they use for their own ends and that some persist in presenting as the real thing. Their religion is an ideological tool of power. Mine is that which proclaims the equality of all people, regardless of their sex or religion. And if I do stress my position as a Muslim woman, it's in the hope that, thanks to this Nobel, all Muslim women will gain confidence in themselves and learn to recognise and struggle for their rights.

Tehran 2003: Shirin Ebadi greets students at Amir Kabir University soon after the award of her Nobel Prize. Credit: AP Photo/ Vahid Salemi

True Islam? Then what is this Islam of the Islamic Revolution that is based on the texts of the hadith *[sayings of the Prophet] and above all the Quran that the ayatollahs are constantly citing?*

Let me reply by giving you a concrete example, my own. In 1979, I was no longer able to continue with my job: Islam, it seems, forbids a woman to be a judge. But after several years of struggle, you see me once again doing the job: this time, Islam permits it. These two contradictory fatwas were both promulgated by the highest Shia authorities in the name of Islam. The only logical conclusion I can come to is that the texts of our religion, as with all texts, can and should be interpreted in accordance with the needs of society and the time we live in . . .

Certain passages in the Quran that concern women are more sensitive. I'm thinking of those that claim the witness of two women is equal to that of a single man. What do you understand by this? To finesse on these verses?

No: you must read the Quran in its entirety; respect the whole. Including those passages that affirm that in certain cases and for certain things, the strict application of the letter of the law is not obligatory: exceptions are always recognised and tolerated. The Quran provides a basic law; experts interpret the rules and adapt them to new situations . . . Of one thing I'm certain: none of our societies today resembles the Arabia of 1,400 years ago for which they were designed.

In brief, you propose nothing less than the reopening of the door of ijtihad – *of interpretation?*

In Shia Islam, the door of *ijtihad* was never closed.

You are a believer, do you also practise your faith? Do you pray five times a day?

Three times a day because I am Shia. Yes, I pray, I observe Ramadan scrupulously, but I see no need to shout this from the rooftops.

So religion is a private matter for you. In which case, you could as well fight your battles in the name of secularism rather than always under the banner of Islam.

Listen: I am a Muslim as are one-sixth of the world's population; one billion people often living in Muslim countries where democracy is not on its top form. I fight in the name of this one billion believers, people who have a faith. I also fight so that they may better understand that their religion is not an enemy of democracy. So I must talk to them of religion; tell them again and again that Islam in itself is not bad.

Why do you think Islam has failed where Christianity has succeeded? That is to say: has accepted secularism and kept religion from encroaching too much on the public sphere?

It's not a matter of religious dogma. Don't forget that over the centuries Christianity encountered the same problems that face Islam today. It took the French Revolution to strip the Catholic Church of its power. This renaissance has not yet happened in Islam.

Do you think that after the election victory of the conservatives in February you will still have elbow room to carry on your struggle?

You know, there have always been conservatives in Iran and there always will be. I intend to carry on doing what I've always done because I believe in it.

Even if it means going back to prison?

I'm not afraid of that. They can do what they have to do and I'll do what I have to do. To tell the truth, I don't believe you can turn back the clock. What Iranian society has accomplished in the last few years can't be taken away. I'm talking about the social advances, about the change in mentalities, in the culture.

And on the veil too, now that Iranian women are wearing it in a far less all-concealing way?

It would be far more useful to encourage women to use their heads than tell them to cover them up. Having said that, the problem confronting Iranian women today is not whether or not to cover their heads, but all those laws that keep them in subjection and that have no relevance to today's reality. The reality is that 63 per cent of students in our universities are girls; only 37 per cent are boys. And still the word of one of these boys is worth that of two of his female colleagues! Iranian women today are studying, working and are a presence in public life.

Is this advance because of the Islamic Revolution?

Madame, Iran has 4,000 years of civilisation. Iran is a country that was ruled by emperors 2,000 years ago. Iran is not the colourful place peddled by the media. Enough of these stories! Are you aware that in Persian, unlike French or Arabic, there are no male and female pronouns, but just a single pronoun to designate both sexes? Nor do we have different words for husband and wife: *memtet* is used for both. This reflects an ancient way of thinking.

Why do you not use the name of your husband Javad Tavassolian?

Because in Iran, even if she wants to, a woman may not take the name of her husband. You find that surprising? I am a human being; I was given a name and an identity at birth; what right has my husband to force his own identity on me? Why do you want a woman to change her name simply because she has married? Why should the man not change his identity on marriage? This business of name-changing at some point in their life has no allure for Iranians.

You have reconciled a knowledge of civil law with the Muslim faith. You could become a reformer of Islam, even set up a school. What prevents you taking this step?

Certainly not the fact that I'm a woman: Grand Ayatollah Saanei, who was attorney general under Khomeini and remains one of the greatest thinkers in Shiism, has said there is nothing to prevent a woman from becoming the Supreme Guide. But I don't think I am sufficiently competent in religious matters to open the way to a new interpretation and serve as a guide to others.

You have criticised the French law banning the wearing of religious symbols at school. But this only refers to the time students spend inside the school premises . . .

My chief opposition to this is its effect on schoolgirls: it penalises them twice over. The first penalty is to have been born a girl, however involuntarily, into a fundamentalist family that forces her to wear the veil. The second is to be excluded from school and denied the benefit of the culture that is her only chance of escaping from it. In the name of fighting the fundamentalists this law is aiding and abetting them. These girls who will be denied both culture and education will be the easiest prey for the fundamentalists: having been excluded, they will get married and bear the fundamentalist of tomorrow. I tell you, this law is meat and drink to all extremists: to the fundamentalists sure, but also to the radicals of the National Front. ❑

Shirin Ebadi *was interviewed for* Le Monde des Religions *by* **Jenane Kareh Tager**

Translated by JVH

A MAN OF HIS WORD

NABEEL YASIN

IRAQ'S LEADING CLERIC GRAND
AYATOLLAH ALI AL-SISTANI IS A MAN TO
BE RECKONED WITH. IF THERE IS ANY
BROKER OF PEACE AND EVENTUAL
DEMOCRACY IN THE COUNTRY, IT IS HE

Iraq's leading Shia cleric Grand Ayatollah Sayyid Ali Husaini al-Sistani appears to play the democratic game rather better than any of country's political parties or other democratic contenders. He combines the ability to dissent with the flexibility needed to accommodate opponents, thus putting the coalition and interim government's intentions to the democratic test. Without question, he has become the key figure in the present turmoil whose opinion is sought by most parties to the conflict.

Al-Sistani has an extraordinary ability to remain silent, surrounding himself with a profound quiet. Throughout my brief meeting with him in a London hospital room in August, he was the listener. He spoke little and even then with extreme caution. He received me as a democratic secular intellectual, evidence of his conviction that Iraq's unity demands accommodation with all views and opinions that share a common purpose: the reconstruction of Iraq, democracy, sovereignty and the rule of law.

Al-Sistani seldom speaks publicly, but when he does, his words have the force of law for Iraq's 12 million or so Shia (there has been no census in Iraq since 1957), who make up 60–65 per cent of the country's population. In the immediate aftermath of Saddam's downfall, many expected a bloodbath of revenge against members of the Baath Party and the thugs of the security agencies. Al-Sistani's fatwas (edicts) and appeals were instrumental in checking personal and mass vendettas. They stress the need to abide by the rule of law and forbid individuals to take the law into their own hands. Respect for public property and the state's law-enforcement agencies are strongly in evidence. A fatwa from the early days of the coalition invasion called for the return of all looted state property to government agencies. As the latter crumbled with the regime's collapse, a further fatwa directed that all stolen items be stored in places like mosques and guarded by teams of locals until they could be returned to their respective departments.

He also forbade the seizure and use of public parks and empty plots of land for house building, and prevented squatting in government buildings or the conversion of these into dwellings. Public property is sacred and not up for grabs by individuals or groups.

He also banned the use of arms stolen from army depots, even for self-defence, stressing that they must remain state property. He called for the stolen weapons with which the country was awash to be collected, stored and overseen by locally organised committees until they could be handed over to the authorities. In the meantime, he forbade non-government outfits and groups from carrying arms or engaging in shoot-outs.

More recently, in July this year, al-Sistani spoke out on the wave of bombing attacks on places of worship belonging to other communities. Declaring such acts totally unacceptable, he called for their religious leaders to be protected and respected. He is aware of the diversity of Iraq's population and of the need to hold this complex ethnic and religious mosaic together.

He has used his influence to play for time until a legitimate, elected authority is in place to discharge its legal and constitutional functions, and is not averse to demonstrating the extent of that influence when the situation calls for it. The dispute with the US pro-consul Paul Bremer over the proposed interim constitution, for instance, was a serious stand-off in which the cleric used his ability to mobilise mass public support and exert his influence on members of the Governing Council to ensure amendments were made despite US persistence.

Meanwhile, he has consistently chosen to deal with the UN, which he regards as the embodiment of international legality, rather than the US occupation authority. Though anxious for elections at the earliest possible opportunity, he acknowledged the international body's verdict that the situation in Iraq made it impossible to hold elections before 2005. Although the outcome does not meet the cleric's demand for early elections, it demonstrates his ability to compromise and his regard for international legality rather than the US agenda in determining Iraq's future political development.

He is not averse, however, to challenging this body too. In June this year, on the eve of the transfer of sovereignty to Iraq's present caretaker government on 30 June, he advised the UN Security Council on the dangers of endorsing Iraq's interim constitution, officially known as the Transitional Administrative Law (TAL), which will govern the country until the voting of a permanent constitution by an elected national assembly. At the insistence of the Kurds, the TAL defines Iraq as a federal state, something the Security Council appeared to have overlooked in Resolution 1546, in which they endorse the forthcoming transfer of sovereignty.

> We have been informed of the attempts to include the so-called 'administrative law for the transitional period' in the new UNSC Resolution on Iraq with a view to giving it a semblance of international legitimacy.
>
> This 'law', which has been drawn up by an unelected council under occupation and under its direct influence, would restrict the national assembly, which is due to be elected early next year, from drawing up the permanent Iraqi constitution . . .
>
> Any attempt to give this 'law' an appearance of legality by including it in the Resolution is contrary to the desire of the Iraqi people and could lead to dangerous consequences.
>
> Kindly convey the position of the Marja'iyya [Iraq's religious hierarchy] in this regard to their Excellencies the honourable members of the Security Council.
>
> *Seal of the Office of Ayatollah al-Sistani in Najaf, 6 June 2004*

As al-Sistani pointed out later, any such endorsement would commit a future government to Kurdish autonomy, rather than the unitary state that is in Iraq's best interests.

In the course of our meeting, al-Sistani told me that his heart was not in the hands of the doctors who were treating him for a heart condition; it was in Iraq dwelling on the tragic events then ensuing in Najaf, seat of the highest Shia authority in the world. I pointed out that democracy was manifest in all his positions and that in his fatwas he seems at home with 400 years of democratic development in Europe. He agreed that Shia Islam is in essence a democratic ideal, especially as laid out in the charter crafted by the fourth caliph Imam Ali in the seventh century, in which he defines the legal limits of power for the man he appointed to rule Egypt.

Al-Sistani was born in 1931 in the Iranian city of Mashad, site of the tomb of the Shia's eighth imam, al-Ridha, killed by the Abbasid Caliph Mamoun, son of Haroon al-Rashid. He comes from a family of prominent clerics and jurists and studied theology at Mashad before moving to Qom in Iran in 1949. He continued his religious learning under the highly respected cleric Ayatollah Hussein al-Baroudjerdi until leaving Qom for Najaf in 1952

Kazemiya, Shia neighbourhood in Baghdad 2004: Grand Ayatollah Ali al-Sistani among the saints and heroes of Shia Islam. Credit: Rex Features

to study under such revered religious clerics as Ayatollah Mohsin al-Hakim and Ayatollah Abu Qassim al-Khoe, the senior and most influential cleric in the Shia hierarchy.

Al-Sistani was tutored by al-Khoe for 10 years, after which he took up religious research and teaching. In 1962, he started to lecture on jurisprudence, turning to teaching the fundaments of Islam three years later. According to his teachers, al-Sistani stood out among his peers for his skill in resolving controversial issues, his shrewdness, insight, keen desire for learning and extensive knowledge in various fields.

Saddam Hussein detained al-Khoe immediately after he had crushed the 1991 Shia uprising in the wake of the US expulsion of Iraq from Kuwait. Al-Sistani was one of six people who secretly buried al-Khoe under cover of darkness in 1992. He said prayers over the body and succeeded the deceased cleric as the highest religious authority for 150 million Shia worldwide.

Al-Sistani is viewed as a moderate among leading Shia clerics in Iran as well as Iraq. He is also seen as a realist, willing to adapt religious doctrine to political facts on the ground. Though he has refused contact with the occupation authority and its pro-consuls Paul Bremer and his succesor John Negroponte, despite repeated lobbying on their behalf by local figures, he has never called for violent resistance to occupation.

Al-Sistani belongs to a school of long-standing Shia tradition in Iraq and Iran that sees the role of the religious establishment as an observer of political developments; it should intervene only when strictly necessary in legal terms, and then decisively. The clergy should not be directly involved in politics any more than the religious establishment should assume a political role in state administration. He has broken ranks decisively with the Iranian clergy since Khomeini's revolution and proclamation of the *velayat-e faqih* doctrine (governance of the religious jurist) as the ultimate and irrevocable authority over all matters, unchecked by parliament and constitution (see p64). While opposed to the *velayat-e faqih* doctrine, he does believe in the clergy's duty to make sure that any Iraqi constitution will not be contrary to the overall teachings of Islam. His stand on the relationship between religion and politics is best illustrated in his reply to a question on a cleric's duties in the present circumstances: should they be involved in administrative affairs? 'Clerics may not be involved in executive and administrative matters. Their role should be confined to direction, guidance and overseeing committees set up to run civil affairs, enforce security and provide public services,' he declared.

Al-Sistani belongs to a traditional *hawza* (seminary), founded in Najaf by Imam Ali, Prophet Mohamed's cousin, which has maintained its independence of government authority for over a thousand years. The *hawza* has featured prominently in Iraq's modern history. It supported the 1920 Iraqi revolt against British occupation which led to the first national Iraqi government a year later. It called for a boycott of the 1924 constituent assembly and non-recognition of the constitution approved by that gathering. To bring the Shia clergy to heel and curb its influence, the authorities banished Shia spiritual leaders to Iran under the pretext that they were non-Iraqis. Decades later, Saddam Hussein used the same pretext to expel millions of Iraqi Shia and dump them on the Iranian border during the Iran–Iraq war.

The heavy price paid by the Shia over the 80 years of Iraq's history as an independent state has taught them a sober understanding of external factors and their impact on regional as well as domestic policy. Little wonder they showed no enthusiam in the defence of a regime that had persecuted the entire community and murdered thousands of their brethren in the 30 years of its rule.

The Saddam regime had sought to end any remaining autonomy enjoyed by the Shia clergy and eliminate its influence over the majority of Iraqis. Millions of Shiites were displaced and deported; thousands of al-Sistani's disciples were expelled. Having crushed the 1991 uprising, Saddam arrested al-Sistani with other clerics and had him tortured at Ar-Razaza camp and the notorious Al-Radwaniya prison. On his release, the Baath regime closed down the Al-Khadra mosque and prohibited the old cleric from praying there. In protest, al-Sistani never left his house until the fall of Saddam. Intelligence documents found after the regime's demise reveal that, like al-Sadr, al-Sistani was marked for assassination.

Al-Sistani combines traditional thinking with modern cultural trends, infusing scripture with a social dimension that reflects changing circumstances. He studied modern law covering Iraqi, Egyptian and French legislation. He has borrowed from modern legal theories and assented to Muslims making use of norms applied in other faiths on the basis of mutual respect. He is known for his respect of the other view, encouraging his students to engage in open debate. Al-Sistani's concern that the rule of law should reflect a humane dimension is evident in his opposition to the notion that punishment is the result of rebellion by a slave against his master. This argument is based, in his view, on the class divisions of ancient society rather than on a legal outlook based on the principle of universal human values.

Prominent clerics are normally stamped by their theological writings and work on matters of concern to Muslims in the field of hermeneutics and exegesis. Al-Sistani has written 44 books on subjects ranging from the judiciary, business contracts and jurisprudence for expatriates to new questions of haj (pilgrimage). He has written on the relative merits of independent judgement and conformism, and guidelines for the young. Much of his work centres on the juristic foundations of Islam. Keeping abreast of social development, al-Sistani has given his consent to interfaith marriage – even to a polytheist.

Al-Sistani has adroitly thwarted a serious internal crisis that faced the Shia community worldwide. Throughout its history, clerics of Iranian origin have always been powerful in the Shia religious establishment. This influence can be traced back to Ayatollah al-Na'ini and Ayatollah Abu al-Hassan al-Asfahani in the first half of the twentieth century. In the 1960s,

12 October 2004 Al-Sadr City, Baghdad: Shia militiamen from Moqtada al-Sadr's Mahdi Army hand in their weapons to Iraqi police. Credit: Sabah Arar/Rex Features

the leading cleric of the day, Mohsin al-Hakim, attempted to redress the balance by involving Iraqi Shia businessmen and merchants in the collection of donations from the faithful as the representative of the clergy.

Taking his lead from this, some years later, the leading cleric of the time, Mohammed Sadiq al-Sadr, who was murdered by Saddam in 1999, took a dramatic step by mandating tribesmen to collect religious donations in a move designed further to curtail the influence of Iranian clerics or clerics of Iranian origin.

Traditionally, Iraqi tribes were under the undisputed influence of the clerics, but by the 1940s this influence was challenged by the emergence of political parties, which slowly replaced the old social structure of clan and tribe as the new unit of loyalty and identity. Al-Sadr's plan hit two birds with one stone: he bestowed on tribesmen a religious status they had never dreamed of, thus reinforcing their attachment to the religious hierarchy; at the same time, he enlarged the religious establishment with Iraqi Arab elements, who now had the right to represent leading clerics and who replaced the Iranians. Powerful tribes followed al-Sadr Senior, a legacy bequeathed to his son Moqtada, leader of the Mahdi army, who has been flexing his military-backed political muscle in and around Najaf.

Al-Sistani has had to use the tribes' traditional loyalty to the Shia religious establishment he represents as a counterbalance to the popularity enjoyed among younger tribesmen and city slum-dwellers by Moqtada al-Sadr. The latter are mostly descendants of tribes in southern Iraq who have fled to the cities to escape Saddam's persecution.

Soon after our meeting in London, al-Sistani returned to Iraq where he used this influence to resolve the confrontation in Najaf between the US and Moqtada's fighters without sacrificing the latter or compromising the coalition forces. Amid tens of thousands of supporters, swiftly mobilised on his return, he marched into the city and entered the mosque, enabling Moqtada to slip out undetected with the crowd. Since then, Moqtada and his young men have been kept in the wings, under the restraining influence of al-Sistani; there has been no further trouble from them.

Al-Sistani's moderate stance, his juristic notion of democracy and his capacity for even-handedness will be a catalyst in building up a constitutional democratic system in a multicultural, multi-ethnic country with a Muslim majority like Iraq. He has demonstrated he can mobilise his followers for effective peaceful action at the right time rather than meaninglessly deploying them all the time. His means to get his message across are popular pressure and the available levers of democracy rather than violence and militancy.

He understands that Iraq's long-term insurance policy is a constitutional democracy committed to the rule of law. The chance Iraqis have today should not be wasted by brinkmanship or military escalation. He will have no truck with Donald Rumsfeld's partial democracy, which would exclude the minority Sunni Muslims now engaged in combat with the Coalition forces in and around the Sunni heartlands of Falluja, Samarra and Tikrit. The most serious threat of breakdown between al-Sistani and the US could come with any attempt by the occupying power to postpone beyond January 2005 the elections al-Sistani has continued to insist on. As Iraq's President Ghazi Alyawer said to another president: 'Al-Sistani is our guarantee of democracy.' ❏

Nabeel Yasin is an Iraqi poet and journalist living in London. He was the only journalist to visit al-Sistani during his visit to London earlier this year

Translated by Abdulilah Nuaimi

EUROPHILE

AFTER TWO CENTURIES OF THE SEPARATION OF CHURCH AND STATE, AND THE UNQUESTIONED SECULARISM OF MODERN EUROPE, THE EUROPEAN UNION FINDS ITSELF PLAGUED BY THE 'RELIGIOUS QUESTION'. THE MAIN ISSUES CENTRE ON THE DESIRE OF CATHOLIC POLAND TO 'RECONVERT' EUROPE, AND THE PRESENCE OF LARGE MUSLIM COMMUNITIES IN THE HEART OF EUROPE ANXIOUS TO ASSERT THEIR RELIGIOUS RIGHTS. AND THEN THERE'S TURKEY...

Sri Swaminarayan Mandir Hindu Temple, Neasden north-west London 2004. Credit: Brett Biedsch

IT'S ALL ABOUT IDENTITY, STUPID

JOSÉ CASANOVA

AFTER TWO CENTURIES OF ENLIGHTENMENT
AND THE MORE RECENT PROGRESS OF
SECULARISM, RELIGION HAS AGAIN REARED
ITS HEAD AS ONE OF THE MORE
CONTROVERSIAL ISSUES IN EUROPE

Since the signing of the Treaty of Rome in 1957 established the EEC and initiated the ongoing process of European integration, Western European societies have undergone a rapid, drastic and seemingly irreversible process of secularisation. In this respect, one can talk of the emergence of a post-Christian Europe. At the same time, the process of European integration, the eastward expansion of the European Union and the drafting of a European constitution have triggered fundamental questions concerning European identity and the role of Christianity in that identity. What constitutes 'Europe'? How and where should one draw the external territorial and the internal cultural boundaries of Europe? The most controversial and anxiety-producing issues, which are rarely confronted openly, are the potential integration of Turkey and the potential integration of non-European immigrants, who in most European countries happen to be overwhelmingly Muslim. It is the interrelation between these phenomena that I would like to explore.

The progressive, though highly uneven, secularisation of Europe is an undeniable social fact. An increasing majority of the European population has ceased to participate in traditional religious practices, at least on a regular basis, while still maintaining relatively high levels of private individual religious beliefs. In this respect, one should perhaps talk of the *unchurching* of the European population and of religious individualisation, rather than of secularisation. Grace Davie has characterised this general European situation as 'believing without belonging'. At the same time, however, large numbers of Europeans, even in the most secular countries, still identify themselves as

Poland 1991: celebrating the visit of Polish Pope John Paul II. Credit: Rex Features

88   INDEX ON CENSORSHIP 4 2004

'Christian': 'belonging without believing', as Danièle Hervieu-Léger puts it. 'Secular' and 'Christian' cultural identities are intertwined in complex and rarely verbalised modes among most Europeans.

The most interesting issue sociologically is not the fact of progressive religious decline among the European population, but the fact that this decline is interpreted through the lenses of the secularisation paradigm and is therefore accompanied by a 'secularist' self-understanding that interprets the decline as 'normal' and 'progressive', that is, as a quasi-normative consequence of being a 'modern' and 'enlightened' European. It is this 'secular' identity shared by European elites and ordinary people alike that paradoxically turns 'religion' and the barely submerged Christian European identity into a thorny and perplexing issue when it comes to delimiting the external geographic boundaries and to defining the internal cultural identity of a European Union.

Four ongoing controversial debates – the role of Catholic Poland, the incorporation of Turkey, the integration of non-European immigrants and the place of God or of the Christian heritage in the text of the new European constitution – illustrate the way in which religion has become a perplexing issue in the constitution of 'Europe'.

The fact that Catholic Poland is 're-joining Europe' at a time when Western Europe is forsaking its Christian civilisational identity has produced a perplexing situation for Catholic Poles and secular Europeans alike. Throughout the communist era, Polish Catholicism went through an extraordinary revival at the very same time that Western European societies were undergoing a drastic process of secularisation. The reintegration of Catholic Poland into secular Europe can be viewed therefore as 'a difficult challenge' and/or as 'a great apostolic assignment'. Anticipating the threat of secularisation, the integralist sectors of Polish Catholicism have adopted a negative attitude towards European integration. Exhorted by the Polish Pope, the leadership of the Polish Church, by contrast, has embraced European integration as a great apostolic assignment.

The anxieties of the 'Europhobes' would seem to be fully justified since the basic premise of the secularisation paradigm, that the more modern a society the more secular it becomes, seems to be a widespread assumption also in Poland. The Polish episcopate, nevertheless, has accepted enthusiastically the papal apostolic assignment and has repeatedly stressed that one of its goals once Poland rejoins Europe is 'to restore Europe for Christianity'. While it may sound preposterous to Western European ears, such a message has found resonance in the tradition of Polish messianism. Barring a radical change in the European secular zeitgeist, however, such an evangelistic effort has little chance of success. Given the loss of demand for religion in Western Europe, the supply of surplus Polish pastoral resources for a Europe-wide evangelising effort is unlikely to prove effective. The at best lukewarm, if not outright hostile, European response to Pope John Paul II's renewed calls for a European Christian revival points to the difficulty of the assignment.

While the threat of a Polish Christian crusade awakens little fear among secular Europeans confident of their ability to assimilate Catholic Poland on their own terms, the prospect of Turkey joining the European Union generates much greater anxieties among Europeans, Christian and post-Christian alike, but of a kind not easily put into words – at least not publicly. Turkey has been patiently knocking on the door of the European club since 1959, only to be told politely to keep waiting, while watching latecomer after latecomer being invited first in successive waves of accession.

The EEC always made clear that candidates for admission would have to meet stringent economic and political conditions. Ireland, the United Kingdom and Denmark formally applied for admission in 1961 but only joined in 1973. Spain and Portugal were unambiguously rebuffed as long as they had authoritarian regimes, but were given clear conditions and definite timetables once their democracies seemed on the road to consolidation. Both joined in 1986. Greece, meanwhile, had already gained admission in 1981 and with it de facto veto power over Turkey's admission. But even after Greece and Turkey entered a quasi-détente and Greece expressed its readiness to sponsor Turkey's admission in exchange for the admission of the entire island of Cyprus, Turkey still did not receive an unambiguous answer, being told once again to go back to the end of the waiting line.

The fall of the Berlin Wall once again rearranged the priorities and the direction of European integration eastward. In 2004, 10 new members – eight ex-communist countries plus Malta and Cyprus – joined the European Union. Practically all the territories of medieval Christendom – that is, of Catholic and Protestant Europe – are now reunited in the new Europe. Only Catholic Croatia and 'neutral' Switzerland are left out, while Orthodox Greece as well as Greek Cyprus are the only religious 'other'. Orthodox Romania and Bulgaria are supposed to be next in line, but without a clear timetable. Now, finally, in October this year, Turkey has been given the go-ahead for negotiations promised for 2005. There is still no timetable, but the prospect of Turkish membership has again unleashed the familiar rhetoric from the rest of Europe.

The first open discussions of Turkey's candidacy during the 2002 Copenhagen summit touched a raw nerve among all kinds of European publics. The widespread debate revealed how much Islam, with all its distorted representations as the 'other' of Western civilisation, was the real issue rather than the extent to which Turkey was ready to meet the same stringent economic and political conditions as all other new members. About Turkey's eagerness to join and willingness to meet the conditions there could be no doubt now that the new, officially no longer 'Islamic' but 'Muslim Democrat', government had reiterated unambiguously the position of all the previous Turkish secularist administrations. Turkey's publics, secularist and Muslim alike, had spoken in unison. The new government was certainly the most representative democratic government in Turkey's modern history. A wide consensus had seemingly been reached among the Turkish population, showing that Turkey, on the issue of joining Europe and thus 'the West', was no longer a 'torn country'.

The dream of Kemal Atatürk, 'Father of the Turks', of begetting a modern Western secular republican Turkish nation state modelled after French republican *laïcité* has proved not easily attainable, at least not on Kemalist secularist terms. But the possibility of a Turkish democratic state, truly representative of its ordinary Muslim population, joining the European Union is today for the first time real. The 'six arrows' of Kemalism (republicanism, nationalism, secularism, statism, populism and reformism) could not lead towards a workable representative democracy. Ultimately, the project of constructing such a nation state from above was bound to fail because it was too secular for the Islamists, too Sunni for the Alevis and too Turkish for the Kurds. A Turkish state in which the collective identities and interests of those groups that constitute the overwhelming majority of the population cannot find public representation cannot possibly be a truly representative democracy, even if it is founded on modern secular republican principles. But Muslim Democracy is as possible and viable today in Turkey as Christian Democracy was half a century ago in Western Europe. The still Muslim, but officially no longer Islamist, party in power has been repeatedly accused of being 'fundamentalist' and of undermining the sacred secularist principles of the Kemalist constitution which bans 'religious' as well as 'ethnic' parties, religion and ethnicity being forms of identity that are not allowed public representation in secular Turkey.

Illustration from the Library of the Crusades *(Gustave Doré 1877): an earlier phase of the Christian–Muslim heritage in Europe. Credit: Ken Welsh / Bridgeman*

One wonders whether democracy does not become an impossible game when potential majorities are not allowed to win elections, and when secular civilian politicians ask the military to come to the rescue of democracy by banning these potential majorities which threaten their secular identity and their power. Practically every continental European country has had religious parties at one time or another. Many of them, particularly the Catholic ones, had dubious democratic credentials until the negative learning experience of fascism turned them into Christian Democratic parties. Unless people are allowed to play the game fairly, it may be difficult for them to appreciate the rules and to acquire a democratic habitus. One wonders who are the real 'fundamentalists' here: Muslims who want to gain public recognition of their identity and demand the right to mobilise in order to advance their ideal and material interests, while respecting the democratic rules of the game; or 'secularists' who view the Muslim veil worn by a duly elected parliamentary representative as a threat to Turkish democracy and as a blasphemous affront against the sacred secularist principles of the Kemalist state? Could the European Union accept the public representation of Islam within its boundaries? Can 'secular' Europe admit 'Muslim' democratic Turkey? Officially, Europe's refusal to accept Turkey so far is mainly based on Turkey's deficient human rights record. But there are not too subtle indications that an outwardly secular Europe is still too Christian when it comes to the possibility of imagining a Muslim country as part of the European community. One wonders whether Turkey represents a threat to Western civilisation or rather an unwelcome reminder of the barely submerged yet inexpressible and anxiety-ridden white European Christian identity.

The widespread public debate in Europe over Turkey's admission showed that Europe was actually the torn country, deeply divided over its cultural identity, unable to answer the question whether European unity, and therefore its external and internal boundaries, should be defined by the common heritage of Christianity and Western civilisation or by its modern secular values of liberalism, universal human rights, political democracy and tolerant and inclusive multiculturalism. Publicly, of course, European liberal secular elites could not share the Pope's definition of European civilisation as essentially Christian. But they also could not verbalise the unspoken cultural requirements that make the integration of Turkey into Europe such a difficult issue. The spectre of millions of Turkish citizens already in Europe but not of Europe, many of them second-generation immigrants, caught between an old country they have left behind and their European host societies unable or unwilling fully to assimilate them, only makes the problem more visible. Guest workers can be successfully incorporated economically. They may even gain voting rights, at least on the local level, and prove to be model or at least ordinary citizens. But can they pass the unwritten rules of cultural European membership or are they to remain strangers? Can the European Union open new conditions for the kind of multiculturalism that its constituent national societies find so difficult to accept?

Throughout the modern era, Western European societies have been immigrant-sending countries, indeed the primary immigrant-sending region in the world. During the colonial phase, European colonists and colonisers, missionaries, entrepreneurs and colonial administrators settled all the corners of the globe. During the age of industrialisation, from the 1800s to the 1920s, it is estimated that c85 million Europeans emigrated to the Americas, to Southern Africa, to Australia and Oceania, 60 per cent of them to the US alone. In the last decades, however, the migration flows have reversed and many Western European societies have become instead centres of global immigration. A comparison with the United States, the paradigmatic immigrant society (despite the fact that from the late 1920s to the late 1960s it also became a society relatively closed to immigration), reveals some characteristic differences in the contemporary Western European experience of immigration.

Although the proportion of foreign immigrants in many European countries (United Kingdom, France, The Netherlands, West Germany before reunification), at approximately 10 per cent, is similar to the proportion of foreign-born in the US, most of these countries still have difficulty viewing themselves as permanent immigrant societies or viewing the native second-generation as nationals, irrespective of their legal status. But it is in the different ways in which they try to accommodate and regulate immigrant religions, particularly Islam, that European societies distinguish themselves not only from the US but also from one another. European societies have markedly different institutional and legal structures regarding religious associations, very diverse policies of state recognition, of state regulation and of state aid to religious groups, as well as diverse norms concerning when and where one may publicly express religious beliefs and practices.

In their dealings with immigrant religions European countries, like the US, tend to replicate their particular model of separation of church and state and the patterns of regulation of their own religious minorities. France's *étatist* secularist model and the political culture of *laïcité* require the strict privatisation of religion, eliminating religion from any public forum, while at the same time pressuring religious groups to organise themselves into a single centralised church-like institutional structure that can be regulated by and serve as interlocutor to the state. This follows the traditional model of the concordat with the Catholic Church. The UK, by contrast, while maintaining the established Church of England, allows greater freedom of religious associations, which deal directly with local authorities and school boards to press for changes in religious education, diet, etc, with little direct appeal to the central government. Germany, following the multi-establishment model, has tried to organise a quasi-official Islamic institution, at times in conjunction with parallel strivings on the part of the Turkish state to regulate its diaspora. But the internal divisions among immigrants from Turkey and the public expression and mobilisation of competing identities (secular and Muslim, Alevi and Kurd) in the German democratic context have undermined any project of institutionalisation from above. The Netherlands, following its traditional pattern of pillarisation seemed, until very recently at least, bent on establishing a state-regulated but self-organised separate Muslim pillar. Lately, however, even the liberal, tolerant Netherlands is expressing second thoughts and seems ready to pass more restrictive legislation setting clear limits to the kinds of un-European, un-modern norms and habits it is ready to tolerate.

If one looks at the European Union as a whole, however, there are two fundamental differences from the situation in the US. In the first place, in Europe immigration and Islam are almost synonymous. The overwhelming majority of immigrants in most European countries, the UK being the main exception, are Muslims and the overwhelming majority of Western European Muslims are immigrants. This identification appears even more pronounced in those cases where the majority of Muslim immigrants tend to come predominantly from a single region of origin: Turkey in the case of Germany, the Maghrib in the case of France. This entails a superimposition of different dimensions of 'otherness' that exacerbates issues of boundaries, accommodation and incorporation. The immigrant, the religious, the racial, and the socio-economic disprivileged 'other' all tend to coincide.

In the US, by contrast, Muslims constitute at most 10 per cent of all new immigrants, a figure that is actually likely to decrease given the strict restrictions to Arab and Muslim immigration imposed after 9/11 by the increasingly repressive US security state. Of the estimated 2.8–8 million Muslims in the US, 30–42 per cent are African-American converts to Islam, making more difficult the characterisation of Islam as a foreign, un-American religion. In addition, the Muslim immigrant communities there are extremely diverse in terms of geographic region of origin, discursive Islamic traditions and socio-economic characteristics.

The second main difference has to do with the role of religion and religious group identities in public life and in the organisation of civil society. Internal differences notwithstanding, Western European societies are deeply secular societies, shaped by the hegemonic knowledge regime of secularism. As liberal democratic societies, they tolerate and respect individual religious freedom. But due to the pressure towards the privatisation of religion, which among European societies has become a given characteristic of the self-definition of a modern secular society, those societies have much greater difficulty in recognising some legitimate role for religion in public life and in the organisation and mobilisation of collective group identities. Muslim-organised collective identities and their public representations become a source of anxiety not only because of their religious otherness as a non-Christian and non-European religion, but more importantly because of their religiousness itself as the 'other' of European secularity. In this context, the temptation to identify Islam and fundamentalism becomes the more pronounced. Islam, by definition, becomes the 'other' of Western secular modernity. Therefore, the problems posed by the incorporation of Muslim immigrants become consciously or unconsciously associated with seemingly related and vexatious issues concerning the role of religion in the public sphere, which European societies assumed they had already solved according to the liberal secular norm of privatisation of religion.

By contrast, Americans are demonstrably more religious than Europeans and therefore there is a certain pressure for immigrants to conform to US religious norms. It is generally the case that immigrants in the US tend to be more religious than they were in their home countries. But even more significantly, today as in the past, religion and public religious denominational identities play an important role in the process of incorporation of the new immigrants.

But US society is entering a new phase. The traditional model of assimilation, turning European nationals into American 'ethnics', can no longer serve as a model of assimilation now that immigration is literally worldwide. The US is bound to become 'the first new global society' made up of all world religions and civilisations at a time when religious civilisational identities are regaining prominence at the global stage.

At the institutional level, expanding religious pluralism is facilitated by the dual clause of the First Amendment. This guarantees the 'non establishment' of religion at the state level, and therefore the strict separation of church and state, and the genuine neutrality of the secular state, as well as the 'free exercise' of religion in civil society, which includes strict restrictions to state intervention and to the administrative regulation of the religious field. It is this combination of a rigidly secular state and the constitutionally protected free exercise of religion in society that distinguishes the US institutional context from the European one.

As liberal democratic systems, all European societies respect the private exercise of religion, including Islam, as an individual human right. It is the public and collective free exercise of Islam as an immigrant religion that most European societies find difficult to tolerate precisely on the grounds that Islam is perceived as an 'un-European' religion. The stated rationales for considering Islam un-European vary significantly across Europe and among social and political groups. For the anti-immigrant, xenophobic, nationalist right, represented by Le Pen's discourse in France and by Jörg Haider in Austria, the message is straightforward. Islam is unwelcome and unassimilable simply because it is a 'foreign' immigrant religion. Such a nativist and usually racist attitude can be differentiated clearly from the conservative Catholic position, paradigmatically expressed by the Cardinal of Bologna when he declared that Italy should welcome immigrants of all races and regions of the world, but should particularly select Catholic immigrants in order to preserve the Catholic identity of the country.

Liberal secular Europeans tend to look askance at such blatant expressions of racist bigotry and religious intolerance. But when it comes to Islam, secular Europeans often reveal the limits and prejudices of modern secularist toleration. One is not likely to hear among liberal politicians and secular intellectuals explicitly xenophobic or anti-religious statements. The politically correct formulation tends to run along such lines as 'we welcome each and all immigrants irrespective of race or religion as long as they are willing to respect and accept our modern liberal secular European norms'. The explicit articulation of those norms may vary from country to country. The

'One veil = One voice' Paris January 2004: French Muslim women from schools and government offices march against the law banning the Islamic headscarf.
Credit: Abbas / Magnum

controversies over the Muslim veil in so many European societies and the overwhelming support among the French citizenry, including apparently among a majority of French Muslims, for the recently passed restrictive legislation prohibiting the wearing of Muslim veils and other ostensibly religious symbols in public schools, as 'a threat to national cohesion', may be an extreme example of illiberal secularism (see p117). But in fact one sees similar trends of restrictive legislation directed at immigrant Muslims in the liberal Netherlands, precisely in the name of protecting its liberal, tolerant traditions from the threat of illiberal, fundamentalist, patriarchal customs reproduced and transmitted to the younger generation by Muslim immigrants.

Revealingly enough, Prime Minister Jean-Pierre Raffarin, in his address to the French legislature defending the banning of ostensibly religious symbols in public schools, made reference in the same breath to France as 'the old land of Christianity' and to the inviolable principle of *laïcité*, exhorting Islam to adapt itself to the principle of secularism as all other religions of France have done before. 'For the most recently arrived, I'm speaking here of Islam, secularism is a chance, the chance to be a religion of France.' The Islamic veil and other religious signs are justifiably banned from public schools, he added, because 'they are taking on a political meaning', while according to the secularist principle of privatisation of religion, 'religion cannot be a political project'. Time will tell whether the restrictive legislation will have the intended effect of stopping the spread of 'radical Islam' or whether it is likely to bring forth the opposite result of radicalising further an already alienated and maladjusted immigrant community.

The positive rationale one hears among liberals in support of such illiberal restriction of the free exercise of religion is usually put in terms of the desirable enforced emancipation of young girls, if necessary against their expressed will, from gender discrimination and from patriarchal control. This was the discourse on which the assassinated politician Pim Fortuyn built his electorally successful anti-immigrant platform in the liberal Netherlands, a campaign that is now bearing fruit in new restrictive legislation. While conservative religious people are expected to tolerate behaviour they may consider morally abhorrent, such as homosexuality, liberal secular Europeans are openly stating that European societies ought not to tolerate religious behaviour or cultural customs that are morally abhorrent in so far as they are contrary to modern, liberal, secular European norms. What makes the intolerant tyranny of the secular liberal majority justifiable in principle is not just the democratic principle of majority rule, but rather the secularist teleological assumption built into theories of modernisation that one set of norms is reactionary, fundamentalist and anti-modern, while the other set is progressive, liberal and modern.

Strictly speaking, modern constitutions do not need transcendent references, nor is there much empirical evidence for the functionalist argument that the standard integration of modern differentiated societies requires some kind of 'civil religion'. In principle, there are three possible ways of addressing the quarrels provoked by the wording of the preamble to the new European constitution. The first option would be to avoid any controversy by relinquishing altogether the very project of drafting a self-defining preamble explaining to the world the political rationale and identity of the European Union. But such an option would be self-defeating in so far as the main rationale and purpose of drafting a new European constitution appears to be an extra-legal one: namely, to contribute to European social integration, to enhance a common European identity and to remedy the democratic deficit.

A second alternative would be the mere enumeration of the basic common values that constitute the European 'overlapping consensus', either as self-evident truths or as a social fact, without entering into the more controversial attempt to establish the normative foundation or to trace the genealogy of those European values. This was the option chosen by the signatories of the Declaration of American Independence when they proclaimed *We Hold These Truths As Self-Evident*. But the strong rhetorical effect of this memorable phrase was predicated on the given belief in a Creator God who had endowed humans with inalienable rights, a belief shared by republican deists, Establishmentarian Protestants and radical-pietist sectarians alike. In our post-Christian and post-modern context it is not that simple to conjure such self-evident 'truths' that require no discursive grounding.

The final and more responsible option would be to face the difficult and polemical task of defining through open and public debate the political identity of the new European Union: Who are we? Where do we come from? What constitutes our spiritual and moral heritage and the boundaries of our collective identities? How flexible internally and how open externally should those boundaries be? This would be under any circumstance an enormously complex task which would entail addressing and coming to terms with the many problematic and contradictory aspects of the European heritage in its intra-national, inter-European and global-colonial dimensions. But such a complex task is made the more difficult by secularist prejudices that preclude not only a critical yet honest and reflexive assessment of the Judaeo-Christian heritage, but even any public official reference to such a heritage, on the grounds that any reference to religion could be divisive and counterproductive, or simply violates secular postulates.

The purpose of my argument is not to imply that the new European constitution ought to make some reference either to some transcendent reality or to the Christian heritage, but simply to point out that the quarrels provoked by the possible incorporation of some religious referent in the constitutional text would seem to indicate that secularist assumptions turn religion into a problem, and thus preclude the possibility of dealing with religious issues in a pragmatic sensible manner.

First, I fully agree with Bronislaw Geremek that any genealogical reconstruction of the idea or social imaginary of Europe that makes reference to Graeco-Roman antiquity and the Enlightenment while erasing any memory of the role of medieval Christendom in the very constitution of Europe as a civilisation evinces either historical ignorance or repressive amnesia.

Second, the inability to recognise Christianity openly as one of the constitutive components of European cultural and political identity means that a great historical opportunity may be missed to add yet a third important historical reconciliation to the already achieved reconciliation between Protestant and Catholics and between warring European nation states: an end to the old battles over Enlightenment, religion and secularism. The perceived threat to secular identities and the biased overreaction to exclude any public reference to Christianity belies the self-serving secularist claims that only secular neutrality can guarantee individual freedoms and cultural pluralism. What the imposed silence signifies is not only the attempt to erase Christianity or any other religion from the public collective memory, but also the exclusion from the public sphere of a central component of the personal identity of many Europeans. To guarantee equal access to the European public sphere and undistorted communication, the European Union would need to become not only post-Christian but also post-secular.

Finally, the privileging of European secular identities and secularist self-understandings in the genealogical affirmation of the common European values of human dignity, equality, freedom and solidarity may not only impede the possibility of gaining a full understanding of the genesis of those values and their complex process of societal institutionalisation and individual internalisation, but also preclude a critical and reflexive self-understanding of those secular identities. David Martin and Danièle Hervieu-Léger have shown that the religious and the secular are inextricably linked throughout modern European history; that the different versions of the European Enlightenment are inextricably linked with different versions of Christianity; and that cultural matrices rooted in particular religious traditions and related institutional arrangements still serve to shape and encode, mostly unconsciously, diverse European secular practices. The conscious and reflexive recognition of such a Christian encoding does not mean that one needs to accept the claims of the Pope or of any other ecclesiastical authority to be the sole guardians or legitimate administrators of the European Christian heritage. It only means to accept the right of every European, native and immigrant, to participate in the ongoing task of definition, renovation and transmission of that heritage. Ironically, as the case of French *laïcité*ism shows, the more secularist self-understandings attempt to repress this religious heritage from the collective conscience, the more it reproduces itself subconsciously and compulsively in public secular codes.

The four issues analysed here – the integration of Catholic Poland in post-Christian Europe, the integration of Turkey into the European Union, the incorporation of non-European immigrants as full members of their European host societies and of the European Union, and the task of writing a new European constitution that both reflects the values of the European people and at the same time allows them to become a self-constituent European demos – are all problematic issues in themselves. But unreflexive secular identities and secularist self-understandings turn those issues into even more perplexing and seemingly intractable 'religious' problems. ❏

José Casanova teaches sociology at New School University, New York. He is the author of Public Religions in the Modern World *(1994) and* The Opus Dei and the Modernisation of Spain *(forthcoming)*

This text emerged from an independent working group named by European Commission President Romano Prodi and chaired by the Rector of Vienna's Institute for Human Sciences, Krsysstof Michalski, and was first published in Transit – Europäische Revue 27 (2004)

LOOKING FOR GOD IN LONDON

All over London, religious buildings are springing up in the most unlikely places. From the heart of the West End to the suburban neighbourhoods, a new place of worship or religious community centre can be spotted as often as a new 'ethnic' restaurant.

They may be grand statements costing hundreds of thousands of pounds and widely publicised in the national media, as was the case with the Hindu

Mandir in Neasden and the earlier Regent's Park mosque. Often they are small affairs, functional or perhaps quietly elegant under the roofs of private homes, as in the case of the Shogyoji Buddhist Temple in Acton, or, as many Jewish communities have done in building their synagogues, in a domestic setting.

For many of these places of worship, the congregation precedes any building activity and the place of worship itself may not be central to the rituals practised within its walls – more a place in which the community can gather socially. But for others, the building is central to the worship, an important and vital statement of the faith.

The buildings represented here are very different from one another – small, understated spaces crowded between shops and office buildings and smattered with the unlovely graffiti that characterises the modern city; or large, recently expanded places on suburban thorough-fares without a soul in sight.

What is evident is that buildings for religious purposes, however modest, are continuing to be built, restored, revamped, or shaped into something new and grander from their more modest origins. It's clear, too, that the old need for faith and community – and increasingly a newer need to claim an identity and make it visible to the community at large – has not been affected by the apparent anonymity of urban life. On the contrary, in the UK, and not only in London, it has been a spur to building, particularly over the past decade or so.

All photographs by Brett Biedscheid 2004

Above: Regent's Park Mosque, central London
Opposite: Romford Road and Upton Lane crossroads, Forest Gate, east London

Ramgarhia Sikh
Gurudwara (Temple)
NEWHAM
Rights
Centre
Radha Krishna
Temple
Namdhari Sangat
(U.K. GURDWARA)

Left: sculpture at the International Pentecostal City Mission Church Inc, Scrubs Lane, north-west London

Below: the International Pentecostal City Mission Church

Opposite: Suleymaniye Mosque, Kingsland Road, north-east London

Above: Evangelical Brotherhood Church, north London

Left: Nanak Community Centre and Gurdwara (Sikh), Croydon, south London

Above: Three Wheels Shin Buddhist House, a branch of the Shogyoji Temple, Japan, west London

Right: synagogue, Pinner, north-west London

ISLAM IN EUROPE
NILÜFER GÖLE

CAN WE IMAGINE A EUROPE THAT ENABLES
US TO DEVELOP A COMMON CITIZENSHIP
DRAWN FROM SECULAR LIBERAL
PLURALISM AS WELL AS FROM THE
VARIETIES OF RELIGIOUS EXPERIENCE?

When we refer to the role of religion in European integration and to Islam in particular, we usually think of it in negative terms, as a hindrance to European integration. A person with a Turkish background, however, would be inclined to tackle this issue in a different and specific way. Since the foundation of the Turkish Republic in 1923, Turkish modernists have been uncompromisingly secular and still are. In consequence, European integration or Europeanness means the final accomplishment of a secular project for those Turks who embrace European values of modernity. From this particular historical and cultural perspective, it is puzzling to think of European citizenship as integration through religion. At the same time, however, it is a challenge to rethink the role of religion in the construction of Europeanness not only from the dominant perspective of the Christian heritage, but also in relation to the Islamic presence.

The presence of Islam through migration in European countries, and also through Turkey's candidacy for the European Union, addresses new issues of difference and tolerance in Western democracies. The discussions on Turkey's candidature during the Copenhagen summit of 2002 illustrated only too well the importance of Islam in European public debate. The question whether European unity should be defined by a common heritage of Christian religion and Western civilisation or in reference to political values, multiculturalism and democratic inclusiveness divided European public opinion. As Turkey moved closer to Europe, public apprehensions surrounding Islam became explicit, as did the need to define and maintain the frontiers of Europe.

If we leave Islam aside for a moment and think of the role of religion in the contemporary modern world, and whether religion can provide us with common values to define European citizenship, one conceptual problem we face is that we no longer can define religion through its institutional repre-

Samsun, Turkey: women shopping in this Black Sea port. Credit: Ian Berry / Magnum

sentations. As others have observed, we are witnessing a process of de-institutionalisation of religion. It is not religion that has disappeared from modern life, but its institutional forms of representation. Religion in the modern world has become a much more personal and spiritual experience. But this does not mean it is limited to the private sphere. People can have religious experience personally and yet belong to a collective group or to collective movements. While religious experience becomes part of 'expressive individualism' – that is, it becomes important to find one's own way as against a model imposed from outside, such as society, the previous generation, religious authority – this will not necessarily mean that the content will be individuating; on the contrary, many will join powerful religious communities.

Yet when we refer to religion in relation to the European project, we usually refer to a past heritage of Christianity rather than the religious practices and values of today.

The process of the deinstitutionalising of religious experience is also valid for Islam. Islam, which has been a binding force among those who belonged to a locality, to a particular confession and to a nation state, has become a point of reference for an imaginary bond between those Muslims who are socially uprooted. In this respect, contemporary Islamism shares some common themes with other modern forms of religious experience because it represents socially disembedded forms of religiosity and becomes a matter of personal choice. Rather than being a descendant of given religious structures, authorities, national and confessional allegiances, the experience of Islam today works as an imaginary horizontal social bonding for Muslim actors in different contexts acting together and simultaneously. Islamism refers to the modern production, elaboration and diffusion of this bonding in spite of the historical distinctions between spiritual Sufi and shariat Islam; Shia and Sunnite Islam; conservative Saudia Arabia and revolutionary Iran.

The contemporary politicisation of Islam engendered a displacement of the authority of the religious classes (ulema) and made way for a democratic opening of the interpretation of religious texts to a public at large that included political militants, Islamic intellectuals and also women. On the other hand, it brought about a vulgarisation of religious knowledge and sources that is used, and more often abused and taken out of context, in the interests of the political ideology of Islamism. Radical Islamism does not subscribe to the traditional interpretations of religion; Islamist discourse is simplistic, anachronistic and cut off from the referential context of the Quran. Activism and terrorism provide, or rather impose, a new source of legitimacy for the Islamic idiom. Who will decide what is licit and illicit in Islam? Who has the authority over the interpretation of religious texts? Who can proclaim a fatwa or declare jihad? These questions become problematic as Islam is detraditionalised in the hands of the Islamists in particular, and in the face of the modern secular world in general.

Islam today is constructed, reinterpreted and carried into public life through political instrumentality and cultural movements, not through religious institutions. But at the same time, the presence of Islam is increasing in public life and in the shaping of the social imagery and daily practices of Muslims. We are observing personal and collective appropriation of Islam.

Even though this does not take place on an institutional, purely political or revolutionary level, we can observe growing claims for its public visibility in Europe and elsewhere.

Being a Muslim and being an Islamist is not the same thing. What we are witnessing is a shift from a Muslim identity to an Islamist identity. The new phenomena connected with Islamism cannot be derived from confessional or national schools of Islam. Contemporary forms of political Islam centre on an affirmative reconstruction of identity, a collective social imaginary. The assertion of a religious self is being carried from the private to the public realm, personally and collectively, in a form of conflictual engagement with Western and secular values of modernity. There is a sociological paradox behind the phenomenon of Islamism. It is not distance from but, on the contrary, familiarity with and proximity to modern forms of life, education and politics that trigger a return to religious identity and its political expressions. Radicalism is mostly a feature of those groups which by their experience of mobility and displacement became acquainted with secular and Western ways of political thinking and urban living through experience in public places such as schools, organisations, the urban habitat and the media. Yet Muslim actors do not conform to the national and secular rules of public spaces; they fulfil and openly claim their religious identity and habits in public.

Islam provides a framework for the orientation of their identity and is a source of orientation and distinction to represent and to achieve a higher form of life. But for that purpose, the radicals would claim, religion needs to be liberated from its traditionally subservient, passive and docile posture in the face of modern power. Religion provides an autonomous, alternative space for the collective self-definition of Muslims in their critical encounter with modernity.

The visibility of religious symbols and performances informs the public of the radical transformation that is taking place: from concealment of Muslimness and its cultural attributes to collective and public disclosure of Islam. By wearing a veil and a beard, by claiming the right to places for prayer and the hours to worship in the workplace, specific food regimes and so on, people become overtly identifiable as Muslims and publicly assertive. They also convey that they are more zealous and meticulous in their religious observance than those who confine their religiosity to the private sphere.

Veiling is usually taken as a sign of the debasement of women's identity, as a sign of their inferiority to men. This sign of passivity and seclusion is now being readopted by those Muslim women who are no longer confined to a traditional role and to an enclosed space. Veiling is both a personal and collective expression of Islamic religiosity. It is personally carried as a bodily sign, but also imagined as a source of collective empowerment and horizontal bondage among those who distinguish themselves as Muslims, more precisely as Islamists. They turn the veiling, an attribute for potential public discredit, into an advantage and change its meaning as they carry it into new, modern spaces. From a symbol of stigma it is reversed into a positive identity affirmation – such as 'black is beautiful' – endowing Muslimness with a higher sense of self; a historical sense of loss of dignity and humiliation is turned into a search for distinction, prestige and power, as exemplified by the Iranian revolution.

The case of young Muslim women in Europe illustrates the ongoing transformation of the symbol meanings of the headscarf. Young migrant girls who adopt the Islamic headscarf in French and German schools are closer in many respects – youth culture, fashion consciousness and language – to their classmates than to their first-generation, home-bound, uneducated mothers. As they adopt, improvise and negotiate the headscarf in the public sphere they are also, albeit unintentionally, altering the symbol of the headscarf and images of Muslim women. These new European Muslims have a double belonging, a double cultural capital. On the one hand they define themselves through their religiosity, on the other they have learned techniques of self-representation in public spaces and gained universal, secular knowledge. Because they have a double cultural capital they can circulate between different activities and spaces such as home, class, youth associations and urban leisure space.

The Islamic presence in public challenges the strict separation between private religion and public secularism. Religion is carried into public life and the profane and sacred realms are intermingled. The regulations governing public spaces become controversial: schools, universities, workplaces and parliament, but also public gardens, cemeteries and beaches become battlegrounds when Muslims invest them and claim religious rules in conformity with Islam.

The political problem we face is the public visibility of religion. We can no longer speak of the public sphere as a pre-established, immutable arena. The inclusion of new social groups necessitates a redefinition of its frontiers and its values. Newcomers reveal the limits of the public sphere as it was constituted and imagined by society and its legislators at a particular time.

Café des Jeunes, Sultan Ahmet Square, Istanbul Turkey: American waffles and a hookah.
Credit: Sipa Press / Rex Features

The headscarf debate in France, for instance, provoked a huge public debate on the school system itself as well as on French secularism, that *laïcité* considered to be a French exception. Protagonists who argued that all religious signs should be banned reminded us of the historical legacy of *laïcité* and the principle of neutrality in the public school system. However, the French government's decision to set up a new French Council for the Muslim Religion had already resulted in a change in the relationship between the French state and Islam. An Islamic religious organisation means the public recognition of the Islamic presence in France and political acknowledgement of Islam as independent from the problem of immigration. It also means a space for religion in the public sphere as well as the space specifically created through a state initiative. Secular concepts and the frontiers of the French public sphere are a subject of public controversy, but the terms of the debate were national and with an emphasis on French exceptionalism rather than with an eye to the future orientation of Europe.

When it comes to discussing these things in relation to Europe, the question is: are we going to handle this issue through a kind of 'didactic democracy', one taught through legislation, a kind of authoritarian intervention in which, for instance, you forbid the veil? (Ironically, this reminds me of Turkish secularism. Historically, this was adopted from French *laïcité*; today, Turkish forms of state control of religion turn out to be a model of reference.) Or do we have other ways of thinking about democracy as a way of inventing new forms of commonality? The definition of a new commonality demands that we reconsider the nature of the public space on a European scale. So far, the public space has been defined by the nation state and by institutionally defined religions; borders were imposed by the very state and religious institutions that Europe is now trying to override. Yet we still take this national public space for granted. Can we open it up? Redefine it as European public space? Not only through means of legislation, but also as an imagined space of shared common values. Conceiving a European public space and a European citizenship could help us to go beyond the national scale and the confrontational definitions of civilisations to focus on daily life experiences and interactions. Why not imagine a European public space as an ethical and physical frame that enables us to develop a common citizenship drawn from liberal pluralism as well as the plurality of religious experience? ❏

Nilüfer Göle is Directeur d'Études at the École des Hautes Études en Science Sociales in Paris

This text emerged from an independent working group named by European Commission President Romano Prodi and chaired by the Rector of Vienna's Institute for Human Sciences, Krzysztof Michalski. The group is charged with identifying the long-term spiritual and cultural perspectives of the enlarged Europe © Author/Institute for Human Sciences

COVER UP
ALMA & LILA LEVY

The Levy sisters Alma and Lila, 16 and 18 respectively and both French Muslims, were excluded from the Lycée Henri-Wallon in Aubervilliers in October 2003 for refusing to take off their headscarves in class. In the following excerpts from their book, published earlier this year by Éditions La Découverte but not yet translated, they talk about the situation and explain their decision. At the time, the French government's decision to ban the headscarf in public places initiated a massive national debate that split families and communities. The majority of French Muslims do not claim the right to wear the headscarf and look on those who do with indifference if not outright hostility. While many favour the new law outlawing it in school, the views of official bodies representing French Muslims remain ambiguous and divided. The contradictions dividing society are reflected within the Levy family: the girls' father is a Jewish lawyer 'without a God'; their mother, a Berber from North Africa, was brought up a Catholic but is now an atheist.

The authorities were expecting trouble in September this year at the start of the new school term when the law came into force. In the event, things passed off better than anyone could have supposed. The kidnapping of two French journalists in Iraq rallied public sympathy in France and French Muslims demonstrated their solidarity as French citizens. Only a handful of girls returned to school wearing the scarf and were dealt with more sympathetically than Alma and Lila with the help of counselling and advice at school. A storm in a teacup was the general verdict, but many are of the opinion that the French Muslim question will not be so easily settled in the long term.

JVH

Alma I started the new school year on Tuesday 3 September, Lila would have started the next day. I arrived at the school gate wearing a scarf that covered my hair, a polo-neck jumper, trousers and a short plain skirt. I had taken off my veil leaving only the scarf covering my hair. The headmaster said, 'To the left, Miss.' There were nine other girls wearing something on their heads, but you could see the chignon, their ears and necks. I was obviously the most covered; I was the 'Iranian' among them. Other girls were sent to join us until by the end there were 14 of us.

Alma and Lila Levy, 2004

The headmaster took us into his office and read us Article 24 of the school's regulations recapitulating the terms of the Bayrou circular [on the new law banning the headscarf and other religious symbols in schools]: 'The wearing by students of discreet symbols of their faith and beliefs, notably religious, is allowed in school; but the wearing of "ostentatious" symbols, which by their very nature are intended to proselytise or single a person out, are forbidden.' We had a right to speak out on this; I wanted to object, but he silenced me (clearly he didn't want the others to benefit from my arguments). Though we were all together in his office, he spoke to each of us individually. 'You (surname and first name), you have a choice: either you take off your veil and go to your class, or you go back home until I have had a chance to talk to your parents on Saturday.'

One by one, we made our exit. The girls were in tears: they thought this really was forbidden. They went up to their classes, some without the headscarf, others promising to remove it the next day. In the end, only two of us were left. The other girl said, 'So! Go and summon my father!' She gave her name as did I and then we left the office. Despite everything, we were sent to the classes we had opted for. As far as I was concerned, everything was fine. Except that when the teacher gave out the cards with the school regulations, he stared at me and said, 'There is a young woman in this class who illustrates perfectly Article 24.' I told him I was not in the least concerned. The headmaster came round to the class to introduce himself. When he saw me, he and the teacher started to shout at me to get out of the classroom, adding that I should at least have had the courtesy to inform him of what I had done. I went out, saying that there had been a misunderstanding. The same thing happened to the other girl.

Véronique Giraud Did you have any hesitation when you were confronted with the alternatives? What did you feel when you saw the other girls taking off their scarves?

Alma Not a moment's hesitation. As I told you, I knew we'd be leaned on but not like that. As to my friends, I thought, 'Poor things.' They slammed the door on the headmaster and insulted him, whereas I remained polite throughout, which seemed only to enrage him further. In the corridor, I met the girl who had also given him a categorical no. She was crying and terrified of her father's reaction. He's a Berber and had already beaten her several times in the summer for wearing her scarf. But since he thought she only wore it out of doors, he didn't envisage any problem at school. But when he got home that same night, after having been called by the headmaster, he beat her badly. Her back was in ribbons. Since then, she takes the scarf off at the gate, and puts it on again in the yard when no one's looking – only to take it off again in the classroom. A number of girls do the same, constantly on the watch, and being dragged off to the headmaster's office if he sees them as he's crossing the yard.

Lila We called our father the moment Alma got home. He was a bit jumpy and told us to go to school the next day as though nothing had happened. The next day, it was my first day back at school and I knew what to expect. My father told me to dress carefully, so I wore black trousers with a short white skirt over them, a pale blue jumper and a white scarf tied at the back of my head. But black or white scarves are completely out at school: too redolent of religion. Last year, Alma was allowed to wear a scarf as long as it wasn't white or black; the teachers even banned navy blue – too close to black.

But Alma hadn't warned me. I got to the place in the yard where our names and courses were pinned up. I found my classroom and started to go up. I didn't know a soul. A man called to me in the corridor and, without even looking at me, told me to report to the headmaster. I asked why and he told me he didn't know – I thought he sounded a bit shifty; if he was summoning me without knowing me it must be because of the scarf! He pointed out the headmaster's office and I was kept waiting there for almost an hour. I told him I had been sent to him but hadn't been told why. He simply said, 'Well, take that thing off your head!' When I said no way, he said he would summon my father. When he heard my name, he flew into a rage: he refused to enrol me, he already had my sister and that was quite enough for him. I told him I was on the list. He then told me to get out, saying that I would be treated the same way as Alma. I went back to see him and said he couldn't exclude me like that but must put the matter to the disciplinary committee. But he said he alone could make the decision. When I finally left his office, he ran after me and escorted me to the gate to make sure I didn't go back to my class as Alma had done. Once I was outside, I called my father, who again suggested I should go back as though I had misunderstood. He thought it impossible that I could be sent away like that.

It took just a week for our readmission the following Monday or Tuesday, but a lot had happened in that time. The day after my first day back, we both went to school at 8am. 'Go home!' We went back every hour. Each time, entry was conditional on our removing our scarves. They said, 'Girls, you must take off a layer.' When we said we already had, that wasn't enough for them: they wanted us to remove everything. The girls who had returned to school had done that . . . .

[*On 26 September 2003, the school's disciplinary committee agreed on the girls' exclusion. This decision was confirmed by the academic appeals committee.*]

VG Have you ever fallen in love? Do you have boyfriends?

Alma I've already told you I'm a boy manqué! I have found someone I like, but not in that way. I found that really messes things up. I've got a girlfriend who goes out with a boy. Even if things didn't go too far and they weren't really in love, I found it disgusting, particularly since she had another the next month. The boys check out their mates, the girls the others, it's a way of showing you are desired. I've seen girls who have no need to go out with this or that boy, but who do it anyway to look like the rest, because that makes them look good . . .

VG You've never wanted a sexual relationship with a boy, not even to hug one, to hold hands, hold him in your arms?

Lila I find the thought grotesque. It reminds me of Beverly Hills and other shows that I hate. Neither Alma nor I have ever been out with a boy. I've never felt a difference between what I feel for a boy and for my sister, or for a girlfriend or for my family. It's always the same kind of affection.

Alma I have a girlfriend who is truly in love and she pours out her heart to me all day about her boyfriend. It's different with the boys; they treat me like a mate, as though I were a boy, and talk to me openly. I've seen both sides and I really think the girls are poor cows. The boys just want to play around, or collect trophies. I've seen these boys of 18 who still want to amuse themselves in this way. I've told them to get a PlayStation if they want to entertain themselves and asked them how they would like it if someone else behaved the same way with their sister or, later, their daughter. Then they stop talking in front of me. All boys want the same thing. Even the nicest among them say that they love their girlfriend, but they don't want to settle down with her. I don't need to amuse myself this way; I don't see the point. One can admire and look at a handsome boy as you would a beautiful girl or a great car. Often, the good-looking boys are too aware of their looks and that makes them loathsome. At our age, you're attracted to things and to people that will not be the same 20 years on. I don't need to waste my time at the mercy of my changing tastes. I'd rather wait.

Lila When someone makes a mistake, it's not only that person who suffers the consequences but everyone around her. We've seen enough of our boy and girlfriends go astray! I've always known that I wouldn't go with a boy unless it was really serious and I was going to marry him. It seems more logical that way.

VG Do you wear the veil and declare your faith because that changes your relationship to boys? If I understand you properly, there are certain taboos for a woman; things thought of as sins.

Paris 2003: French Muslim women retain the scarf in the streets after the ban on wearing it in 'public places'. Credit: Rex Features

Lila And for men!

VG Yes. But a woman cannot be discovered alone with a man . . .

Lila And by the same token, nor can a man! Before you go out with a boy, you should first have visited him, shaken his hand, given him a kiss. That's where temptation lies and it gets so easy to give in. If you avoid temptation, you can avoid the sin. Before marriage, a man and woman should not be alone, nor should they touch each other. Nor should they go around together. There's no instance of that in Islam.

VG What do you think of people who have sex before marriage?

Alma We're not trying to impose our way of life or views on anyone else. Personally, I don't think it's right, but it doesn't bother me what other people do. It's forbidden in Islam, but only for Muslims.

VG But suppose you were crazy about someone, what would you do before the wedding was announced? Would you kiss him, hold his hand?

Lila Nothing. You have to wait. But it only takes a couple of minutes to announce a wedding! And we can see each other, go for walks – just not alone. Some scholars say that people who are engaged can walk together in public places; others disagree. I'd never go to the cinema with a boy: it's dark, no one's paying any attention to you and it encourages sin. Seduction should come after marriage. It's even strongly advised. The couple get dressed up for each other, play and laugh together. There are books that give advice on all that. If a wife makes herself attractive for her husband, she will reap the benefit, and vice versa. A Companion of the Prophet laughed at him when he saw him tidying his hair and his beard before going home. The Prophet replied that he hadn't the slightest interest in looking handsome outside when his wife was at home preparing herself for his return. And in a country like France, given what men see in the street and on posters, if women don't make that effort, they've lost at the outset! It's not like that in a society where they don't see any other woman. Men and women both have their weaknesses, and it's in indulging them at home that they can get the greatest pleasure. Besides, Islam advises people to avoid monotony and gives practical advice on how to make a marriage last. There is no limit to seduction after marriage!

In the same way, though modesty prevents a male and female from shaking hands, it actually depends enormously on the particular situation. The gesture means different things in different countries. It's a matter of culture: the same thing doesn't have the same meaning universally. In France, a girl and a boy may kiss on the cheek without it going any further; in the Maghrib, on the other hand, better stick to the handshake since the peck on the cheek means something quite different. In Afghanistan, even to look at someone or shake a hand can be totally out of place. You always have to consider the context. Each of us is different, sees things differently and interprets them differently. When we do something, we know how it affects us, what we intend, but we've no idea what it means for the other person. If a Muslim man holds out his hand, knowing that he shouldn't, I reckon that's a provocation. But if it's a man who doesn't know the rules, I'll shake his hand – at least the first time. If I see him again, I'll explain why I prefer not to do this.

Yves Sintomer Why has God required women to cover their heads? Is it simply a matter of modesty?

Alma Men are also instructed to be modest! When they play football in shorts, they are disobeying the *hadith* [traditions]. Men should be covered from their navel to their knees and, unless they work in the mines or in intense heat, they should cover their upper body and shoulders – ideally, it should be from their wrists to their ankles.

Lila The Prophet said that the best garment for a man is the one that covers most. If you look at Aladdin, when you see men with bare chests, they are wearing baggy pants that come up to their chest and at least down to their knees.

YS But they don't cover their head, or nape of their neck, or ears. Why don't the same rules apply to them?

Lila It would be difficult to cover your ears without covering your hair. But it's stressed over and over again that we should not confuse men and women: if they wore exactly the same clothes, that would complicate things, lead to mistakes. However, they are advised to cover their heads. The traditions of the Prophets would rather they didn't walk around bare-headed. But if we're being logical – and I'm not sure this has anything to do with logic – it's difficult for a man to conceal his neck and his ears with a hat, a *chechia* [man's hat worn in North Africa] or a turban.

VG But why don't we ever see a veiled man?

Alma As we've told you already, men and women should make their differences apparent. Everyone in his rightful place.

VG So what is a man's place? Or a woman's?

Lila That's a huge question! But one thing's for sure: while there are places like Saudi Arabia where women can't drive or do certain jobs, this has nothing to do with anything in the Quran. In some countries – or in certain circles or families – when children of both sexes live at home with their parents, the boy will be sent to school while the girl is kept at home to help in the house. You have to understand that from a religious point of view, it is very serious not to put your son and daughter on an equal footing. It is categorically forbidden not to give the same rights to all your children. We're not talking here about what we think personally, but about what is written in the Quran and Sunna [sayings of the Prophet]: 'Bring up your children without discriminating between them.' Education should be equal; time for study and for helping in the house should be shared. Teaching a daughter to read and write, to learn – whether it is religious knowledge or learning generally – equally with a son, will bring merit.

There is no profession, not a single activity that is forbidden to a woman. In the end, a woman has fewer obligations than a man. While he is obliged to feed his family, the woman has the right to work for a wage and to keep whatever she earns. She can do what she likes with that money while the man must use what he earns to keep the family. He has no right to the money earned by his wife, but she has every right to his. It's this that allows a man to forbid his wife to do certain things, and I don't think she has any right to go against his wishes. It's justified by the fact that if, say, the wife has an accident or whatever, the husband is responsible for looking after her. In the same way, if he goes off leaving his wife to starve in his absence, he is to blame in the sight of God. He must feed and clothe her as well as he can.

Alma The Prophet helped his wives around the house. His daughter Fatima was married to her father's cousin, Ali [fourth Caliph of Islam], and because they were so poor, she helped him in his work. These are the people we should take as our examples. Having said that, though, frankly I'd prefer to stay at home and look after my children than work in a mine. You might even think it unfair that a man has to work and guarantee his family's livelihood! Why is it the woman who gives birth and feeds the baby? Because God created us this way. ❑

VARIETIES OF EXPERIENCE
DANIEL STEWART

The complexity of the legislation covering religious freedom around the world is compounded by its variation from region to region, country to country. In general, the gap between law and practice means that knowledge of the law is in no sense a reliable indication of an individual's ability to believe and worship freely.

Having said that, a working understanding of the laws and regulations of governments worldwide is an important introduction to government attitudes on the subject. The myriad of variables that form part of this picture are reflected in the *Index Index* that follows, our first on varieties of discrimination and persecution on religious grounds, rather than free expression in the media.

The religious demographics aim to give a lightning indication of the larger pieces of the religious mosaic in each country; groups with less than 1 per cent of the population are not recorded. The lack of detailed information in some cases means that the categories remain less precise than we would have wished.

A similar caveat is necessary on the sources of much of our information: these are far more abundant on Christianity than on any other, a simple reflection of the effort put into monitoring by Christian groups as opposed to those of other religions.

The inclusion of statistics on the military, educational and holiday observance in a country illustrates the extent to which religious groups are present – or not – in the public sphere.

The lists of organisations that are banned, monitored or under other forms of restriction indicate government attitudes towards the day-to-day functioning of various groups, while the combination of registration requirements and government sponsorship of interfaith dialogue indicates the role governments play in controlling religious practice and the administration of religion nationally.

There are many more variables and minutiae of legislation affecting religion and its practice globally. Here, the aim is only to give a broad picture of the comparative degrees of freedom and non-freedom of religious expression from country to country. ❏

Daniel Stewart *was a volunteer researcher with* Index *over the summer*

A censorship chronicle incorporating information from ACPress.net, Adventist News Network), African Church Information Service, African News Agency (Afrol), the Age, Agencia Efe, Agence France-Press (AFP), AlertNet, Ananova, Angola Press, www. AsiaNews.it, Asharq al-Awsat, assyrianchristians.com, Amnesty International (AI), Associated Press (AP), Baha'i World News Service, BBC, Bulawayo Standard, Catholic News, CBS News Catholic World News, Christian Monitor, Committee to Protect Journalists (CPJ), Compass, La Crónica, East African Standard, Cubanet, Dawn, El Universal, Euro-Asian Jewish Congress (www.eajc.org, www. equality.ie, www.forf.org, Frontline, Forum 18, Freedom House, HCJB World Radio, Human Rights Watch (HRW), Ghanaian Chronicle, Globe & Mail, www.icrf.com, www.iglesia.net, Integridad Network, International Pen, International Religious Freedom Report, www.icrf.com, Inter Press Service (IPS), Lusaka Post, Ma'ariv, MOJO, NRC Handelsblad, Independent Catholic News, Nicaragua Network, www.pastornet.net.au, www.persecution.org, Public Broadcasting Service (PBS), Radio Cooperativa, www.religiousfreedom.com, www.religionnewsblog.com, Religion Today, Reporters Sans Frontières (RSF), www.risu.org, Reuters, RFL/Radio Liberty, San Francisco Chronicle, Sri Lanka Project Briefing, The Sunday Times, The Tablet, TamilNet, Tibetan Information Network (TIN), This Day, UNCHR, US Commission on International Religious Freedom, US State Department, Washington Post, Welt am Sonntag, World Evangelical Alliance, World Radio Network, www.worthynews.com, www.uwrn. org, Writers in Prison (WiPC), Zenit, and other sources including members of the International Freedom of Expression eXchange (IFEX).

KEY

1   *Religious membership as % of population*
2   *Constitutionally specified state religion*
3   *Consitutional secular state*
4   *Religion favoured by state*
5   *Religion linked to state*
6   *Employment of clergy in military*

7   *National holidays recognised:*
7a   *for two or more religions*
7b   *for one religion only*
8   *Freedom of worship:*
8a   *constitutional*
8b   *limited constitutional provision*
8c   *all legislation derives from Sharia*
9   *Limitations:*
9a   *banned activities*
9b   *monitored activities*
9c   *required practices*
10   *Religious instruction:*
10a   *not allowed in state schools*
10b   *privately funded religious schools banned*
10c   *religious instruction in one religion mandatory*
10d   *mandated for all religions*
10e   *for all religions but opt-out available*
11   *Government-sponsored religious unity group:*
11a   *Meets frequently*
11b   *infrequent or one-off*
12   *Registration with government:*
12a   *required of all religious groups*
12b   *required for benefits*
12c   *registration requirements*
13   *Religious discrimination banned by law*
14   *Application of religious law in courts:*
14a   *personal status and family law of religious groups implemented*
14b   *specific religious-based law/courts in designated areas for particular religions*
15   *Public worship limited by government*

AFGHANISTAN

Proportion of religious adherence (1): Muslim (Sunni) 84%, Muslim (Shia) 15%
Constitutionally specified state religion (2): Islam
Religion favoured by state (4): Islam
National holidays recognised (7a): Islam (Sunni and Shia)
Freedom of worship (8a): constitution provides for this
Banned activities (9a): Propagation of information offensive to religions; conversion from Islam; propagation of Taliban doctrines/organisation
Religious instruction (10e): Islamic instruction allowed for but opt-out permitted

Government-sponsored religious unity group (11a) Meets frequently
Extent of application of religious law in courts (14b): Shari'a applied to 'serious' crimes, including blasphemy and apostasy
Afghanistan's new constitution technically allows for religious freedom but relations between Sunni and Shia Muslims remain strained. Critics of US policy blame the US strategy of allowing local warlords virtual freedom from the rule of law in exchange for support in clamping down on the enemies of the US. (HRRAC)
In January 2003, the governor of Helmand province confiscated approximately 200 shops owned by **Hazara Shia Muslims** in Lashkar Gah and distributed them to other residents. He also blocked the Hazara/Shia community's attempts to build a mosque in Lashkar Gah. Afghanistan's Human Rights Commission and the UN won agreement on compensation for the Hazaras, but disbursement of the funds was incomplete. (US State Department)
In October 2003, a grenade was thrown at Afghanistan's last functioning **Sikh temple** in Kabul. There were no casualties; no suspects were apprehended. (US State Department)

ALBANIA

Proportion of religious adherence (1): Albanian Orthodox 25%, Roman Catholic10%, None 20%, Muslim (Sunni) 32%, Muslim (other) 13%
National holidays recognised (7a): for two or more religions
Freedom of worship (8a): constitution provides for this
Religious instruction (10a): not allowed in public schools
Registration with government (12b): required in order to gain benefits
In January 2003, the Islamic Community of Albania's general secretary, **Sali Tivari**, a key figure in the country's Islamic community was shot dead at the community's headquarters. (US State Department)
In June 2003, state legal officials stepped in to prevent university staff from barring a female **Muslim student** from wearing a

headscarf in her graduation photo in June 2003. Wearing religious symbols is not illegal, but banned in the strongly secular Albanian school system. (US State Department)

ALGERIA

Proportion of religious adherence (1): Muslim (Sunni) 98%, Muslim (other) 1%
Constitutionally specified state religion (2): Islam
Legislation (8c): all legislation derives from Shari'a law and must not contradict designated religious practice
Banned activities (9a): Proselytising and use of mosques outside of regular prayer hours
Monitored activities (9b): the designation of imams; importation of non-Islamic texts;
Religious instruction (10c): Islamic religious instruction mandatory
National holidays recognised (7b): only Islamic holidays
Religious discrimination (13): Law bans this
Extent of application of religious law in courts (14b): Shari'a law for many family and personal law matters applies to all
Limits on public worship (15): applies only to Muslims
Article 2 of Algeria's 1996 constitution designates Islam as 'the religion of the State'. Article 36 makes freedom of religious belief 'inviolable'; Article 42 bans the founding of political parties on a religious basis; and Article 73 rules that only a Muslim can become president. (www.algeria-un.org)
An October US government report noted a 'generally amicable relationship among religions in society [that] contributed to religious freedom; however, differences remain within the country's Muslim majority about the interpretation and practice of Islam. Moderate Islamists have publicly criticised acts of violence committed in the name of Islam. (US State Department)

ANGOLA

Proportion of religious adherence (1): Roman Catholic 45%, Protestant 40%, 10% (indigenous/animist)

Secular state (3): religion and state are explicitly separated by the constitution
Freedom of worship (8b): constitution provides for this but in accordance with public order and the national interest
Banned religions (9a): non-Christian religions are officially banned under colonial-era law
Monitored activities (9b): 'new religions and cults'
*Registration with government (12aii**):* required of all religious groups
Limits on public worship (15): public worship not allowed outside designated areas
In July 2004, Reverend Mateus Justino Chaves, head of a Baptist seminary in Huambo province, appealed to mainstream Christians to resist the spread of foreign religious sects in Angola. Chaves accused these of trying to 'implant the cultures and beliefs' of their home nations in Angola. (Angola Press)

ARGENTINA

Proportion of religious adherence (1): Roman Catholic 88%, Protestant 7%, Muslim 1.5%, Jewish 1%, none 1.5%
Constitutionally specified state religion (2): Roman Catholicism
Religion favoured by state (4): Roman Catholicism
National holidays recognised (7a): for two or more religions
Freedom of worship (8a): constitution provides for this
Religious instruction (10e): instruction allowed for all religions but opt-out permitted
Government-sponsored religious unity group (11a) Meets frequently
State benefits available for religious groups (12bii):* some available after registration (see note)
In March 2004, anti-Semites daubed swastikas on the walls of a **Jewish youth group** in the city of Rosario. Trade unionists meeting Tucumán province officials on July 30 shouted anti-Semitic abuse against governor **José Alperovich** and called for 'the expulsion of all Jews from the province'. (ADF)
In July 2004, the Argentine Federation of Evangelical Churches

(FAIE) protested against government rules requiring registration of new congregations. FAIE said the rules, which do not apply to the Roman Catholic Church, were discriminatory and breached the country's constitution. (Integridad Network)

ARMENIA

Proportion of religious adherence (1): Armenian Orthodox 80%, Roman Catholic 5%, indigenous/animist 1%, none 7%, Muslim 2.5%, Christian (other) 2%
Secular state (3): religion and state are explicitly separated by the constitution
Religion favoured by state (4): Armenian Orthodox
Banned activities (9a): Jehovah's Witnesses must register themselves; only the Armenian Orthodox church is permitted to proselytise
Religious instruction (10e): Armenian Orthodox doctrines
Government-sponsored religious unity group (11b) infrequent or one-off meetings
Registration with government (12a): required of all religious groups except Armenian Orthodox
In February 2004, citing a 2003 secret order (No 551-A) that bans members of 'religious minorities' from serving as police officers, Jehovah's Witness **Zemfira Voskanyan** was dismissed from the Lori regional police. Human rights groups have called the secret order 'unconstitutional'. (Forum 18)
In 2004, **Jehovah's Witnesses** were denied state registration for the twelfth time since 1995. Scores of Witnesses are in jail for refusing military service on conscientious grounds. (Forum 18)

AUSTRALIA

Proportion of religious adherence (1): Roman Catholic 26%, Anglican 20%, Protestant 13%, Christian (other) 9%, none 15%, Buddhist 1.7%, Muslim 1.3%, indigenous/animist 0.03%
Secular state (3): religion and state are explicitly separated by the constitution
Freedom of worship (8a): constitution provides for this

'They that can give up essential liberty to obtain a little temporary safety deserve neither liberty nor safety' Benjamin Franklin

UMBERTO ECO ON

EUROPE

PHILIP PULLMAN ON

READING

SARA MAITLAND ON

RELIGION

... all in INDEX

SUBSCRIBE & SAVE

SUBSCRIBE & SAVE

Religious instruction (10a): not allowed in state schools
Religious discrimination (13): law bans this in seven of Australia's eight states
10a
The city of Melbourne was ordered to apologise for discriminating against the **Falun Gong** by barring it from the city's 2003 'Moomba' Parade, reportedly under pressure from the Chinese government. Judge John Bowman ordered the city council to publish an apology in three Chinese-language newspapers. (ICRF)

AUSTRIA

Proportion of religious adherence (1): Roman Catholic 74%, Lutheran 5%, Muslim 4%, none 14%, Orthodox 1.5%
Freedom of worship (8a): constitution provides for this
Government-sponsored religious unity group (11b) infrequent or one-off meetings
State benefits available for religious groups (12aii★★★): some available after registration which is compulsory for all religious groups which are divided into three hierarchical categories for fiscal and educational benefits (see note)
Banned religions (9a): Unification Church — ban applies to the sect and any associated political party
Monitored religions (9b): 'Sects' and cults, including the Church of Scientology
Religious instruction (10e): recognised religions designated as level one in the hierarchy

AZERBAIJAN

Proportion of religious adherence (1): Muslim (Shia) 56%, Muslim (Sunni) 24%, none 10%, Russian Orthodox 4.3%, Christian (other) 1%
Freedom of worship (8b): constitution provides for this if there is no threat to public order or stability
Banned activities (9a): proselytising by foreigners, religious leaders' interference in politics, political parties' interference in religious activities
Religious instruction (10a): not allowed in public schools
Government-sponsored religious unity

group *(11a)* Meets frequently
Registration with government (12a): required of all religious groups
Angered by his support for religious and political freedoms, the Azeri government removed **Iman Ilgar Ibrahimoglu** from his position at Baku's Juma Mosque, triggering a summer of protest. Police raided the mosque on 30 June, beating and arresting 27 people including 11 women. Baptist pastor Ilya Zenchenko and Adventist pastor Yahya Zavrichko condemned the action. (Forum 18)

BAHRAIN

Proportion of religious adherence (1): Muslim (Shia) 75%, Muslim (Sunni) 24%
Constitutionally specified state religion (2): Islam
Freedom of worship (8a): constitution provides for this
Legislation (8c): all legislation derives from Shari'a law and must not contradict designated religious practice
Banned activities (9a): anti-Islamic writings and internet sites
Monitored activities (9a): proselytising
Registration with government (12aii★): required of all religious groups
Extent of application of religious law in courts (14b): inheritance
In April 2004, the Ministry of Information banned Mel Gibson's film *The Passion of the Christ.* Sharia law forbids the depiction of Jesus, known to Muslims as the Prophet Isa (US State Department)
In the past, there has been tension between the Shi'a community and the Sunni majority though things are rather better now. In 2002, the government licensed the first school to provide students with a Shi'a religious curriculum. (US State Department)
In 2003, the Ministry of Interior lifted its ban on policewomen wearing Muslim headscarves. Also in 2003, by royal decree, the king allowed women to drive while fully veiled. (US State Department)

BANGLADESH

Proportion of religious adherence (1): Muslim (Sunni) 88%, Hindu 10%, Christian 0.7%, Buddhist 0.6%
Constitutionally specified state religion (2): Islam
Religion linked to state (5): Islam
National holidays recognised (7a): for two or more religions
Freedom of worship (8b): constitution provides for this if there is no threat to public order or morality
Restrictions on religious groups (9a): Christian Khasis not recognised as legal landowners
Monitored activities (9b): foreign missionaries
Religious instruction (10d): mandatory in a choice of religions
Extent of application of religious law in courts (14a): personal status and family law to be conducted in courts and laws of individuals' religious groups
On 31 October 2003 **Shah Alam**, Imam of the Ahmadi mosque in the village of Raghanathpur Bak in Jessore, was beaten to death in front of his family by a mob, reportedly for refusing to renounce his Ahmadi faith. (AI)
On 8 January 2004 the government banned all publications, including the Quran, by the Muslim **Ahmadi** sect citing 'objectionable materials... that hurt or might hurt the sentiments of the majority Muslim population'. (AI)
Writer **Taslima Nasreen** commented in February 2004 on the years she has spent under threat: 'If I have to omit my views on religion, then it is as good as censoring my life. Not just Islam, I believe no religion gives women freedom. But since I lived in an Islamic society, that was what I wrote most about.' (*Frontline*)

BELARUS

Proportion of religious adherence (1): Belarusian Orthodox 50%, Roman Catholic 12%, Protestant 3%, Christian (other) 6%, none 27%
Religion favoured by the state (4): Belarusian Orthodox church
Freedom of worship (8b): Cooperation between the state and religious organisations 'is regulated with regard for their influence on

the formation of spiritual, cultural, and country traditions of the Belarusian people'.'
Monitored activities (9b): foreign organisations
State benefits available for religious groups (12c): groups are divided into three hierarchical categories, for benefits; nontraditional religions are described as sects, forbidden to register, and subject to harassment.
Public worship (15): limited by government
Only the official Orthodox church escapes discrimination in Belarus. Baptists **Vasili Bilas**, **Leonid Martynovich** and **Nikolai Krynts** were fined 153 Euro for singing hymns and distributing literature in a hospital at Easter. The **Greek Catholic Church** was refused registration because a 2002 law on religion requires the head of the church to be based in Belarus and its primate to be a Belarusian citizen. **Hare Krishna** devotees are routinely arrested and fined $40 for parading in the street. Anti-Semitism is rife. In January 2004 the doors of the Jewish Community House in Polotsk were daubed with the words 'Death to Jews'. Neo-fascist groups from the neighbouring town of Nowopolotysk were blamed. (Euro-Asian Jewish Congress, Forum 18)

BELGIUM

Proportion of religious adherence (1): Roman Catholic 50%, none 15%, Muslim 3%, Protestant 1.5%, Laic 8%
Freedom of worship (8a): constitution provides for this
Monitored activities (9b): Currently 189 groups are on a 'harmful sects' list and subject to careful scrutiny.
Religious instruction (10e): instruction allowed for all religions but opt-out permitted
State benefits available for religious groups (12cii):* government decides whether to recognise religions, which leads to subsidies for education in public schools.

BHUTAN

Proportion of religious adherence (1): Buddhist 70%, Hindu 20%, Muslim 1%, Christian 0.7%

Constitutionally specified state religion (2): Buddhism
Religion favoured by the state (4): Buddhism
National holidays recognised (7a) for two or more religions
Freedom of worship (8a): constitution provides for this
Banned activities (9a): proselytising; propagation of non-Buddhist religious texts
Required practices (9c): traditional Buddhist dress to be worn in all public places
Religious instruction (10e): Buddhism – government says this is not enforced in schools; NGOs disagree
Government-sponsored religious unity group (11b) infrequent or one-off meetings
Extent of application of religious law in courts (14a): personal status and family law to be conducted in courts and laws of individuals' religious groups
Public worship (15): limited by government
The law provides for freedom of religion but in practice the government limits this. Dissidents claim that Buddhist texts are the only printed religious materials allowed into the country and that the tiny **Christian** minority is persecuted. The government denies these claims and says its citizens are free to practise any religion openly. On Easter 2004, **three 'house churches'** in the southern district of Sarpang were raided at. Homeowners were warned against hosting the services and although no arrests were made, three pastors and an elder were summoned by the authorities. (Compass, Zenit)

BOLIVIA

Proportion of religious adherence (1): Roman Catholic 78%, Protestant 16%, Baha'i 3%, none 2.5% (indigenous/animist 60% – overlap)
Constitutionally specified state religion (2): Roman Catholicism
Religion favoured by the state (4): Roman Catholicism
Freedom of worship (8a): constitution provides for this
Banned activities/religions (9a): State president and vice-president can-

not be ministers of religions and must resign their religious posts 60 days before running for any national office. Hari Krishnas are a banned religion
Monitored organisations (9b): Unification Church
*Religious instruction (10e):*Roman Catholicism
State benefits available for religious groups (12c): only Roman Catholic church exempt from registration
Religious discrimination (13): Law bans this
On 28 February 2004, Quechua Indians destroyed an **evangelical church building** in the village of Chucarasi and beat a **congregational elder** unconscious, blaming their Christian neighbours for a hailstorm that damaged crops. (*Christian Monitor*, HCJB World Radio)

BOSNIA-HERZEGOVINA

Proportion of religious adherence (1): Muslim 40, Serbian Orthodox 31%, Roman Catholic 15%, Protestant 4%, none 5%
Freedom of worship (8a): constitution provides for this
Religious instruction (10e): in regional majority religion only, plus pressure for all to take classes
Required practices (9c): ethnic political office quotas overlap as religious quotas
On 18 March 2004 arsonists attacked the **Serbian Orthodox Church of the Holy Mother of God in Bugojno** in central Bosnia, reportedly in reaction to continuing ethnic violence in Kosovo. Interior Minister Mevludin Halilovic condemned the attack and several people were arrested. (Forum 18)
On 21 March 2004 in the Bosnian-Serb ruled part of the country, a bomb was thrown at a **mosque in Orahova, near Gradiska**. It was the anniversary of the day in 1993 when the original mosque was destroyed. It was rebuilt and reopened last year as Bosnian Muslims expelled during the Balkan wars returned to their original homes. (Forum 18)

BOTSWANA

Proportion of religious adherence (1): Christian 55%, indigenous/animist 40%, Muslim 1%, Hindu 1%
National holidays recognised (7b): Christian
Freedom of worship (8b): constitution provides for this, but provision can be suspended in the interests of national defence, public safety, public order, public morality, or public health; however, any suspension of religious freedom by the government must be deemed reasonably justifiable in a democratic society.
State benefits available for religious groups (12a): registration required of all religious groups
Reacting to the consecration of gay priest **Gene Robinson** as bishop-coadjutor of the diocese of New Hampshire in the US, Bishop of Botswana the Reverend Theophilus Naledi said that homosexuality was 'ungodly, unnatural and unbiblical'. (African Church Information Service)
A dispute over the ordination of the first woman priest of the Dutch Reformed Church in Botswana split the denomination, with a small group – mostly women – who opposing the ordination of **Reverend Monnie Kgosiemang** in 2004. The critics aim to get the ordination annulled in the high court. (ENI)

BRAZIL

Proportion of religious adherence (1): Roman Catholic 72%, Pentecostal 12%, Pentecostal/Baptist 3%, none 7%, indigenous/animist 4%
Secular state (3): religion and state are explicitly separated by the constitution
Freedom of worship (8a): constitution provides for this
Monitored activities (9b):-Entry to indigenous lands for religious groups
Religious discrimination (13): Law bans this
Government-sponsored religious unity group (11a) Meets frequently
The Catholic Bishop of Caicó, Jaime Vieira Rocha, complained in September 2004 that **evangelical 'sects'** were increasing their influence on Brazilian politics. He noted that the Universal Church of the Kingdom of God planned to deploy 500 candidates in municipal elections in October 2004. Evangelical pastor **João Monteiro de Castro** was assassinated in Río de Janeiro on 6 July 2004, possibly for political reasons. He was a local council member for the conservative Partido del Frente Liberal and was planning to stand again in the upcoming municipal elections. (EFE, Integridad Network, Zenit, ACPress.net))
In August 2004 a São Paulo appeals court reversed the convictions of Baptist pastor **Joaquim de Andrade** and Anglican deacon **Aldo dos Santos Menez**, accused of violating Brazil's anti-hate speech law by distributing leaflets allegedly critical of the Afro-Brazilian religions Umbanda and Candomble. (*Religion Today*)

BULGARIA

Proportion of religious adherence (1): Bulgarian Orthodox 82%, Muslim 12%, Roman Catholic 1.5%, Protestant 2%, none 1%, Jewish 0.8%
Constitutionally specified state religion (2): Bulgarian Orthodox
Freedom of worship (8a): constitution provides for this
Banned activities (9a): political parties established on religious grounds
Religious instruction (10e): mainly Bulgarian Orthodox but opt-out available
State benefits available for religious groups (12c): only Bulgarian Orthodox exempt from registration
Public worship (15): limited by government
The state finally intervened directly in the decades-long dispute between Orthodox church supporters of the mainstream Patriarch Maksim and the dissident Metropolitan Inokenty. On 21 July 2004 police forcibly expelled members of the alternative Orthodox synod from about 250 churches they use. More than ten priests and 100 worshippers were injured in the raids. (Forum 18)
In March 2004, the Bulgarian government agreed to pay US$9,800 compensation to Jehovah's Witness preachers **Alfred** and **Edith Lohat** and allow them to live in Bulgaria. In return the couple will drop a court action against Bulgaria in the European Court of Human Rights in Strasbourg. The couple's lawyer said that while the sum was 'not a very big figure (it) has symbolic moral value'. (ENI)

BURMA

Proportion of religious adherence (1): Buddhist 88%, Baptist 3%, Roman Cathgolic 1%, Muslim 4%, indigenous/animist 1%
Religion linked to state (5): Buddhism
National holidays recognised (7a): for two or more religions
Freedom of worship (8b): constitution provides for this, but provision can be limited by law and public interest
Banned activities (9a): all imported texts censored; missionaries; minorities' proselytising, religious instruction, building permits strictly controlled
*Religious instruction (10e):*Buddhist, with limited opt-out; government-supported forced conversions of Christians to Buddhism
Registration with government (12a): required of all religious groups
State censors oversee local publication of the Bible, the Koran and Christian and Muslim publications generally. Censors refer to a list of more than 100 words banned from Christian or Islamic publications, because they are indigenous terms long used in Buddhist literature but since adopted by all faiths. Groups that translate and publish non-Buddhist religious texts are appealing against the ban. (US State Department)

BURUNDI

Proportion of religious adherence (1): Roman Catholic 60%, Muslim 10%, indigenous/animist 10%, Protestant 15%
National holidays recognised (7b): Roman Catholic
Freedom of worship (8b): constitution provides for this, but provision can be limited by law and public interest

State benefits available for religious groups (12ai★): registration required of all religious groups
Religious discrimination (13): Law bans this
On 8 August Burundi's senior Anglican priest, **Bishop Pie Ntukamazina**, narrowly escaped kidnap. A spokesman blamed the rebel Hutu Forces for National Liberation (FNL) for the attack. In December 2003, the government blamed the FNL for the murder of Vatican envoy **Michael Courtney**, a charge the rebels deny. (AlertNet)

CAMBODIA

Proportion of religious adherence (1): Buddhist 93%, Muslim 4%, Christian 1%, indigenous/animist 1%
Constitutionally specified state religion (2): Buddhism
National holidays recognised (7b): Buddhist
Freedom of worship (8a): constitution provides for this
Banned activities (9a): public proselytising; visit of Dalai Lama
Government-sponsored religious unity group (11b) infrequent or one-off meetings
Registration with government (12b): required in order to gain benefits
In July 2003, a mob of angry villagers severely damaged a **Christian church** in Svey Rieng Province, blaming the construction of the church several years earlier for the area's drought. In August 2003, a tribal group in Rattanakiri Province demanded that a Christian group stop conducting conversion activities in their villages. (US State Dept)
On 26 July, 31 members of the **Christian tribal Montagnard** community claimed they had been forced to hide in the jungle, living off tubers and rainwater, after being forced to flee Vietnam's central plains when demonstrations against religious oppression and land confiscation turned violent in April. (www.AsiaNews.it)

CAMEROON

Proportion of religious adherence (1): Roman Catholic 20%, Protestant 20%, Muslim 20%, indigenous/animist 40%

Secular state (3): religion and state are explicitly separated by the constitution
National holidays recognised (7a): for two or more religions
Freedom of worship (8a): constitution provides for this
Banned activities (9a): witchcraft
Religious instruction (10a): not allowed in public schools
State benefits available for religious groups (12aii★): registration required of all religious groups
Religious discrimination (13): Law bans this
Community activist Garga Aoudou alleged in August that the northern provincial capital of Garoua had experienced an increase in anti-Christian propaganda that called on Muslims to refuse to rent homes to Christians. Bishop Yves Steven of Maroua says that some Christian families have been driven out of their homes by Muslim extremists. (World Evangelical Alliance)
The practice of witchcraft is a criminal offence in Cameroon, although people are generally prosecuted only in conjunction with another offence, such as murder. In April 2002, the government banned the **Ma'alah**, a non-traditional religious body, following the March 2002 death of a six-year-old girl whose mother and others members had been beaten to death in the belief that they were beating out demonic possession. Both the government and the girl's father have since sued the mother and her accomplices. (US State Department)

CANADA

Proportion of religious adherence (1): Roman Catholic 43%, Protestant 29%, Muslim 2%, Jewish 1%, Buddhist 1%, 11, Sikh 1%, none 10%
National holidays recognised (7b): Christian
Freedom of worship (8a): constitution provides for this and professes supremacy of God
Religious instruction (10): Provincial governments determine educational policy, so variations exist

CENTRAL AFRICAN REPUBLIC

Proportion of religious adherence (1): Roman Catholic 50%, Muslim 15%, indigenous/animist 35%
National holidays recognised (7b): Christianity
Freedom of worship (8b): constitution provides for this,but prohibits religious fundamentalism or intolerance
Banned activities/organisations (9a): Unification Church, 'subversive' religious groups; witchcraft;
Religious instruction (10e): open to all religions
Government-sponsored religious unity group (11b) infrequent or one-off meetings
Registration with government (12ci★): smaller indigenous groups exempt from registration

CHAD

Proportion of religious adherence (1): Muslim 54%, Christian 32%, indigenous/animist 10%
Secular state (3): religion and state are explicitly separated by the constitution
Freedom of worship (8a): constitution provides for this
Religion linked to state (5): Islam
National holidays recognised (7a): for two or more religions
Banned activities/organisations (9a): Faid al-Djaria (a sufi Muslim group)
Faid al-Djaria fundamentalist groups
Religious instruction (10a): not allowed in public schools
Registration with government (12aii★★): required of all religious groups
In February 2003, a church run by the **Church of Christian Assemblies** in Chad in the predominantly Muslim town of Abeche was burnt down, the most serious of a series of attacks fuelled by a long-running dispute between the church and Abeche's Islamic Affairs Committee. (US State Deparment)
In July 2002, the Superior Council of Islamic Affairs rebuked **Mahamadou Mahamat** (aka Sheikh Faki Suzuki) and **Haroun Idriss Abou-Mandela** after they

participated in a weekly religious affairs show aired by private radio FM Alnassr. Both had been previously banned from preaching by the council. (US State Department)

CHILE

Proportion of religious adherence (1): Roman Catholic 70%, Pentecostal 13%, Protestant 2%, none 8%, 8b-In line with good morals, customs, or the public order.
Secular state (3): religion and state are explicitly separated by the constitution
Religion favoured by the state (4): Roman Catholicism
Employment of clergy in military (6): restricted to Roman Catholic priests
National holidays recognised (7b): Christian
Religious instruction (10e): instruction available mainly in Roman Catholic doctrine, but opt-out possible
Registration with government (12bi★★): required in order to gain benefits
Religious discrimination (13): Law bans this
In July 2003, members of the dissident Baptist group Valientes de David set fire to a statue of the Virgin of Carmen in Alto Hospicio claiming that a local festival held there was 'a pagan event' and the statue 'an idol' and that the festival was a pagan event. (*The Tablet, La Crónica*)
On 24 July 2004, priest **Faustino Gazziero** was killed during a service in Santiago's metropolitan cathedral. A 24-year-old man who cut Gazziero's throat told investigators that he was a member of a satanic sect who had gone to the cathedral to kill any priest who might be there. (BBC, Radio Cooperativa)

CHINA

Proportion of religious adherence (1): none 75%, Buddhist 9%, Muslim 1.5%, Christian 5%, indigenous/animist 9%
Freedom of worship (8a): constitution provides for this
Banned activities (9a): cults, especially Falun Gong; foreign 'control' of religious groups;

simultaneous Communist Party membership and religious affiliation
Monitored activities (9b): all religious activity
Religious instruction (10e): not permitted — instruction in atheism is mandated
Registration with government (12ciii★★★): required of the five recognised religions — Buddhism, Roman Catholicism, Protestantism, Taoism
Public worship (15): limited by government to approved sites
The Chinese government now routinely blocks internet access to sites related to **Falun Gong**, the Tibetan Buddhist leader **Dalai Lama**, certain branches of **Islam**, the covert **Christian 'house churches'** and mainstream Christian bodies, including the **Vatican**. (Freedom House)
On June 18, **Jiang Zongxiu** was reportedly beaten to death in jail on the day of her arrest for 'spreading rumours and inciting to disturb social order' in Guizhou province. The 34-year-old farmer had been handing out Bibles; these are banned in bookshops. (www.AsiaNews.it)
On 14 May, Catholic priests **Lu Genjun** and **Cheng Xiaoli** were briefly arrested in An Guo, Hebei province. The two had been charged with 'disturbing public order' after they held a course in natural family planning and theology that had not been authorised by the state Bureau of Religious Affairs. (Freedom House)

COLOMBIA

Proportion of religious adherence (1): Roman Catholic 81%, Protestant 3, Christian (other) 10%, none 2%
Secular state (3): religion and state are explicitly separated by the constitution
Religion linked to state (5): Roman Catholicism
Employment of clergy in military (6): restricted to Roman Catholic priests
Freedom of worship (8a): constitution provides for this
Monitored activities (9b): proselytising to indigenous peoples
Religious instruction (10e): available for all religions

Registration with government (12c): required of all non-Roman Catholic groups
Religious discrimination (13): Law bans this
Catholic and evangelical churches, especially those in rural communities are on the frontline of a war between the rebel Revolutionary Armed Forces of Colombia (FARC) and the pro-state paramilitary Self-Defence Forces of Colombia (AUC). Scores of attacks, targeted assassinations, kidnappings and extortion demands have claimed the lives of more than 60 Catholic priests, nuns and lay workers since 1993. (Fides)
Among the dead in 2004: pastor **Miguel Mariano Posada**, church secretary **Ana Bernice Giraldo Velaquez** and two community members, killed by a group of 25 men in a church near the town of Tierralta in north-east Colombia; priest **Cesar Dario Peña**, killed while held by FARC forces; priest **Saulo Carreño** from Saravena in Arauca department and secretary **Maritza Linares** killed by two gunmen on bicycles after visiting sick parishioners in hospital. (*Catholic World News*)

CONGO REPUBLIC

Proportion of religious adherence (1): Roman Catholic 45%, Christian (other) 5%, Muslim 1%, none 8%, indigenous/animist 35%
National holidays recognised (7b): Christian
Freedom of worship (8a): constitution provides for this
Monitored activities (9b): messianic groups aligned with opposition political parties
Registration with government (12a): required of all religious groups
Religious discrimination (13): Law bans this
In March 2003, the government and the Ninja rebel militia group, led by self-proclaimed prophet Frederic Bistangou (aka Pasteur Ntumi), signed a peace accord. Subsequently, there have been no reports of abuse or desecration of churches as alleged in previous years. (US State Department)

CONGO DRC

Proportion of religious adherence (1): Roman Catholic 55%, Protestant 25%, indigenous/animist 17%, Muslim 3%
Government-sponsored religious unity group (11a) Meets frequently
Registration with government (12a): required of all religious groups
Because of civil war, no constitution in place.
Archbishop Dirokpa Balufuga Fidele and Congo Kinshasa bishops signed a statement condemning homosexuality in reaction to a worldwide appeal from the Anglican church calling for an open debate on the issue of the church and homosexuality, which the Congo DRC bishop claimed was 'ravaging the Western world' (Afrol)

COSTA RICA

Proportion of religious adherence (1): Roman Catholic 72%, Protestant 19%, none 10%
8b-Does not impugn universal morality or proper behaviour.
Constitutionally specified state religion (2): Roman Catholicism
National holidays recognised (7a): for two or more religions
Banned activities (9a): clergy running for public office
Religious instruction (10e): allowed for Roman Catholic doctrine but opt-out available

CÔTE D'IVOIRE

Proportion of religious adherence (1): Muslim 38%, Roman Catholic 19%, indigenous/animist 12%, Protestant 7%, Christian (other) 3%, none 18%
Religion favoured by the state (4): Christianity
National holidays recognised (7a): for two or more religions
Freedom of worship (8a): constitution provides for this
Religious instruction (10e): allowed for Protestant, Roman Catholic and Muslim doctrine
Government-sponsored religious unity group (11a) Meets frequently
Registration with government (12cii★): required, indigenous.animist groups exempt
Monitored activities (9b): minority religious groups with possible politically subversive behaviour

CROATIA

Proportion of religious adherence (1): Roman Catholic 85%, Serbian Orthodox 6%, Muslim 2%, Jewish 1%, none 2%
Religion linked to state (5): Roman Catholicism
National holidays recognised (7a): for two or more religions
Religious instruction (10e): mainly Roman Catholic, schools need a specified minimum of minority religious adherents to warrant additional instruction
Registration with government (12a): required of all religious groups
The legacy of the 1993 Balkan war between Muslim, Orthodox Serb and Catholic Croatians lingers despite improvements in recent years. Orthodox churches are frequently desecrated with fascist Ustasha symbols; local resistance to the rebuilding of war-damaged mosques can hold up the work for years. (International Religious Freedom Report, www.icrf.com)

CUBA

Proportion of religious adherence (1): Roman Catholic 42%, Baptist 2%, Pentecostal 1%, Christian (other) 2%, none 37% (Santeria – 60% overlap)
Secular state (3): religion and state are explicitly separated by the constitution
Freedom of worship (8b): constitution provides for this, within bounds of respect for the law
Banned activities (9a): access to Internet by many religious groups, incl. Roman Catholics
Monitored activities (9b): humanitarian activities seen as the responsibility of the government
Religious instruction (10a): not allowed in public schools
In a pastoral letter published in September 2003, Cuban bishops expressed their concern at what they described as 'a subtle struggle against the Church: she is treated as a private entity or a marginal entity that might drain force or energy away from the revolution'. (*Independent Catholic News*, Cubanet)
Christian groups are campaigning for the release of jailed Christian dissidents, among them the

founder of the Lawton Foundation for Human Rights, **Dr Oscar Elías Biscet**, and the blind lawyer **Juan Carlos González Leiva**. (US Commission on International Religious Freedom, *Independent Catholic News*, Cubanet)

CZECH REPUBLIC

Proportion of religious adherence (1): none 52%, Roman Catholic 15%, Protestant 5%, Christian (other) 3%
Freedom of worship (8a): constitution provides for this
Religious instruction (10a): not allowed in public schools
Government-sponsored religious unity group (11b) infrequent or one-off meetings
Registration with government (12bii★): in order to register with the state, a religious group must be able to prove that it has at least 10,000 adult members. Smaller religious groups that fail the test are denied legal status and are thus unable to own property. (www.icrf.com)

DENMARK

Proportion of religious adherence (1): Lutheran 85%, none 9%, Muslim 3%, Christian (other) 2%
Constitutionally specified state religion (2): Lutheranism
Freedom of worship (8a): constitution provides for this
Religion favoured by state (4): Lutheranism
Banned activities (9a): adherence to Church of Scientology
Religious instruction (10e): allowed for Luheran doctrine but opt-out available
Registration with government (12bi★): required in order to gain benefits

EAST TIMOR

Proportion of religious adherence (1): Roman Catholic 90%, Protestant 2%, Muslim 3%, (indigenous/animist 40% overlap)
Secular state (3): religion and state are explicitly separated by the constitution
Religion linked to state (5): Roman Catholicism
National holidays recognised (7b): fRoman Catholic

Freedom of worship (8a): constitution provides for this
Banned activities (9a): foreigners providing religious assistance to security and defence forces
Religious discrimination (13): Law bans this
Registration with government (12ci*): only required if most or all members are foreigners.

In late 2003, groups of Catholic youths stoned a **mosque in Los Palos** and threatened its small local Muslim population. The situation was resolved when local Catholic and Islamic leaders from Dili jointly held meetings in Los Palos to discuss the importance of religious tolerance. (US State Department)

ECUADOR

Proportion of religious adherence (1): Roman Catholic 93%, Protestant 2%, Christian (other) 2%, none 1% (indigenous/animist 40% overlap)
Religion linked to state (5): Roman Catholicism
Freedom of worship (8b): constitution provides for this but professes supremacy of God, and limits 'those proscribed by law to protect and respect the diversity, plurality, security, and rights of others.'
Banned activities (9a): state president and members of congress cannot be ministers of religion.
Religious instruction (10a): not allowed in public schools

EGYPT

Proportion of religious adherence (1): Muslim (Sunni) 90%, Muslim (Shia) 1%, Coptic Christian 5%, Christian (other) 3%
Constitutionally specified state religion (2): Islam
Religion favoured by state (4): Islam
National holidays recognised (7a): for two or more religions
Legislation (8c): all legislation derives from Shari'a law and must not contradict designated religious practice
Banned activities (9a): adherence to Baha'i faith, 'ridiculing of a heavenly religion', political parties based on religion
Monitored activities (9b): all mosque activities are monitored to combat extremism

Religious instruction (10d): mandated and available for all religions
Registration with government (12a): to qualify for registration, religious groups must not pose a threat or upset national unity
Religious discrimination (13): Law bans this
Extent of application of religious law in courts (14a): personal status and family law to be conducted in courts and laws of individuals' religious groups

Egypt's political establishment makes a point of embracing its ancient minority Coptic Christian community, but Christian voices in the West have criticised the treatment of the **Copts** in Egypt in the past, notably the massacre of 21 Copts during riots in Al-Kosheh village in January 2000. (AI)
On 7 January 2003, Egypt officially marked the day of Coptic Christmas as a national day of celebration for the first time. (UNCHR)

EL SALVADOR

Proportion of religious adherence (1): Roman Catholic 60%, Protestant 18%, Christian (other) 2%, none 17%
Religion favoured by state (4): Roman Catholicism
Freedom of worship (8b): constitution provides for this but within the bounds of public order and public
Religious instruction (10a): not allowed in public schools
Registration with government (12ci*): all religions but Roman Catholicism required to register
Religious discrimination (13): Law bans this
Legal requirements (9c): the state president, vice-president, cabinet members, supreme court justices, magistrates, the public defender, attorney general and other top government officials must be laypeople.
On 7 September 2004, the Catholic Church in El Salvador asked for the 1980 murder of Archbishop **Oscar Romero** to be reinvestigated. The call came four years after a federal judge in California ruled that retired Salvadorian air force captain Alvaro Rafael Saravia was liable to pay

US$10 million in damages for conspiracy to kill Romero. Saravia, who apparently lives in the US, did not respond to the lawsuit. (Reuters, *Catholic News*, AP)

ERITREA

Proportion of religious adherence (1): Muslim (Sunni) 50%, Orthodox 40%, Roman Catholic 5%, Protestant 2%, indigenous/animist 2%
12ciii (***) -R/D/B/AA exempted
Banned activities (9a): political activity by religious groups; faith groups may fund but not implement development groups; foreigners traveling to Eritrea to meet with religious groups;
Monitored activities (9b): Jehovah's Witnesses severely limited; radical Muslim groups;
Registration with government (12c): Orthodox, Muslim, Roman Catholic and Evangelical Protestants exempt

The state stepped up a two-year government crackdown on evangelical Christians by detaining **Haile Naizgi** of the **Full Gospel Church**, **Kifle Gebremeskel** of the **Eritrean Evangelical Alliance** and Pastor **Tesfatsion Hagos** of the **Rema Evangelical Church** in Asmara along with singer **Helen Berhane**, 29. She has reportedly refused demands that she recant her faith. (AI, Compass)
In August 2003, scores of teenage schoolchildren were beaten and detained by the military after being found with Bibles in the Tigrinya language. They were promised freedom if they renounced their faith and joined the majority Eritrean Orthodox Coptic Church. Only three other faiths are legal, the Catholic Church, Muslims and the (Lutheran) Evangelical Church of Eritrea. All others were effectively banned in May 2002. (Afrol, AI)

ETHIOPIA

Proportion of religious adherence (1): Orthodox 40%, Evangelical Protestant 8%, Muslim 45%
Secular state (3): religion and state are explicitly separated by the constitution

National holidays recognised (7a): for two or more religions

Freedom of worship (8b): constitution provides for this but limited by interest of the state and the revolution, pubic morality or the freedom of other citizens

Banned activities (9a): religious groups forming political parties; defamation of religions and religious leaders; wearing headscarves in school

Monitored activities (9b): Bible importation

Registration with government (12a): required of all religions

FINLAND

Proportion of religious adherence (1): Lutheran 86%, national Orthodox 1%, Pentecostal 1%, none 7%

Constitutionally specified state religion (2): Lutheranism/national Orthodox

Freedom of worship (8a): constitution provides for this

Religious instruction (10e): for all religions but opt-out available

Government-sponsored religious unity group (11b) infrequent or one-off meetings

Registration with government (12bi*): required to gain benefits; not required for 'traditional churches'

Religious discrimination (13): law bans this

Christian, Jewish and Islamic leaders in Finland planned a permanent forum in February and hope to promote inter-faith cooperation at a local level. '(ENI)

FRANCE

Proportion of religious adherence (1): Roman Catholic 65%, Muslim 7%, Protestant 2%, Jewish 1%, Buddhist 1%, Christian (other) 3%, none 12%

Secular state (3): religion and state are explicitly separated by the constitution

National holidays recognised (7a): for two or more religions

Freedom of worship (8a): constitution provides for this

Banned activities (9a): in schools wearing of Muslim headscarves, Jewish skullcaps, large Christian crucifixes and other conspicuous religious ornamentation

Monitored activities (9b): 'Sects/cults', including Church of Scientology and Jehovah's Witnesses

*Religious instruction (10a):*not allowed in public schools

Government-sponsored religious unity group (11a): meets frequently

Registration with government (12b): required in order to gain benefits

Religious discrimination (13): law bans this

Jewish graves have been desecrated throughout 2004 with anti-semitic grafitti. French President Jacques Chirac declared that 'When a Jew is attacked in France, it is an attack on the whole of France'; Prime Minister Jean-Pierre Raffarin promised the 'heaviest penalties'. (BBC)

Muslim cemeteries have also been defaced with Nazi swastikas and SS inscriptions. After the attacks, interior minister Dominique de Villepin announced the creation of an inter-faith committee 'to promote mutual understanding'. (Al-Jazeera)

The announcement of a plan to ban religious signifiers such as Muslim headscarves and Jewish skullcaps from traditionally secular French schools provoked an outcry and threats of mass peaceful civil disobedience. Ironically the kidnap of two French journalists in Iraq by Islamist extremists effectively killed the campaign in France. (BBC and see p117)

GEORGIA

Proportion of religious adherence (1): national Orthodox 73%, Greek, Russian and Armenian Orthodox 6%, Muslim 5%

Secular state (3): religion and state are explicitly separated by the constitution

Religion linked to state (5): national Orthodox

Freedom of worship (8a): constitution provides for this

Monitored activities (9b): foreign missionaries and all non-Orthodox missionaries.

The Georgian Orthodox church took against British writers: in June 2003 it protested against a performance of a play based on William Shakespeare's love sonnets as 'blatant pornography'. And

in February 2004, the church complained that JK Rowling's *Harry Potter* books were 'anti-Christian'. (FT)

In March 2004, four months after President Mikheil Saakashvili came to power in the so-called 'Rose Revolution', notorious excommunicated Orthodox priest Vasil Mkalavishvili (aka Father Basil) was finally arrested after leading a campaign of intimidation and violence against religious minorities for six years. (Forum 18)

Since Saakashvili came to power, minority religious groups said that the building of non-Orthodox places of worship was still being blocked and the new government was stalling on giving religious minorities legal recognition. Jehovah's Witness lawyer Manuchar Tsimintia said they were now holding conventions without facing attack from Orthodox vigilantes. 'This is the first year we have been able to do this for five years,' he said. (Forum 18 and see p218)

GERMANY

Proportion of religious adherence (1): Lutheran 24%, Protestant 9%, Roman Catholic 33%, Muslim 4%, Orthodox 1.5%, Christian (other) 1%, non 20%

Freedom of worship (8a): constitution provides for this

Banned activities (9a): visits to Germany by leaders of the Unification Church; Church of Scientology adherents joining three major political parties

Monitored activities (9b): Church of Scientology and 'sects and cults'

Religious instruction (10e): mainly provided by Protestant and Roman Catholic schools, opt-out available

Government-sponsored religious unity group (11b) infrequent or one-off meetings

Registration with government (12ci**): Not required for major faiths, including Lutheranism, Roman Catholicism and Judaism; denied to Jehovah's Witnesses and Church of Scientology

Germany's first university centre to train teachers in Islam for religious education in schools was officially opened in January 2004 at the University of Münster in northwestern Germany. (ENI) President Johannes Rau drew fire in January 2004 after saying that all religious signs – including Christian symbols – should be banned from schools if the wearing of Islamic headscarves is prohibited. 'If one bans the headscarf in schools as a religious symbol it is difficult to defend the monk's habit,' Rau, a prominent Protestant layperson said. (*Welt am Sonntag*)

Neo-Nazi groups from Germany have been responsible for defiling Jewish graves across the German border in Alsace. They are banned from meeting publicly in Germany. (*Le Monde*)

GHANA

Proportion of religious adherence (1): Christian 60%, Muslim 20%, indigenous/animist 10%
Freedom of worship (8a): constitution provides for this
Religious instruction (10e): mainly provided by Christian schools, opt-out available
Government-sponsored religious unity group (11a) Meets frequently
Registration with government (12bii*): necessary to gain benefits
Khalid Ahmad of the Ahmadi Muslim Elders' Association appealed to the elders of all Ghana's faiths to preach against same-sex marriages and to treat the concept as a challenge to be opposed. (*Ghanaian Chronicle*)

GREECE

Proportion of religious adherence (1): Greek Orthodox 95%, Christian (other) 1%, Muslim 1%
Constitutionally specified state religion (2): Greek Orthodox
Religion favoured by state (4): Greek Orthodox
Freedom of worship (8a): constitution provides for this
Banned activities (9a): proselytising, Church of Scientology
Limits on public worship (15): cannot disturb public order or offend moral principles.
Religious instruction (10c): mandatory for Greek Orthodox adherents only

GUATEMALA

Proportion of religious adherence (1): Roman Catholic 55%, Evangelical Protestants 40%, (indigenous/animist 40% overlap)
Religion favoured by state (4): Roman Catholic
Freedom of worship (8a): constitution provides for this
Religious instruction (10e): provided for all religionsl
The government has failed to carry out proposed constitutional guarantees to Indigenous beliefs and sacred sites
On 12 February 2003, Guatemala's Supreme Court upheld the convictions of a priest and three members of the military for the 1998 murder of Catholic bishop **Juan Gerardi**, a few days after he had reported on human rights violations during the country's 36-year civil war. (AP, Guatemala Solidarity Campaign)
On 14 December 2003, unknown gunmen assassinated Catholic priest **José María Ruiz Furlan** as left his church in a poor quarter of Guatemala City. The 72-year-old was a staunch defender of the poor and had twice run for mayor of the city in 1978 and 1982. (BBC, AI)

HAITI

Proportion of religious adherence (1): Roman Catholic 78%, Baptist 10%, Pentecostal 4%, Christian (other) 3%, none 2%, (overlap of Vodou with other religions)
Religion linked to state (5): Roman Catholic
Freedom of worship (8a): constitution provides for this assuming there is no disturbance of law and order
Religious instruction (10e): mainly Roman Catholic
Registration with government (12a): required of all religions
In April 2003, the Haitian government officially approved **Vodou** as a religion and gave practitioners legal authority to perform baptisms and marriages. C70% of Haiti's 8 million people practise Vodou to some extent, among them many Roman Catholics and adherents of other Christian denominations. (AP, BBC, ASSIST News Service)

On 13 September 2004, Evangelical pastor **Jean Moles Lovinsky Bertomieux** was shot dead on his way to work in Port-au-Prince. Bertomieux hosted a popular religious breakfast show at Radio Caraibes. He had made an unsuccessful bid for the lower house of Parliament for the National Congress of Democratic Movements Party in 1995 but was said not to have been overtly political on the radio. (AP)

HONDURAS

Proportion of religious adherence (1): Roman Catholic 75%, Evangelical Protestant 14%, Protestant 6%
Religion linked to state (5): Roman Catholic
Employment of clergy in military (6): restricted to Roman Catholic priests
Freedom of worship (8b): constitution provides for this but in line with law or public policy
Banned activities (9a): Ministers cannot hold public office or use religious beliefs for political motives; Unification Church
There were reports of discriminatory attitudes in the media and in government statements against persons of Arab descent, both first-generation immigrants and those whose families have resided in the country for generations and in spite of the fact that the vast majority of Arabs in the country are Christian. (US State Department)

INDIA

Proportion of religious adherence (1): Hindu 82%, Muslim (Sunni) 11%, Muslim (Shia) 1%, Christian 2.3%, Sikh 2%, Jain 0.5%
Secular state (3): religion and state are explicitly separated by the constitution
National holidays recognised (7a): for two or more religions
Freedom of worship (8a): constitution provides for this
Banned activities (9a): groups that promote intercommunity friction, terrorism or sedition, or break the Foreign Contribution Act; Students Islamic Movement of India; Deendar Anjuman, a Muslim group; using religious site for political purpose; 'forcing/allur-

ing' conversion in several states; foreigners cannot speak publicly against other religions.
*Religious instruction (10a):*not allowed in public schools
Religious discrimination (13): law bans this
Extent of application of religious law in courts (14a): personal status and family law to be conducted in courts and laws of individuals' religious groups
The Congress Party election victory over the incumbent Bharatiya Janata Party (BJP) marked the end of a period of ascendancy for Hindu extremism, though it did not stop criticism of party leader Sonia Gandhi's Italian Roman Catholic origins. She quickly stepped down to protect the government from the effects of extremist propaganda. The Congress victory also slowed the spread of 'anti-conversion' laws, used by supporters of the extremist Hindu groups to target minority Christian communities and to block missionary work. Until its repeal, all conversions had to be registered in Tamil Nadu state; if police rejected the paperwork, both the converter and the converted could be jailed. (Compass)
After six Hindus were arrested for forcibly shaving the heads of nine **Christian converts** in Kilipal village, Orissa state, one of the victims, **Pastor Subas Samal** and a colleague were arrested on 29 May. Charged with 'conversion by inducement', under the state's Freedom of Religion Act they were released on bail on 14 July (Compass)
On 9 August the Supreme Court indicated its determination to ensure that victims of rape and murder in the 2002 **anti-Muslim pogrom** – at least 2,000 victims – in Gujarat get justice. The bench suggested the Gujarat government appoint a new public prosecutor and order police in Gujarat to deliver up the main suspects to trial. (IPS)

INDONESIA

Proportion of religious adherence (1): Muslim (Sunni) 64%, Muslim (Shia) 1%, Protestant 6%, Roman Catholic 4%, Hindu 3%, Buddhist

1%, Confucian 1%, (indigenous/animist 20% overlap)
Employment of clergy in military (6): the five *recognised religions are allowed*
National holidays recognised (7a): for two or more religions
Freedom of worship (8a): constitution provides for this but refers to belief in one Supreme God
Banned activies (9a): atheism
Monitored activities (9b): radical Muslim groups; attempting to convert others is severely limited; ID cards have one of the five recognised religion indicated on them
Religious instruction (10e): is allowed and is mainly Muslim
Government-sponsored religious unity group (11a) Meets frequently
Registration with government (12ciii): required, but only five groups – Muslims, Hindus, Buddhists, Roman Catholics and Protestants are recognised as religions officially. The rest are classified as 'cultural groups'.
Extent of application of religious law in courts (14b): or Muslims only Shari'a law has been introduced in Aceh province.
Inter-religious violence broke out in Maluku and North Maluku provinces in April 2004 after supporters of the mainly Christian Maluku Sovereignty Front gathered in Ambon to mark the anniversary of the separatist movement. The UN offices, hundreds of homes, the Nasaret Protestant Church, a Muslim school and parts of the Christian University of Maluku were destroyed in sporadic fighting that left at least 40 dead and more than 300 injured. (US State Department)

IRAN

Proportion of religious adherence (1): Muslim (Shia) 89%, Muslim (Sunni) 10%
Constitutionally specified state religion (2): Shia Islam
Employment of clergy in military (6): restricted to Muslims
Legislation (8c): all legislation derives from Shari'a law and must not contradict designated religious practice

Banned activities (9a): religious minorities are not permitted to stand for election to representative bodies or high government/military posts; conversion from Islam; Baha'i barred from almost any function, employment, etc.; proselytising to Muslims; anti-Muslim publication or speech
Religious instruction (10c): mandatory in Islamic doctrine
Registration with government (12ciii★★★): only Islam, Judaism, Christianity and Zoroastrianism recognised
The grave of Quddus, a prominent figure in early Baha'i history, and sacred to the **Baha'i** faith, was destroyed despite protests. Destruction began in February 2004 but was halted after local Baha'is demanded to see a legal permit for the demolition work. The destruction continued in secret and was completed by April 2004. (Baha'i World News Service)
Many of Iran's remaining **Zoroastrians** made their annual pilgrimage in May to the temple of Chak-Chak near the city of Yazd. Zoroastrianism is a permitted faith in Iran, but many of their rituals are banned and many believers have emigrated to join coreligionists among India's Parsi community. Since 1979, their numbers have halved. (WRN, AFP)

IRAQ

Proportion of religious adherence (1): Muslim (Shia) 62%, Muslim (Sunni) 33%, Christian 2%
Freedom of worship (8a): constitution provides for this
Among the scores of Iraqi and foreign kidnap victims murdered in Iraq, South Korean interpreter **Kim Sun-il** was reportedly singled out for his faith. In a internet statement attributed to alleged killers Tawhid wa al-Jihad (Unification & Holy War) said Kim was an 'infidel' who studied theology and 'was preparing to become a missionary in the Islamic world.' His employers, Gana Trading, donate 10% of their profits to Christian missionary work. (*Korea Times*)
Violence against Iraq's small but established **Christian commu-**

nity has been on the increase recently. A wave of car bombings targeted five churches in Baghdad and Mosul, killing 12 and injuring at least 66 more, and church leaders and individual families have been targeted by armed factions. The situation has been complicated by the large number of US evangelist Christian groups that flooded into Iraq shortly after the fall of the Saddam regime and mixed the provision of aid to desperate Iraqis with a policy of seeking converts. Some were led by public critics of Islam, such as Franklin Graham of the aid group Samaritan's Purse. The kidnap threat has since driven most out of the country. More than 50 Christian aid groups had their names removed from public files in Baghdad for security reasons. (www.assyrianchristians.com, WRN, *The Age*)

IRELAND

Proportion of religious adherence (1): Roman Catholic 88%, Anglican 3%, none 3%, Christian (other) 1.5

Freedom of worship (8a): constitution provides for this

Religious discrimination (13): law bans this

National holidays recognised (7a): Roman Catholic

Banned activities (9a): publication of blasphemous materials

Religious instruction (10e): mainly Roman Catholic but opt-out permitted

In September 2003, Ireland's Equality Authority said that faith-linked schools could legally refuse to admit students not of their religion, if the school could prove that refusal was essential to maintain the ethos and culture of the school. (www.equality.ie)

ISRAEL

Proportion of religious adherence (1): Jewish 80%, Muslim 16%, Christian 2%, Druze 2%

Constitutionally specified state religion (2): Judaism

Religion favoured by state (4): Judaism

National holidays recognised (7b): Jewish

Freedom of worship (8a): no formal constitution, but law provides for freedom of religion

Banned activities(9a): Offering material benefits as part of proselytising; Mormons voluntarily banned from proselytising

Religious instruction (10e): mainly Jewish but opt-out permitted

Registration with government (12ai**): required of all religious groups

Extent of application of religious law in courts (14a): personal status and family law to be conducted in courts and laws of individuals' religious groups but some opportunity for Muslims and Christians to use civil courts instead in some instances

'Women of the Wall', a 14-year-old organisation seeking equal rights for women to recite from the Torah at Jerusalem's Wailing Wall, say there is no prohibition against women praying in Jewish law, but Orthodox parliamentarians tried to amend public behaviour laws to include a three-year jail sentence for women wearing shawls or citing the Torah near the Wall. (WRN, *Guardian*)

In January 2004, Israel approved the appointment of the Greek Orthodox patriarch of the Holy Land, Irineos I, ending a struggle for recognition of more than two years. (ENI)

The **Armenian Orthodox Patriarch**, Torkom Manoogian, complained that his people are being harassed by what he called 'extremist Jews' in Jerusalem's Old City. 'They spit on us and swear at us when our people walk down the street,' Archbishop Manoogian told Israeli interior minister Avraham Poraz in January 2004. (ENI)

ITALY

Proportion of religious adherence (1): Roman Catholic 87%, Muslim 1.5%, Protestant 1%, none 8%

Secular state (3): religion and state are explicitly separated by the constitution

Religion favoured by state (4): Roman Catholicism

Freedom of worship (8a): no formal constitution, but law provides for freedom of religion

Religious instruction (10e): mainly Roman Catholic but opt-out permitted

Registration with government (12bii*): required in order to gain benefits

JAMAICA

Proportion of religious adherence (1): Church of God 24%, Seventh Day Adventist 11%, Pentecostal 10%, Baptist 7%, Anglican 4%, Roman Catholic 2%, United Church 2%, Methodist 2%, none 22%, Rastafarian 2%

National holidays recognised (7b): Christian

Freedom of worship (8b): constitution provides for this but limited by defence, public safety, public order, public morality, or public health, or for the purpose of protecting the rights of other persons, including the right to observe and practise one's religion without the unsolicited intervention of members of any other religion.

Banned activies (9a): marijuana use, one of the religious practices of Rastafarianism

Registration with government (12ai*): required of all religions

In February 2003, Rastafarian priest Dilipi Campagnie won a case against prison authorities who had barred him from using a prison chapel to baptise inmate Kevin Hall. Lawyers for the litigants said the settlement would pave the way for Rastafarians to petition parliament to grant their churches tax-exempt status, to allow them to perform weddings and to use marijuana as part of their sacraments. Rastafarians and evangelical Christians have been accused of tolerating if not condoning anti-homosexual rhetoric and violence in Jamaica. In January 2004, around 30,000 people attended a huge stage show and Rastafarian celebration in St. Elizabeth, where some of Jamaica's most celebrated artists, performed anti-homosexual songs urging the killing and rape of gays. (*Globe & Mail, Guardian*, AP, BBC, AI)

JAPAN

Proportion of religious adherence (1): Shintoism/Buddhism 70%, none 12%, Christian 3%, 'new reli-

gions' (including indigenous/animist, Unification Church, Church of Scientology) 8%
Freedom of worship (8a): constitution provides for this
Banned activities (9a): visit to the country by Reverend Sun Moon, founder/leader of the Unification Church; Aleph, formerly Aum Shinrikyo.
Monitored activities (9b): 'New religions, sects and cults', following 1995 Metro gas attack by Aum Shinrikyo group.
Religious instruction (10a): not allowed in public schools
Registration with government (12b): required in order to gain benefits
The Aum Shinrikyo group, which under messianic leader Shoko Asahara released nerve gas on the Tokyo subway in 1995, remains in existence, renamed Aleph and supposedly repurposed to humanitarian objectives. The Japanese security services say the group is still violent; its members say they have developed business to raise compensation funds for victims of the 1995 attack. (www.religiousfreedom.com)

JORDAN

Proportion of religious adherence (1): Muslim (Sunni) 95%, Christian 3%
Constitutionally specified state religion (2): Sunni Islam
Employment of clergy in military (6): Muslims
National holidays recognised (7a): for two or more religions
Freedom of worship (8b): constitution provides for this but consistent with public order and morality
Banned activities (9a): proselytising to Muslims; converts from Islam not recognised; use of religious places of worship for political purposes;
Legal requirements (9c): nine seats in parliament allocated to Christians
Religious instruction (10c): Islamic religious instruction for Muslims only
Religious instruction (10e): for all religions but opt-out available for Christians
Government-sponsored religious unity group (11a): Meets frequently
State benefits available for religious

groups (12c): registration not required for Muslims, Druze and Baha'i not recognised
Extent of application of religious law in courts (14a): personal status and family law to be conducted in courts and laws of individuals' religious groups; Druze and Baha'i use Shari'a courts
In January 2003, it was reported that **Siham Qandah**, a Christian widow, had been ordered by a Jordanian court to hand over her two children to be raised as Muslims or be jailed for a month. Her husband had allegedly converted to Islam before his death, making his children Muslims in the eyes of the law. Qandah had to find a Muslim to become her children's legal guardian. (Compass)

KAZAKHSTAN

Proportion of religious adherence (1): Muslim (Sunni) 58%, Russian Orthodox 35%, Evangelical Protestant 2%, Lutheran 2%, Baptists 2%, Protestant 2%
Secular state (3): religion and state are explicitly separated by the constitution
Banned activities (9a): extremist groups
Monitored religions (9b): proselytising by Protestants
Government-sponsored religious unity group (11a): Meets frequently
State benefits available for religious groups (12b): some available after registration which is compulsory for all religious groups
At least five **Baptist churches** were raided, fined or closed for refusing to register with the state over the past year. Pastor Pyotr Panafidin argued in court in May that the constitution and the law on religion did not require it. The court disagreed and fined him twice the minimum monthly wage. Jehovah's Witnesses, who in earlier years faced similar fines after some of their congregations were denied registration, advised the Baptists to follow their example and register. (Forum 18)

KENYA

Proportion of religious adherence (1): Protestant 35%, Roman Catholic 28%, Hindu 1%, Muslim 12%, Indigenous/animist 21%

National holidays recognised (7a): for two or more religions
Freedom of worship (8a): constitution provides for this
Banned activities (9a): Islamic Party of Kenya; witchcraft
Religious instruction (10e): available to all
State benefits available for religious groups (12c): only new religions must register
Extent of application of religious law in courts (14b): Muslims have access to special courts for most family law and personal status matters and increasing number of civil matters
On 13 June, Muslims rioted after the police arrested a cleric for inciting religious hatred during a speech in Bura. During the riots five churches were destroyed. To quell the riot, the Muslim cleric was released by order of an MP and no one was charged over the church burnings. (www.pastornet.net.au)
Opposition MP Billow Kerrow accused the Kenyan government of discriminating against nongovernmental organisations and humanitarian aid groups run by Muslims, allegedly under US pressure. Assistant home affairs minister Noah Arap Too denied the charges that had followed the closure of the **Africa Muslim Agency** aid group and the deportation of two of its directors. (*East African Standard*)
In March, Kenyan Christians protested against the perceived entrenchment of Islamic law in a constitutional review that provided special Muslim courts known as Kadhis courts. (ENI)

KUWAIT

Proportion of religious adherence (1): Muslim (Sunni) 45%, Muslim (Shia) 30%, Muslim (other) 8%, Christian 10%
Constitutionally specified state religion (2): Islam
Religion favoured by the state (4): Islam
National holidays recognised (7b): only Islamic holidays
Freedom of worship (8b): constitution provides for this providing there is no conflict with public policy or morals

Legislation (8c): all legislation derives from Shari'a law and must not contradict designated religious practice
Banned activities (9a): proselytising to Muslims; non-Muslims may not be naturalised; defamation of religion; non-Muslim publishing companies or training of clergy
Religious instruction (10c): Islamic instruction for Muslims only
State benefits available for religious groups (12c): some available after registration which is compulsory for religious groups
On 20 January 2004, the writer **Yasser al-Habib** was sentenced to a year in jail for allegedly defaming companions of the Prophet Mohammed in a public lecture, but then released in an amnesty to mark Kuwaiti National Day. Wahhabi members of the national assembly, angered by his use of Wahhabi texts in his research, pressured the justice minister to re-arrest him. He went into hiding and was later sentenced *in absentia* to 10 years in jail. (PEN-WiPC)

KYRGYZSTAN

Proportion of religious adherence (1): Muslim (Sunni) 76%, Russian Orthodox 12%, Protestant 4%
Secular state (3): religion and state are explicitly separated by the constitution
National holidays recognised (7a): for two or more religions
Freedom of worship (8a): constitution provides for this
*Banned activi*ties (9a): political parties based on religious grounds; Islamic extremist groups, including Hizb ut-Tahrir
Monitored activities (9b): activities of religious groups that jeopardise the state
Religious instruction (10a): not allowed in state schools (under debate)
Government-sponsored religious unity group (11a) meets frequently
State benefits available for religious groups (12aii★★★): some available after registration which is compulsory for all religious groups
Religious discrimination (13): law bans this
In March, conservative Muslims in Karasuu in the southern Osh

region protested the presence of a male obstetrician in a local maternity hospital. A number requested divorces after learning that a man delivered their children. Officials say female obstetricians also worked in the hospital. (US State Dept.)

LAOS

Proportion of religious adherence (1): Buddhist 45%, Indigenous/animist 43%, Christian 2%, None 2%
Religion favoured by state (4): Buddhism
Freedom of worship (8b): constitution provides for this, but nothing must create divisions between religious groups, must conform to all laws and customs
*Banned activi*ties (9a): home religious services; celebration of several Christian holidays; foreigners proselytising
Monitored activities (9b): all religious practice
Religious instruction (10a): not allowed in state schools
Religious instruction (10b): no religiously private funded schools allowed
Government-sponsored religious unity group (11b): infrequent or one-off meetings

On 11 August, Nouhak Phoumsavan, an advisor to the president, held a meeting in Savannakhet City to stop **Christians** gathering in home churches throughout the province. Christians are only allowed to assemble in church buildings that have government permits. Some groups allege that Christians have been threatened and their livestock confiscated, and others coerced into renouncing their faith. (www.worthynews.com)

LATVIA

Proportion of religious adherence (1): Roman Catholic 20%, Lutheran 17%, Latvian Orthodox (and Old Believers) 16%, Evangelical Protestants 2%, Protestant 3%, None 34%
Religion linked to state (5): Traditional religions (Orthodox/ Roman Catholic/Lutheran/Baptists/Jews/Old Believers)

National holidays recognised (7b): for Protestants only
Freedom of worship (8a): constitution provides for this
Monitored activities (9b): passport must have ethnicities printed, including Jewish as ethnicity
Religious instruction (10e): for traditional religions (see above)
Government-sponsored religious unity group (11a): Meets frequently
Registration with government (12b): required in order to gain benefits

On 28 August 2003, **Archbishop Viktor Kontuzorov** of the Autonomous True Orthodox Church was injured in a suspected arson attack on his church in Daugavpils. Kontozurov said he had received several threats prior to the fire. (Forum 18)
On 13 September 2003, the **Jewish cemetery** on Lizuma Street in Riga was vandalised. Chief of state police, Yanis Zashchirinskis insisted that the destruction of the cemetery had been an act of simple hooliganism and was not connected to anti-Semitism (www. eajc.org)

LEBANON

Proportion of religious adherence (1): Muslim 70%, Christian (Maronite) 23%
National holidays recognised (7a): for two or more religions
Freedom of worship (8b): constitution provides for this, but limited by public order
Required practices (9c): President must be Maronite Christian, Prime Minister must be Sunni Muslim, Speaker of Parliament must be Shia Muslim; religious affiliation on ID cards
Religious instruction (10e): for Christians and Muslims
State benefits available for religious groups (12c): registration allowed for 18 recognised groups
Extent of application of religious law in courts (14a): personal status and family law to be conducted in courts and laws of individuals' religious groups

Religious groups not officially recognised by Lebanon's multi-faith government face legal obstacles. **Baha'is, Buddhists,**

Hindus, and some evangelist churches may own property and hold services without interference, but have limited marriage, divorce and inheritance rights. Foreign Protestant Christian churches must register with the Evangelical Synod, but it has refused to accept new members since 1975. (US State Dept)
A bomb attack in the city of Tripoli that killed an Arab convert to Christianity, **Jamil Ahmed al-Rifai**, was 'almost 100 per cent' due to religious hostility, said attack survivor Gerrit 'Joep' Griffioen, a Dutch missionary. (Compass)

LIBYA

Proportion of religious adherence (1): Muslim (Sunni) 97%, Christian 2%
Religion linked to state (5): Islam
Monitored activities (9b): Islamic fundamentalism; all Islamic teaching and practice to be in line with government interpretations
After the revolution that brought Colonel Muammar Qaddafi to power in 1969, over 60,000 Libyan Jews left the country, mostly for Israel. Their families now demand the right to visit their country. On 6 January, Knesset member Jila Jamlil called on Qaddafi to allow Israeli Jews of Libyan descent into the country. (*Ma'ariv*)

LIECHTENSTEIN

Proportion of religious adherence (1): Roman Catholic 78%, Protestant 7%, *Muslim* 3%, None 2%
Constitutionally specified state religion (2): Roman Catholic
Religion linked to state (5): Roman Catholic
Freedom of worship (8a): constitution provides for this
Religious instruction (10e): for Catholics and Protestants
Government-sponsored religious unity group (11a): Meets frequently
Religious discrimination (13): law bans this
Senior Roman Catholic cleric Markus Walser, vicar-general of Liechtenstein's Vaduz diocese has rejected suggestions that church

and state can be separated under ongoing constitutional reforms. 'The constitution states that the Catholic Church is the church of this country … Discussions have been underway for 30 to 40 years about possible changes.' (ENI)

LITHUANIA

Proportion of religious adherence (1): Roman Catholic 79%, Lithuanian Orthodox (and Old Believers) 4%, Protestant 2%, None 10%
National holidays recognised (7a): for Christians only
Freedom of worship (8b): constitution provides for this, but can be limited by law when necessary to protect the safety of society, public order, a person's health or morals, or the fundamental rights and freedoms of others
Monitored activities (9b): 'Sects'
Religious instruction (10e): for all traditional religions
Government-sponsored religious unity group (11b): infrequent or one-off meetings
State benefits available for religious groups (12c): divides groups into four hierarchal categories, traditional religions (Latin Rite Catholics, Greek Rite Catholics, Evangelical Lutherans, Evangelical Reformed Church members, Orthodox Christians (Moscow Patriarchate), Old Believers, Jews, Sunni Muslims and Karaites) do not need to register
In February 2004, the national daily *Respublika* published a series of anti-Semitic editorials titled 'Who Rules the World?' The country's prosecutor general considered charging the paper's editor with incitement to ethnic and racial hatred. In April, parliament formed a working group to strengthen laws punishing incitement of anti-Semitism, racism, and xenophobia. The **Jewish community** of Lithuania argued that while most school textbooks accurately and fairly present the Holocaust, some perpetuate unfavorable stereotypes of Lithuania's pre-WWII Jewish community and thereby promote intolerance. (US State Dept)

MACEDONIA

Proportion of religious adherence (1): Macedonian Orthodox 66%, Muslim 30%, Roman Catholic 1%, Protestant 2%
Freedom of worship (8a): constitution provides for this
Banned activities (9a): Unification Church as a religious group
Monitored activities (9b): contribution collections limited to religious places of worship
Religious instruction (10e): for all religions but opt-out available
Government-sponsored religious unity group (11b): infrequent or one-off meetings
State benefits available for religious groups (12a): registration required of all religious groups
Public worship (15): only established places of worship without permit
A campaign led by Bishop Jovan and the Serbian Orthodox Church against the independence of the breakaway Macedonian Orthodox Church was widely resisted by public, press and government. In January 2004, parliament unanimously voted in support of the Macedonian Church's independence; the government sided with the Macedonian Church by using the law to target Macedonian Church clergy who refused to break with the Serbian church. (Forum 18)
In February, two explosions occurred in Bitola: one at a furniture store owned by an ethnic Macedonian Muslim and the other at **the Asan Baba mosque**. During unrest in Kosovo in March 2004, several Molotov cocktails were thrown at a **mosque in Kumanovo** causing only minimal damage. Later, **two churches** in the Tetovo region were said to have been vandalised following Easter services. (US State Dept)

MADAGASCAR

Proportion of religious adherence (1): Indigenous/animist 40%, Roman Catholic 23%, Christian (Reform) 15%, Lutheran 6%, Anglican 6%, Muslim 8%
Religion linked to state (5): Christian
Freedom of worship (8a): constitution provides for this

Monitored activities (9b): restrictions on Unification Church
Registration with government (12b): required in order to gain benefits
Religious discrimination (13): law bans this

Religious leaders opposed Madagascar's 2004 plan to distribute 15 million free condoms in 2005 as an HIV/AIDS prevention method. Armand Razafimahefa, former head of the island's Protestant church said the plan would encourage promiscuity and suggested that the campaign funds go to HIV vaccine research instead. (AFP)

MALAWI

Proportion of religious adherence (1): Roman Catholic 25%, Presbyterian 20%, Evangelical Protestants 10%, Protestants 15%, Muslim (Sunni) 20%, Indigenous/animist 4%
Freedom of worship (8a): constitution provides for this
Religious instruction (10e): for Christians
Government-sponsored religious unity group (11a): Meets frequently
State benefits available for religious groups (12a): registration required of all religious groups

On 3 June, with allegations of 'hate speech' flying between rival Christian and Muslim broadcasters, the government ordered community radio stations to stop carrying news programmes. The ban was aimed at the Catholic station **Radio Maria**, as well **as Radio Islam**, **Transworld Radio**, **Radio Calvary Church** and **MIJ 90.3**, all of which interview people of all political tendencies. (RSF)

Archbishop Bernard Malango who heads the Anglican Church in Malawi, Zimbabwe, Zambia and Botswana urged clergymen with political ambitions to resign from their church posts before taking part in politics. 'The role of the church is a prophetic one. Those indulging in politics, directly or indirectly, are doing so against the will of the church,' cautioned Malango in March 2004. (ENI)

MALAYSIA

Proportion of religious adherence (1): Muslim (Sunni) 60%, Buddhist 19%, Hindu 6%, Confucianism/Taoism 3%
Constitutionally specified state religion (2): Islam — Malay person is defined as a Muslim
Religion favoured by state (4): Islam
National holidays recognised (7a): for two or more religions
Freedom of worship (8a): constitution provides for this
Banned activities (9a): deviant interpretations of Islam, including strict scrutiny of small Shia population; proselytising to Muslims
Monitored activities (9b): remarks or publications that could incite religious disharmony

On 21 July 2004, **Daud Mamat**, **Kamariah Ali**, and **Mad Yacob Ismail** from Kelantan, lost their appeal to the High Court against a local Sharia court that had convicted them of apostasy for converting from Islam. They had previously argued that they had the constitutional right to practise their own religious beliefs, and that since they were no longer Muslims, a Sharia court could not charge them. (Assist News)

MAURITANIA

ortion of religious adherence (1): Muslim (Sunni) 99%
Constitutionally specified state religion (2): Islam
Religion favoured by state (4): Islam
National holidays recognised (7b): for Muslims only
Legislation (8c): all legislation derives from Shari'a law and must not contradict designated religious practice
Banned activities (9a): proselytising by non-Muslims; distribution of non-Islamic materials; use of mosques for non-religious purposes
Required practices (9c): President, Constitutional Court and High Council of Magistrates must all be Muslims
Religious instruction (10c): Islamic religious instruction mandatory

Although there is no specific law against proselytising, in practice the government prohibits it through the use of Article 11 of the Press Act. This bans publication of material that 'contradicts or otherwise threatens Islamic principles'. In May 2003, the government banned Arab-language newspaper *al-Raya*, noted for its Islamist leanings, under this law. (US State Dept)

After a May 2003 crackdown on Islamic activists, the government closed a number of Saudi- and Gulf-funded **Islamic schools** and charities. It also closed an Islamic charity association in late April for its alleged connections to local Islamic activists. ISERI, the state-supported Institute for Islamic Science, Studies, and Research, remained open and fully funded. (US State Dept)

MEXICO

Proportion of religious adherence (1): Roman Catholic 88%, Pentecostal 1.5%, Evangelical Protestants 2.5%, Protestant 2%, (indigenous/animist overlap), None 4%
Secular state (3): religion and state are explicitly separated by the constitution
National holidays recognised (7b): for Christians only
Freedom of worship (8a): constitution provides for this
Banned activities (9a): clergy cannot hold public office, support candidates, or oppose laws of the state
Religious instruction (10a): not allowed in state schools
Government-sponsored religious unity group (11a): Meets frequently
Registration with government (12ai):* required of all religious groups
Religious discrimination (13): law bans this

In November 2003, politically secular Mexico modified its religious association law to let public officials attend church services, but only in a private capacity. The change followed a year of debate surrounding President Vicente Fox's decision to kiss Pope John Paul's ring during the Pope's visit to Mexico in 2002. (AP)

MOLDOVA

Proportion of religious adherence (1): Moldovan Orthodox 70%, Christian (Old Believers) 4%, Protestant 1%, Roman Catholic 1%, None 20%

Freedom of worship (8a): constitution provides for this
Banned activities (9a): 'abusive' proselytising
Religious instruction (10e): for all religions
Registration with government (12a): required of all religious groups
On 5 March 2004, Chisinau police closed down a **Muslim community centre** detained several Muslims and expelled three Syrian citizens from the country. Community leader **Talgat Masaev** has been repeatedly fined for leading a faith group without state registration. However, Muslim and non-Moldovan Orthodox Church communities have been repeatedly denied state registration, despite the Russian Orthodox Church Abroad winning a high court appeal against the practice. The case is now before the European Court of Human Rights, which fined Moldova in 2002 for denying the Romanian Orthodox Church the right to register. (Forum 18)

MOROCCO (AND WESTERN SAHARA)

Proportion of religious adherence (1): Muslim (Sunni) 99%
Constitutionally specified state religion (2): Islam
National holidays recognised (7b): for Muslims only
Banned activities (9a): proselytising to Muslims; Arabic bibles
Monitored activities (9b): limits placed on Muslim groups whose activities exceed 'religious bounds' ie Baha'i
Religious instruction (10e): for Muslims and Jews
Government-sponsored religious unity group (11a): Meets frequently
Extent of application of religious law in courts (14a): personal status and family law to be conducted in courts and laws of individuals' religious groups
Public worship (15): limits on public worship by government
Since the 16 May 2003 bombings by an Islamic fundamentalist group in Casablanca, the authorities have strictly monitored the activities of Moroccan **Imams**. Several have been among more than 6,000 people questioned and

2,000 jailed for their religious and political activities. In this new environment, the state reformed the family code (*Moudawana*), raising the age of marital consent to 18, reinforcing divorce rights and giving men and women legal equality as parents. The law was passed unanimously early in 2004 with little opposition from the state-endorsed Islamist PJD party. Three years earlier, similar plans brought a million protestors on to the streets in Casablanca. (US State Dept, www.pbs.org)

MOZAMBIQUE

Proportion of religious adherence (1): Roman Catholic 14%, Protestant 11%, Muslim 10%, Christian (other) 7%, (Indigenous/animist overlap) 80%
Secular state (3): religion and state are explicitly separated by the constitution
Freedom of worship (8a): constitution provides for this
Banned activities (9a): religious groups from forming political parties; political parties from espousing religious propaganda
Religious instruction (10a): not allowed in state schools
Government-sponsored religious unity group (11a): Meets frequently
Registration with government (12a): required of all religious groups
Brazilian Lutheran missionary **Doraci Edinger** was murdered after she had supported Catholic nuns investigating organ and child trafficking in the Nampula region. Her body was found on 23 February. The Lutheran World Federation expressed its concern over 'apparent delays' in the investigation. (Afrol)

NEPAL

Proportion of religious adherence (1): Hindu 81%, Buddhist 11%, Muslim 4%, Indigenous/animist 3%, Christian 1%
Religion favoured by state (4): Hindu
National holidays recognised (7b): for Hindus only
Freedom of worship (8a): constitution provides for this
Banned activities (9a): converting others or proselytising
Monitored activities (9b): Islamic schools (*madrassas*) must register

Religious discrimination (13): law bans this
Following the murder of 12 Nepali workers in Iraq by alleged Islamists, crowds stormed the main mosque in Kathmandu chanting 'down with Islam' on 1 September. One man was killed by police and another killed when the mob turned on the city's Egyptian embassy. About 3.5 per cent of Nepal's population is Muslim. (Reuters)

NETHERLANDS

Proportion of religious adherence (1): Roman Catholic 32%, Protestant 16%, Muslim 6%, None 40%
Secular state (3): religion and state are explicitly separated by the constitution
Freedom of worship (8b): constitution provides for this, but limited by health hazards, traffic safety, and risk of public disorder
Banned activities (9a): wearing of burqas in school
Government-sponsored religious unity group (11a): Meets frequently
Registration with government (12b): required in order to gain benefits
Religious discrimination (13): law bans this

NICARAGUA

Proportion of religious adherence (1): Roman Catholic 73%, Evangelical Protestant 15%, Christian 3%, None 8%
Religion favoured by state (4): Roman Catholic
Freedom of worship (8a): constitution provides for this
Registration with government (12bi):* required in order to gain benefits
Religious discrimination (13): law bans this
In February 2003, the Auxiliary Bishop of Mangua, Jorge Solorzano excommunicated a number of people, including the child's parents, who had helped a nine year old rape victim have an abortion. The Church later withdrew the decision after an internet campaign led 26,000 Catholics to sign a petition reading 'I also want to be excommunicated in the face of the excommunication of Rosa's parents in Nicaragua because all of us have contributed actively in

making the interruption of Rosa's pregnancy possible.' (CBS News, BBC, Nicaragua Network)

NIGERIA

Proportion of religious adherence (1): Muslim (Sunni) 46%, Muslim (Shia) 4%, Christian 40%, Indigenous/animist 10%
National holidays recognised (7a): for two or more religions
Freedom of worship (8a): constitution provides for this
Banned activities (9a): sporadically for religious advertisements; religious organisations on primary school grounds
Religious instruction (10d): mandated and available for Muslims and Christians
Government-sponsored religious unity group (11b): infrequent or one-off meetings
Registration with government (12b): required in order to gain benefits
Religious discrimination (13): law bans this
Extent of application of religious law in courts (14b): religious based law/courts in designated areas, for designated religions and citizens
Public worship (15): limits on public worship by government
An inter-religious centre established by Nigeria's Anglican Communion, aimed at creating a suitable environment for adherents of both Christianity and Islam to study each other's religions, turned out its first graduates in January 2004. Graduates included clergy, lawyers, medical doctors, university teachers from various parts of the north of Nigeria. Students from Chad and Sudan were among these. (ENI)
The Anglican Church of Nigeria, which reportedly administers to one-third of the world's Anglicans, roundly rejected the election of the gay canon **Gene Robinson** as Bishop of New Hampshire in the US. In March 2003, Nigerian Archbishop Peter Akinola refused to attend a meeting of fellow church leaders alongside US churchmen who had consented to the ordaining of gay clergy. (Afrol)
In September 2003, **Amina Lawal** was acquitted of adultery by a Sharia appeals court in Nigeria on procedural grounds. If the

conviction had stood, she would have been buried up to her chest and stoned to death. Another woman, **Fatima Usman**, remains under death sentence for adultery. No stonings have yet been carried out, but a Sharia court did order the surgical removal of the left eye of one **Ahmed Tejsan** after he partially blinded a friend. **Abubakar Ali**, had a hand amputated for stealing. (freedomhouse.org)
Christian fundamentalists were urged to stop destroying relics from the country's traditional tribal faiths and show 'mutual respect and understanding'. Traditional faith leader Igwe Promise Eze, said some of the recently destroyed artifacts had been the focus of tribal devotions for four centuries. (*This Day*)

NORTH KOREA

Proportion of religious adherence (1): None 73%, Christian 2%, Buddhist 2%, Indigenous/animist 5%
Freedom of worship (8b): religion should not be used for purposes of dragging in foreign powers or endangering public security
Banned activities (9a): proselytising
North Korea, though a closed society, is more open to Christianity than outsiders may think, claimed Dr Kim Yong-Beck of the Presbyterian Church of South Korea in August. He reported that new churches are being built and theological schools opened. (ENI)

PAKISTAN

Proportion of religious adherence (1): Muslim (Sunni) 88%, Muslim (Shia) 8%, Hindu 2%, Christian 1.5%, Ahmadis 0.2%
Constitutionally specified state religion (2): Islam
Religion favoured by state (4): Islam
National holidays recognised (7b): for Muslims only
Banned activities (9a): proselytising by Ahmadis; actions or speech derogatory to Islam
Monitored activities (9b): Madrassas (religious schools) must register; Ahmadi faith severely restricted; Islamic extremists; restricts distribution of Christian images
Religious instruction (10c): Islamic instruction, only available to Muslims

Religious instruction (10e): permitted for non-Muslims but little provision in reality
Government-sponsored religious unity group (11b): infrequent or one-off meetings
Extent of application of religious law in courts (14b): for marriages, respective faiths; Shari'a law applies in many situations to all citizens, criminal and civil
Public worship (15): limits on public worship by government, for Ahmadis in particular
Anwer Masih, a Christian, was arrested for blasphemy by police in the town of Shadhra. He had made comments about a neighbour's beard, unaware that the man had become a Muslim. A day later, on 29 November 2003, the neighbour turned up at the head of a mob of 100 Islamist militants from a city 70 miles away. Masih was arrested the next day. Commenting on the case in December, the *Daily Times* noted that 'so far not a single conviction under the blasphemy law has been upheld in the higher courts'. (Compass, Daily Times)
Karachi police arrested one suspect and seized a cache of powerful explosives from a group linked to an attack on a Bible Society shop on 15 January that injured at least 13 people. At the time, seven attacks targeting Pakistan's **Christian churches and institutions** had killed 42 and injured more than 100 since September 2001 when the government threw its support behind the US-led war on al-Qaida supporters in the region. (Compass, BBC)

PALESTINE

Proportion of religious adherence (1): Muslim (Sunni) 98%, Protestant 2% (Jewish settlers present)
Constitutionally specified state religion (2): Islam
Religion favoured by state (4): Islam
National holidays recognised (7b): for Muslims only
Legislation (8c): all legislation derives from Shari'a law and must not contradict designated religious practice
Required practices (9c): citizen must be affiliated with a religion
Religious instruction (10d): man-

dated and available for Muslims and Christians

State benefits available for religious groups (12): Recognition only given to the three monotheistic beliefs: Judaism/Islam/Christianity

Extent of application of religious law in courts (14a): personal status and family law to be conducted in courts and laws of individuals' religious groups **Nader Sadakah**, one of the country's tiny remaining Samaritan community of 660, was shunned for his membership of the Popular Front for the Liberation of Palestine (PFLP), a left-wing PLO faction. In July 2004, Hosni Wasif, a Samaritan high priest in Nablus, said Israeli authorities had begun to take a hard line against Samaritans because of Sadakah's activities. 'By joining a left-wing faction he left our religion,' he said. 'The entire sect sees him as an apostate.' Samaritans descended from the ancient Israelite tribes but broke away from mainstream Judaism 2,800 years ago. (AP, WRN)

PANAMA

Proportion of religious adherence (1): Roman Catholic 81%, Evangelical Protestants 9%, Christian (other) 3%

Religion linked to state (5): Roman Catholic

Freedom of worship (8b): constitution provides for this, but provision limited by Christian morality and public order

Banned activities (9a): ministers of religion can only hold public office in roles related to social assistance, education, or scientific research

Monitored activities (9b): Unification Church limited in some ways

Religious instruction (10e): for Catholics

Anglican Bishop Julio Murray of Panama warned presidential candidates, ahead of the 2 May national election, to limit their election promises and curb attempts 'to dupe the people with proposals difficult to fulfill'. 'Considering the realities of growing unemployment, lack of social security, rampant violence and

public corruption, we need viable proposals and not mere electoral promises', said Murray. (ENI)

PHILIPPINES

Proportion of religious adherence (1): Roman Catholic 78%, Protestant 7%, Christian (other) 4%, Muslim 8%, Indigenous/animist 1%

Secular state (3): religion and state are explicitly separated by the constitution

Religion linked to state (5): Roman Catholic

National holidays recognised (7a): for two or more religions

Freedom of worship (8a): constitution provides for this

Monitored activities (9b): Madrassas

Religious instruction (10e): for all religions but opt-out available

Government-sponsored religious unity group (11a): Meets frequently

Registration with government (12b): required in order to gain benefits

Extent of application of religious law in courts (14b): religious based law/courts in designated areas, for designated religions and citizens; Shari'a law for Muslims in civil matters only

Church leaders appealed to President Gloria Macapagal-Arroyo to re-institute a moratorium on the death penalty, in a bid to halt the scheduled 30 January 2004 execution of two convicted kidnappers. 'As Christians, we have to uphold the absolute dominion of God over human life,' Roman Catholic Bishop Vicente Navarra of the Bacolod diocese in central Philippines said. (ENI. AI)

POLAND

Proportion of religious adherence (1): Roman Catholic 96%, Orthodox 2%, Protestant 1%

Secular state (3): religion and state are explicitly separated by the constitution

Religion linked to state (5): Roman Catholic

National holidays recognised (7b): for Catholics only

Freedom of worship (8a): constitution provides for this

Monitored activities (9b): Unification Church declared 'sect'

Religious instruction (10e): should be provided in four recognised

religions: Roman Catholic/ Protestant/Orthodox/Jewish

Government-sponsored religious unity group (11b): infrequent or one-off meetings

Registration with government (12b): required in order to gain benefits

On 20 February 2004, Witold Murczkieicz, crime prevention chief for the Gdansk region, ordered police to list and monitor minority religious organisations, among them **Baptists, Pentecostals, Adventists** and **Jehovah's Witnesses**. Police later questioned Pentecostal pastor **Tomasz Ropiejko** and pastor **Rober Miksa** of Gdansk's First Baptist Church about their activities. (Forum 18)

In January 2004, church leaders in Poland lamented the state of inter-church relations. 'Looking at our mutual ties and wider church politics, I don't see any great rapprochement,' said Metropolitan Sawa, the head of Poland's 570 000-member Orthodox church. 'Though there are unresolved issues between us, and many levels of dialogue, we don't note much movement or activity.' (ENI)

QATAR

Proportion of religious adherence (1): Muslim (Sunni) 95%, Muslim (Shia) 1%

Constitutionally specified state religion (2): Islam

Religion favoured by state (4): Islam

National holidays recognised (7b): for Muslims only

Freedom of worship (8b): constitution provides for this, but provision limited by protecting the public system and public behaviour

Legislation (8c): all legislation derives from Shari'a law and must not contradict designated religious practice

Banned activities (9a): non-Muslims from proselytising or public worship; conversion by Muslims; publication, importation and distribution of non-religious books and materials

Monitored activities (9b): Hindus/Buddhists/Baha'is less free than Muslims or Christians

Required practices (9c): all citizens Muslim

Religious instruction (10c): Islamic instruction mandatory
State benefits available for religious groups (12c): Arbitrary determination of ability to register
Religious discrimination (13): law bans this
Public worship (15): limits on public worship by government
In January 2003, Indian Christian **Stanislas Chellappa** and his family were deported, apparently because of his role as pastor to a small congregation of Tamil-speaking Christian migrant workers in Doha. Similarly, Filipino churchman **Nemencio Mendoza Bonton** was deported after 20 years residency in Qatar, reportedly in connection with his role as senior pastor of the Qatar International Christian Ministries. (Compass, www.hrwf.net)

ROMANIA

Proportion of religious adherence (1): Romanian Orthodox 87%, Roman Catholic 5%, Protestant 7%
Religion favoured by state (4): Romanian Orthodox
National holidays recognised (7b): for Romanian Orthodox only
Freedom of worship (8a): constitution provides for this
Monitored activities (9b): proselytising by non-Romanian Orthodox
Religious instruction (10e): only seventeen groups allowed to teach beliefs
Government-sponsored religious unity group (11b): infrequent or one-off meetings
Registration with government (12a): hierarchy of registration and benefits, only seventeen groups recognised as religious groups, others as cultural/charitable foundations
In August 2004, Romanian Orthodox priest **Agapie Aurel Rusu** was reportedly punished for delivering a five-hour funeral service. He was told to live in seclusion for a month on just bread and water. Zenovie Mosoiu, spokesman for the Orthodox Church in Brasov said that normally a service cannot take more than an hour with the priest's sermon included. (Ananova)

RUSSIA

Proportion of religious adherence (1): Russian Orthodox 52%, Muslim 14%, Protestant 2%, Roman Catholic 2%, Jews 0.5%, None 25%
Secular state (3): religion and state are explicitly separated by the constitution
Religion favoured by state (4): Russian Orthodox
Employment of clergy in military (6): Muslims banned
National holidays recognised (7a): for two or more religions
Freedom of worship (8a): constitution provides for this
Banned activities (9a): 'Sects and cults'
Monitored activities (9b): religious 'groups' severely restricted; non-registered groups can be 'liquidated' or 'banned'; all non-Russian Orthodox viewed as threat to nation; very difficult for foreigners to gain visas
Religious instruction (10e): Mainly Russian Orthodox
State benefits available for religious groups (12c): 4 religions recognised as traditional: Russian Orthodox/Judaism/Islam/Buddhism; hierarchy of recognition
Religious discrimination (13): law bans this
During 2002 and 2003, one person was killed and several injured by **anti-semitic** signs planted around the country and booby-trapped with explosives. The bombs were set to go off if anyone tried to remove the signs, a deliberate targeting of Jews and sympathisers. (www.eajc.org)
On 1 April 2004, **Sergei Popov**, **Aleksandr Takhteyev** and **Yevgeni Perov** were sacked by their employers on the Russian Pacific island of Sakhalin for being Jehovah's Witnesses. The Nevada Company alleged that their faith made them a security threat. Popov claimed one manager believed the trio would rob the firm 'if told so by their religious superiors'. (Forum 18)
The director of the Andrei Sakharov museum, **Yury Samodurov** and artists **Lyudmila Vasilovskaya** and **Anna Mikhalchuk** face up to five years in jail for inciting religious hatred

with an exhibition entitled *Caution: Religion* shown in February 2003. It had featured a sculpture of an orthodox church made of vodka bottles among other controversial items and was largely destroyed by a group of vandals after four days. The attackers were later acquitted by a Moscow court. (www.wwrn.org)

RWANDA

Proportion of religious adherence (1): Roman Catholic 49%, Protestant 30%, Anglican 8%, Muslim 4%
National holidays recognised (7a): for two or more religions
Freedom of worship (8a): constitution provides for this
Banned activities (9a): no political organisations based on religion
Monitored activities (9b): regulates all public meetings
Religious instruction (10e): available to all
Registration with government (12a): required of all religious groups
Public worship (15): limits on public worship by government
Archbishop Emmanuel Kolini, Primate of the Episcopal Church of Rwanda, has established The Interfaith Commission for Reintegration of Rwanda. The Archbishop heads the organisation, his deputy is Rwanda's Islamic leader, Shehe Mufti Habimana Saleh. (Afrol)

SAUDI ARABIA

Proportion of religious adherence (1): Muslim (Sunni) 85%, Muslim (Shia) 8%, Roman Catholic 3%, Christian 1%
Constitutionally specified state religion (2): Islam
Religion favoured by state (4): Islam
National holidays recognised (7b): Islam (Sunni)
Legislation (8c): all legislation derives from Shari'a law and must not contradict designated religious practice
Banned activities (9a): Proselytising of any non-Islamic religion, public worship, publication of materials; conversion from Islam; non-Islamic clergy from entering country; most Sunni practices
Monitored activities (9b): Religious 'extremism'

Required practices (9c): Non-citizens must carry religious-affiliated ID cards; No constitution; all citizens are Muslim
Religious instruction (10b): No non-Islamic schools funded by religious groups
Religious instruction (10c): Islamic instruction mandatory
Government-sponsored religious unity group (11b): Infrequent or one-off government sponsored inter-faith meetings
Extent of application of religious law in courts (14b): Shia Muslims have extremely limited access to Shia judges, although permitted by law
In March 2004, 37-year-old Saudi school teacher **Mohammed al-Suhami** was jailed for three years and given 300 lashes for blasphemy. His own students testified against him, alleging that by describing love as 'a great and noble feeling' he was promoting homosexuality and leading them to decadence by speaking favourably about music. (*Asharq al-Awsat*)
A new Saudi school textbook, *Monotheism and Fiqh,* demonises the West and Christians and Jews in particular, reported the Saudi Institute, a Washington-based pro-reform group in a July 2004 study. (*Guardian*)
Saudi Arabia's highest religious authority has issued an edict barring the use of mobile phones with built-in cameras, blaming them for 'spreading obscenity' after a ban on their sale and import failed to dent their popularity. Religious authorities complain camera phones are misused to photograph women without their knowledge. (AP)
In October the US government unexpectedly accused Saudi Arabia of 'particularly severe violations' of religious freedom and warned that the country faced US sanctions as a result. It also cited the use of 'violent anti-Jewish and anti-Christian language' by state-sponsored Imams. (*Washington Post*)

SERBIA & MONTENEGRO

Proportion of religious adherence (1): Serbian Orthodox 78%, Muslim

5%, Roman Catholic 4%, Protestant 1%, None 6%
Religion favoured by state (4): Serbian Orthodox
Employment of clergy in military (6): Serbian Orthodox (subject to change)
Freedom of worship (8a): constitution provides for this
Religious instruction (10e): Religious instruction allowed for but opt-out permitted; Serbian Orthodox/Muslim/Roman Catholic/Christian (Reform)/Evangelical Protestants/Jewish
Government-sponsored religious unity group (11b): Infrequent or one-off government sponsored inter-faith meetings
At least 28 people were killed, and about 1,000 injured across Kosovo in violence between **Kosovo Albanians** and **Kosovo Serbs**, resulting in the destruction of some 30 Orthodox churches and monasteries in Kosovo and retaliatory arson attacks on mosques in Belgrade and Nis. In a bid to ease tensions Anastasios, Archbishop of Tirana, offered US$600 000 for the restoration of a church and mosque in Kosovo. 'The burning of churches and mosques, does not promote justice and peace, and certainly neither progress,' said Anastasios, Orthodox Archbishop of Tirana and Albania. (ENI, Forum 18)
In July 2004 Serbia's Ministry of Religious Affairs tabled a new draft law on religion that will give full rights only to religious communities recognised by the parliament of the former Yugoslavia between 1918 and 1941 - the Serbian Orthodox Church, Catholics, Muslims, Jews, Lutherans and the Hungarian Reformed Church. Other religious communities would be denied the right to state financial support, to perform marriages and funerals. (Forum 18)

SINGAPORE

Proportion of religious adherence (1): Buddhist/Taoist/Indigenous/animist 45%, Muslim 15%, Hindu 4%, Roman Catholic 4%, Protestant 8%, Christian 2%, None 8%
National holidays recognised (7a):

Government recognises holidays from two or more religions
Freedom of worship (8b): Limited by other laws relating to public order, public health or morality
Banned activities (9a): Unification Church, Jehovah's Witnesses; no controversial religious speech
Monitored activities (9b): Religious leaders or groups engaged in political activity, insensitive proselytising, subversive activities
Religious instruction (10a): No religious instruction in public schools allowed
Government-sponsored religious unity group (11b): Infrequent or one-off government sponsored inter-faith meetings
Registration with government (12a): required of all religious groups
During 2003, five conscientious objectors to military service were imprisoned; 19 others continued to serve their sentences. All were members of the banned **Jehovah's Witnesses** religious group. (AI)

SLOVAKIA

Proportion of religious adherence (1): Roman Catholic 73%, Lutheran 7%, Orthodox 1%, Christian (Reform) 2%, None 13%
Religion linked to state (5): Roman Catholic
National holidays recognised (7b): Government recognises Christian holidays only
Monitored activities (9b): Sects and Cults
Religious instruction (10e): open to all religions
Registration with government (12b): required in order to gain benefits
In January 2003, a **Jewish cemetery** in Banovce nad Bebravou was desecrated and 35 tombs were destroyed, the fourth such attack on the cemetery. The town is the birthplace of the pro-Nazi WWII Slovak leader and Catholic priest Jozef Tiso. The vandals received suspended sentences of four-seven months. (www.icrf.com)

SLOVENIA

Proportion of religious adherence (1): Roman Catholic 64%, Evangelical Protestants 1%, Orthodox 2.5%, Muslim 2.5%, None 15%

Freedom of worship (8a): constitution provides for this
Religious instruction (10e): religious instruction debated; only schools supported by religious groups teach it currently
Government-sponsored religious unity group (11a): meets frequently
Registration with government (12b): required in order to gain benefits (subject to change)
On 7 August 2003, the Calvary Chapel Protestant church in Celje became the first new religious community to be granted registration in Slovenia since 1999. The registration of the Tibetan Buddhist Dharmaling association followed on 22 August. (Forum 18) Muslims in Slovenia protested after state-run television refused to concede free airtime for live programmes for Muslim communities during Ramadan. (www.forf.org)

SPAIN

Proportion of religious adherence (1): Roman Catholic 82%, Muslim 2.5%, None 13%
Secular state (3): religion and state are explicitly separated by the constitution
Religion linked to state (5): Roman Catholic
National holidays recognised (7a): only Christian holidays recognised
Freedom of worship (8b): limited by maintenance of public order
Religious instruction (10e): Religious instruction for all allowed for but opt-out permitted
Registration with government (12a): required of all religious groups
Religious discrimination (13): Law bans this
Spanish Protestants protested religious discrimination ahead of parliamentary elections on 14 March. 'Very few things have improved in the matter of religious freedom in our country' since the restoration of democracy, said Mariano Blazquez, executive secretary of the Federation of Evangelical Religious Entities of Spain. Blazquez said **Protestants** did not enjoy the same tax exemptions as the Roman Catholic Church. (Adventist Press Service)

SOMALIA

(No functioning government)
Proportion of religious adherence (1): Muslim (Sunni) 95%, Muslim (others) 3%, Christian 1%
Banned activities (9a): Proseltyzing by non-Muslims
Extent of application of religious law in courts (14b): Some laws based on Shar'ia, regional differences
No Constitution
There were several attacks against **non-Muslim international relief workers** in 2003; in April 2004, thousands of citizens marched through the streets of Mogadishu and in the southern coastal town of Merca protesting against alleged attempts by aid agencies to spread Christianity. Protesters set ablaze hundreds of cartons containing goods, some marked only as gifts from the 'Swiss Church'. (US State Dept.) In March 2004, warlord Mohamed Omar Habeb **banned women from wearing veils** and jailed at least 17 women who violated the decree. He alleged that the full body covers were being used by men to conceal weapons. Habeb later released the women following an outcry by Islamic scholars. (US State Dept.)

SOUTH AFRICA

Proportion of religious adherence (1): Christian (African Independent) 35%, Christian (Dutch Reform) 10%, Roman Catholic 9%, Methodist 8%, Anglican 4%, Lutheran 3%, Presbyterian 2%, Baptists 1%, Christian (Congregational) 1%, Christian (Other) 3%, Hindu 1.5%, Muslim 1.5%, None 10%, Indigenous/animist 5%
National holidays recognised (7b): only Christian holidays recognised
Freedom of worship (8a): constitution provides for this
Monitored activities (9b): Rising Islamist extremist groups
Religious instruction (10e): Religious instruction for all allowed for but opt-out permitted
Scores of right-wing white supremacist Christian faith groups are being founded by Christians who believe that black majority rule is God's punishment for the disobedience by the Afrikaner people. Reverend Willie Smith,

formerly a Baptist minister for 26 years, founded Lewende Hoop (Living Hope) in the late 1990s and said: 'Our leaders sold us out. They want us to mix with the other races. But it is not working. The other churches are preaching that you must love all. But we don't want that.' (www.religioustolerance.org)
A government task-force evaluating the number of public holidays warned that that no holiday should be regarded as sacred in multiracial South Africa. The Johannesburg *Sunday Times* quoted Muslim leader Sheikh Achmat Sedick as describing Christmas and Easter as 'legacies of apartheid'. (*Sunday Times*)

SOUTH KOREA

Proportion of religious adherence (1): Buddhist 22%, Protestant 18%, Roman Catholic 6%, None 50%
Secular state (3): religion and state are explicitly separated by the constitution
Freedom of worship (8a): constitution provides for this
Religious instruction (10a): not allowed in public schools
Government-sponsored religious unity group (11a): Meets frequently

SRI LANKA

Proportion of religious adherence (1): Buddhist 70%, Hindu 15%, Roman Catholic 6%, Protestant 2%, Muslim 7%
Religion linked to state (5): Buddhism
National holidays recognised (7a): for two or more religions
Freedom of worship (8a): constitution provides for this
Banned activities (9a): Jesuits banned from allowing entrance of new clergy in last 30 years
Religious instruction (10d): mandated and available for designated religions:
Buddhist/Muslim/Hindu/Christian
Government-sponsored religious unity group (11a): Meets frequently
Extent of application of religious law in courts (14a): personal status and family law to be conducted in courts and laws of individuals' religious groups

The National Christian Evangelical Alliance of Sri Lanka (NCEASL) blamed a series of attacks on Christian churches from summer 2003 on supporters of anti-conversion laws sought by Buddhist nationalists and some Hindu groups. It said that 136 Christian places of worship had been attacked between January 2003 and January 2004. On 8 February, the Anuradhapura office of the **Christian** humanitarian agency World Vision was firebombed. Three Buddhist monks and a university professor were charged with this attack. (Sri Lanka Project Briefing, TamilNet, *Frontline* and see p190)

In June the attorney general ordered a ban on the sale of bikinis decorated with Buddha images after a Buddhist monk, the Venerable Daranaagama Kusaladhamma Thera, petitioned the Supreme Court for the ban. On 18 June, foreign minister Lakshman Kadirgamar made appealed for an end to the commercial exploitation of the image of the Buddha. (BBC, Daily News)

SUDAN

Proportion of religious adherence (1): Muslim (Sunni) 70%, Indigenous/animist 10%, Christian 15%
Religion favoured by the state (4): Islam
Employment of clergy in military (6): restricted to Muslims
Legislation (8c): all legislation derives from Shari'a law and must not contradict designated religious practice
Banned activities (9a): Conversion from Islam; proselytising by non-Muslims; Christians forbidden from burial in Muslim cemeteries; non-Muslims may only adopt non-Muslim children; abandoned children deemed Muslim only
Monitored activities (9b): Religious publications
Religious instruction (10d): mandated and available for Islam for Muslims in the North; choice of Islamic or Christian elsewhere
Government-sponsored religious unity group (11b):
Registration with government (12a): all religious groups

Extent of application of religious law in courts (14a): personal status and family law to be conducted in courts and laws of individuals' religious groups

SWEDEN

Proportion of religious adherence (1): Lutheran 78%, Catholic 1.5%, Orthodox 1%, Muslim 2.5%, None 15%
Secular state (3): religion and state are explicitly separated by the constitution
Freedom of worship (8a): constitution provides for this
Religious instruction (10d): General religious instruction
Government-sponsored religious unity group (11a): Meets frequently
Religious discrimination (13): Law bans this

Lutheran Bishop of Stockholm Bishop Caroline Krook defended her decision to officially open the city's four day 'Stockholm Pride' gay and lesbian festival in July saying that a faithful partnership for life is a gift from God. (ENI)

A Swedish court jailed Pentecostal Ake Green for a month in prison in June 2004 for incitement. He had described homosexuality as 'a horrible cancerous tumour in the body of society'. (ENI)

SWITZERLAND

Proportion of religious adherence (1): Roman Catholic 42%, Protestant 33%, Orthodox 2%, Muslim 4%, None 11%
Separation of church and state in Constitution (3): Cantons (regional demarcations) have different laws on relationship between church and state
Freedom of worship (8a): constitution provides for this
Banned activities/religions (9a): Jesuits; proselytising in an intrusive manner; ritual slaughter of animals, part of some religions
Religious instruction (10e): Mainly dominant religion of the canton
Religious discrimination (13): Law bans this

SYRIA

Proportion of religious adherence (1): Muslim (Sunni) 74%, Muslim (other) 16%, Christian 10%

Religion favoured by the state (4): Islam
National holidays recognised (7a) for two or more religions
Freedom of worship (8a): constitution provides for this
Banned activities/religions (9a): Jews are banned from being in the military and being employed by the government
Monitored activities (9b): Proselytising discouraged; militant Islamic groups and individuals
Required practices (9c): Jews must show their affiliation on ID cards and passports; President of the country must be Muslim
Religious instruction (10d): mandated and available for Christians and Muslims
Registration with government (12aii*): required of all religious groups
Extent of application of religious law in courts (14a): personal status and family law to be conducted in courts and laws of individuals' religious groups

After a series of bombings in Turkey in 2003, Syria expelled 22 Turks, three of whom were among some 1,000 foreign students who attend Damascus's Abu Nour Foundation each year to study Arabic and Islam. In March 2004, Syria said it would no longer allow new foreign students to register at Islamic schools. (BBC)

TAJIKISTAN

Proportion of religious adherence (1): Muslim (Sunni) 88%, Muslim (Shia) 5%, Muslim (other) 2%, Russian Orthodox 1.5%, None 2%
Secular state (3): religion and state are explicitly separated by the constitution
National holidays recognised (7b) only Islamic holidays
Freedom of worship (8a): constitution provides for this
Banned activities/religions (9a): Members of Hizb ut-Tahrir; political parties may not get support from religious groups; government printing presses may not print in Arabic
Monitored activities (9b): Militant Islamic groups and individuals; religious groups commenting on

political matters; imams must be tested for religious knowledge
Religious instruction (10a): not allowed in public schools
Registration with government (12aii**): required of all religious groups
Extent of application of religious law in courts (14a): personal status and family law to be conducted in courts and laws of individuals' religious groups
The last of Tajikistan's **Jewish** community, fewer than 500, have been ordered to vacate Dushanbe's century-old synagogue, the last in the country, to make way for a new presidential palace. The government has offered an alternative plot for a new synagogue, but the community cannot afford it. (RFL/Radio Liberty)

TANZANIA

Proportion of religious adherence (1): Catholic 25%, Protestant 15%, Muslim (Sunni) 27%, Muslim (Shia) 3%, Indigenous/animist 15%
National holidays recognised (7a): for two or more religions
Freedom of worship (8b): limited by checks of public order and safety
Banned activities/religions (9a): Preaching or distribution of materials that are inflammatory; religious groups involved with politics; political parties' use of religious language
Religious instruction (10e): General
Registration with government (12ai*): required of all religious groups
Religious discrimination (13): Law bans this
Extent of application of religious law in courts (14a): Muslims can choose Shari'a law for family and personal status
Some 20 people from Makete, Iringa region, have been charged with murdering seven men they suspected of practicing witchcraft, it was reported in August 2004. Among the accused are village leaders and other local officials who ordered the killings, according to the police. (BBC)

THAILAND

Proportion of religious adherence (1): Buddhist 85%, Muslim 8%, Christian 2%, Indigenous/animist 3%
Religion favoured by state (4): Buddhism
Banned activities/religions (9a): Insulting Buddha; female Muslims banned from wearing the headscarf when in civil service uniform
Monitored activities (9b): Some Falun Gong on immigration 'blacklist'
Required practices (9c): the Monarch must be a Buddhist
Religious instruction (10d): mandatory in Buddhism and Islam
Government-sponsored religious unity group (11a): Meets frequently
State benefits available for religious groups (12ci*): group must be accepted into one of 7 officially recognised groups (Buddhist, Muslim, Roman Catholic, Protestant); government has not registered any new groups since 1984
Religious discrimination (13): Law bans this
On 22 May 2004, Buddhist **Sieng Patkaoe** was decapitated by men with machetes as he worked on his rubber plantation in the southern province of Narathiwat. A note pinned to his body read: 'If innocent Malayu (the predominant ethnic group in the Muslim South) continue to be arrested, we will murder more Buddhists'. (www.religionnewsblog.com)

TIBET

Proportion of religious adherence (1): Buddhist 99%
Freedom of worship (8a): constitution provides for this
Banned activities/religions (9a): No political dissent in the form of religious practice; ownership of photographs of the Dalai Lama; government employees from entering monasteries
Monitored activities (9b): Dalai Lama declared a criminal by Chinese government; limits building of Buddhist monasteries as sites of political dissent; weeding out anti-government nuns and monks; limits on foreign visitors
In October 2003, Tibetan monk **Nyima Dragpa** of Dawu County in Sichuan Province's Kardze Prefecture died from tor-

ture while serving a nine-year sentence for state subversion. (TIN)
On February 24, authorities released Tibetan Buddhist nun **Phuntsog Nyidrol** from prison. She had served eight years for taking part in a peaceful demonstration in support of the Dalai Lama in 1989. Authorities extended her sentence after she and other nuns recorded songs about their devotion to Tibet and the Dalai Lama in 1993. (TIN)

TRINIDAD & TOBAGO

Proportion of religious adherence (1): Roman Catholic 29%, Hindu 24%, Muslim 6%, Anglican 11%, Pentecostal 7%, Seventh Day Adventists 4%, Baptists 3%, Presbytarian 3%, (Indigenous/animist overlap 5%)
National holidays recognised (7a): for two or more religions
Freedom of worship (8a): constitution provides for this
Banned activities/religions (9a): No act or speech that insults a person on religious grounds
Monitored activities (9b): Jamaat al Muslimeen, Jamaat al Murabiteen Waajihatul Islaamiyyah all radical Islamist groups
Religious instruction (10e): instruction allowed for all religions
Government-sponsored religious unity group (11b): infrequent or one-off meetings
Registration with government (12bi**): required in order to gain benefits
Religious discrimination (13): Law bans this

TUNISIA

Proportion of religious adherence (1): Muslim 98%
Constitutionally specified state religion (2): Islam
National holidays recognised (7b): Islamic holidays only
Freedom of worship (8b): constitution provides for this but in accordance with public order
Banned activities/religions (9a): No political parties based on religion; proseltyzing; wearing of headscarves in government offices; Arabic language Christian texts;

Muslims banned from marrying non-Muslims
Monitored activities (9b): Baha'i; only government-approved personnel may preach in mosques, and mosques may not be used outside official ceremonies; Islamist fundamentalists; converts from Islam will be punished; all religious publications
Required practices (9c): President must be a Muslim
Religious instruction (10c): Islamic religious instruction mandatory
Registration with government (12bi**): recognises only Muslims, and Christian and Jewish groups established before 1956
Extent of application of religious law in courts (14a): Islamic law in some family cases only
In August 1992, 265 alleged members of the **Islamist al-Nahda** movement were jailed for plotting a coup. AI criticised the trials for 'vague and imprecise' charges and reliance on 'uncorroborated police statements ... extorted under duress'. Some 100 remain in jail imprisoned solely for the peaceful exercise of their beliefs. (AI)

TURKEY

Proportion of religious adherence (1): Muslim (Sunni) 80%, Muslim (Shia) 5%, Alevi 12%, Armenian 1%
Secular state (3): religion and state are explicitly separated by the constitution
Freedom of worship (8b): limited by existence and integrity of secular state
Banned activities/religions (9a): Insulting a religion recognised by the state; debasing its property or interfering with its services; religious fundamentalism; mystical Sufi religious social orders (tarikats); wearing of headscarves by civil servants or at universities;
Monitored activities (9b): Eastern Orthodox churches
Required practices (9c): Religious affiliation on ID cards
Religious instruction (10c): Islamic, Greek Orthodox/Armenian, Jews exempt; 8 years of secular education compulsory
State benefits available for religious groups (12cii*): state determines

whether group is religious or cultural; Alevis cultural only
Religious discrimination (13): Law bans this
Public worship (15): limited by government; designated places only
On 14 May, Turkey's pro-Islamic government adopted a new education law intended to end the second-class status given to qualifications from religious high schools in applications to university. The religious training schools or *Imam Hatips* were downgraded to 'technical schools' in 1997 under pressure from the military, who suspected they were becoming focal points for Islamist radicals and sought to deter young people from attending them. (Al-Jazeera)
On 11 June, Kurdish imams petitioned the government to allow them to deliver sermons in Kurdish, following the launch of Kurdish-language broadcasts on state radio and television and the opening in April of private courses to teach Kurdish. (*Kurdistan Observer*)
On 30 June, the European Court of Human Rights ruled in Turkey's favour in two cases concerning women excluded from higher education for wearing the headscarf. The ECHR permitted the ban in Turkey as necessary to preserve public order and the rights of women who chose not to wear headscarves. The ban has effectively excluded thousands of women from higher education while hundreds of woman teachers have lost their jobs. (HRW)

TURKMENISTAN

Proportion of religious adherence (1): Muslim (Sunni) 81%, Muslim (Shia) 3%, Russian Orthodox 4%, Christian 1%, None 2%
Religion linked to state (5): Islam (Sunni)
National holidays recognised (7a): Islamic holidays only
Freedom of worship (8a): constitution provides for this
Banned activities/religions (9a): Imams from formal teaching in madrassas; importing foreign language newspapers and journals
Monitored activities (9b): Tight control on Islamic fundamentalism;

Seventh Day Adventists/Jehovah's Witnesses limited in ability to educate their children in their beliefs
Religious instruction (10c): 'Rukhnama', President Niyazov's spiritual guidebook on Turkmen culture and heritage
Registration with government (12aiii***): Change enacted in March 2004, for the first time does not limit registration toSunni Muslims and Greek Orthodox. Effects still to be determined.
In an April 2003 report, the UN Commission on Human Rights cited Turkmen state 'restrictions on the exercise of freedom of thought, conscience and religion ... including the harassment and persecution of members of independent faith groups and the discriminatory use of the registration procedures for such groups'. (UNCHR)
On 2 March 2004, the state-approved Sunni Imam **Nasrullah ibn Ibadullah**, the country's chief mufti, was sentenced to 22 years in prison on charges related to his reported refusal to use the *Rukhnama*, a book written by President Saparmurat Niazov. On March 29, Niazov ordered that no new mosques are to be built in the country. (RFE/Radio Liberty)
Secret police raided a **Baptist** bible study meeting on 4 August, arrested the participants for three hours, confiscated the bibles and hymn books, and threatened 'a big problem' if Baptist meetings continued. The raid contradicts a much-trumpeted 'liberalisation' of the law on religion that granted the Baptist church state registration and official recognition. (Forum 18)

UGANDA

Proportion of religious adherence (1): Roman Catholic 30%, Anglican 30%, Christian (other) 6%, Muslim (Sunni) 14%, Muslim (Shia) 2%, Indigenous/animist 8%
National holidays recognised (7a): for two or more religions
Monitored activities (9b): 'Cults'
Religious instruction (10a): not allowed in public schools
Registration with government (12aii*): registration required of all religious groups

On 14 February, a government minister accused the Catholic-run Radio Ecclesia of 'defamation and false propaganda against official personalities and public institutions' and 'terrorist discourse'. Supporters staged a demonstration three days later, calling on the government to stop putting pressure on news media considered to be pro-opposition. (RSF)

The Japan-based Niwano Peace Foundation awarded its annual US$185,000 prize to the Acholi Religious Leaders' Peace Initiative that seeks social justice and an end to the conflict in Uganda. The peace prize is awarded annually for contributions to world peace by promoting inter-religious cooperation. (ENI)

UKRAINE

Proportion of religious adherence (1): Ukrainian Orthodox 48%, Orthodox/Catholic 10%, Roman Catholic 2%, Protestant 2%
National holidays recognised (7b): only Christian holidays
Monitored activities (9b): Restricts activities of non-native religious groups (native groups recognised as Orthodox, Roman Catholic and Jewish)
Religious instruction (10a): not allowed in public schools (subject to change)
Registration with government (12aii★): registration required of all religious groups

On 28 January 2004, a court closed the opposition daily **Silski Visti** for publishing advertisements for an anti-Semitic publication, an order that was widely seen as politically motivated. Yevhen Chervonenko, vice president of the Eurasian Jewish Congress and a Ukrainian MP called the closure a 'calculated provocation by the presidential administration against the media.' (CPJ)

On 30 March, Ukrainian MPs appealed to Viktor Bondarenko, head of the National Committee on Religious Matters, on behalf of Nigerian Pentecostal minister **Sunday Adelaja**, whose application for a new residency permit had been refused. MPs said the constitutional rights of thousands of citizens to freedom of religion would be threatened if Adelaja was deported. (www.risu.org)

UNITED ARAB EMIRATES

Proportion of religious adherence (1): Muslim (Sunni) 59%, Muslim (Shia) 3%, Hindu 20%, Christian 8%, Buddhist 4%
Constitutionally specified state religion (2): Islam
Religion favoured by state (4): Islam
National holidays recognised (7b): only Islamic holidays
Legislation (8b): constitution provides for this, subject to public order and morals, within established customs
Legislation (8c): all legislation derives from Shari'a law and must not contradict designated religious practice
Banned activities (9a): non-Islamic proselytising or distributing religious materials
Monitored activities (9b): all Sunni Muslim mosques; all sermons monitored
Religious instruction (10c): Islamic religious instruction for Muslims only
State benefits available for religious groups (12ci★): Only Muslims can register
Extent of application of religious law in courts (14b): Secular courts for civil matters; Shari'a law for family and criminal matters
Limits on public worship (15): limited by government

UNITED KINGDOM

Proportion of religious adherence (1): (Wales, England, Scotland): Anglican 35%, Roman Catholic 10%, Protestant 9%, Christian (other) 10%, Muslim 3%, Hindu 1%, None 16%
(Northern Ireland): Protestant 53%, Roman Catholic 44%
Constitutionally specified state religion (2): Anglican (England); Presbyterian (Scotland)
Freedom of worship (8a): constitution provides for this
Banned activities (9a): crimes against religious targets bring a higher sentence than same crime with no indication of this motivation; national broadcasting licenses not available to groups wholly or mainly religious in character; travel by Reverend Moon, leader of the Unification Church, banned; blasphemy against Anglican doctrine
Monitored activities (9b): Church of Scientology not recognised as a charity, all others are
Required practices (9c): Monarch must be an Anglican
Religious instruction (10d): locally-based syllabi, must reflect Christian basis; daily act of worship required, can be waived if deemed inappropriate
Government-sponsored religious unity group (11a) Meets frequently
Religious discrimination (13): Law bans this

A report by the Commission on British Muslims and Islamophobia warned in June 2004 that failure to tackle racist images of Muslims could create 'time bombs, of bitterness and resentment'. Police stop and search practices topped the grievance list of British Muslims. Those surveyed by the BBC blamed the media for anti-Muslim prejudice. (BBC)

A BBC TV documentary in July 2004 showed members of the far-right British National Party describing **Islam** as a 'wicked religion' and admitting to assaults on Muslims. (Al-Jazeera)

In January 200, the Northern Irish Ulster rugby team played England's Leicester Tigers on a Saturday, instead of Sunday after protests led by Ian Paisley, head of the province's Democratic Unionist Party and moderator of the Free Presbyterian Church. (ENI)

On 4 October, the UK banned religious discrimination, particularly against Hindus and Muslims. The new measures are to ensure that providers of goods, services, premises etc, cannot refuse someone because of their religion or belief. (*The Times*)

UNITED STATES OF AMERICA

Proportion of religious adherence (1): Roman Catholic 25%, Baptists 16%, Lutheran 4.5%, Methodist 7%, Evangelical Protestants 5%, Protestant 19%, Jews 2%, Muslim 1.5%, None 14%

Secular state (3): religion and state are explicitly separated by the constitution
Freedom of worship (8a): constitution provides for this
Monitored activities (9b): 'Cults'; travel by Reverend Moon, leader of the Unification Church
Religious instruction (10a): not allowed in state schools
Registration with government (12bi★): required in order to gain benefits
Native American jail inmate **Billy Soza Warsoldier** claimed he lost privileges because his Cahuilla tribal faith prohibited him from cutting his hair unless a family member dies. His case was taken up by the American Civil Liberties Union in April 2004. Warsoldier has lost visitation rights and is banned from receiving quarterly packages and attending vocational courses. (AP)
A Canadian Amish man, **Daniel Zehr** refused to have a photo taken of him when he applied for legal residence in the US in April 2004. He is a member an Old Order Amish sect that takes literally the Bible's prohibition of graven images. Zehr's lawyers argue that he has a First Amendment right to freedom of religion that allows him to object being photographed. (AP)
The Council on American-Islamic Relations complained about **anti-Muslim** rhetoric by conservative radio talk show hosts in April 2004. One host, Michael Graham of WMAL in Washington DC, said on 1 April 2004: 'I don't wanna say we should kill 'em all (Muslims), but unless there's reform (within Islam) , there aren't a lot of other solutions that work in the ground struggle for survival'. (AP)
Gay couples in the US state of Massachusetts began to exchange marriage vows in April 2004, making the US one of a few countries where homosexuals can legally wed, but the issue divided the nation's churches. 'Marriage is necessarily monogamous and heterosexual,' US Orthodox church leaders said. 'Today, however, this divine purpose is increasingly questioned, challenged or denied, even within some faith communi-

ties, as social and political pressures work to normalise, legalise and even sanctify same-sex unions.' (ENI)

UZBEKISTAN

Proportion of religious adherence (1): Muslim 78%, Russian Orthodox 8%, Christian 2%
Secular state (3): religion and state are explicitly separated by the constitution
Religion linked to state (5): Islam
Freedom of worship (8b): constitution provides for this but limited by national security
Banned activities (9a): Islamic extremists; Hizb ut-Tahrir; proselytising; private teaching of religious principles; no recognised religious centre means no right to train religious personnel – only seven groups have centres; religious groups cannot form political parties or social movements
Monitored activities (9b): government censor has to approve all publications; Unification Church effectively banned
Religious instruction (10a): not allowed in public schools
Registration with government (12aiii★★★): some available after registration which is compulsory for all religious groups
Public worship (15): limited to recognised locations
On 30 October 2003, HRW urged the US to include Uzbekistan on its list of Countries of Particular Concern (CPC), because of its continued disregard for the International Religious Freedom Act by the legal and practical suppression of religious beliefs, the systematic torture and 'other flagrant denials of the right to life, liberty or the security of persons'. **Independent Muslims** outside government-controlled organisations are continually harassed, arrested and abused, often under the pretext of clamping down on extremism. HRW also report frequent torture against religious prisoners, often for the crime of praying, and observing religious practices such as fasting. (HRW, US State Dept.)
Jehovah's Witnesses are the most persecuted religious group in Uzbekistan. The Internal Affairs

Ministry has classified them as a 'radical extremist organisation', and has included them in a list of 'illegal extremist religious organisations active on Uzbek territory along with groups such as **Hizb-ut-Tahrir** and **Satanists**. (Forum 18)

VENEZUELA

Proportion of religious adherence (1): Roman Catholic 68%, Protestant 28%, None 2%
Religion favoured by state (4): Roman Catholicism
Employment of clergy in military (6): Roman Catholic
Freedom of worship (8b): constitution provides for this but must not violate public morality/decency/order
Monitored activities (9b): Sects and 'Cults', especially the Unification Church
Government-sponsored religious unity group (11b): infrequent or one-off meetings
Registration with government (12ai★★): registration required of all religious groups
On 6 December 2003, a crowd shouting slogans in favour of President Hugo Chávez decapitated a statue of the Virgin Mary in a square, in a part of Caracas popular with the opposition and dissident members of the army. Five days later, unidentified arsonists set the Roman Catholic Church 'El Carmen' in Teques on fire. While Venezuela's bishops blamed Chávez supporters, the government alleged that infiltrators from the opposition had carried out the attacks. (www.iglesia.net)

VIETNAM

Proportion of religious adherence (1): Buddhist 50%, Roman Catholic 9%, Indigenous/animist 10%, Protestant 2%, None %
Freedom of worship (8a): constitution provides for this
Restrictions on religious groups (9b): all aspects of religious groups strictly monitored
Registration with government (12aiii★★★): officially recognised religions: Buddhism/Roman Catholic/Protestant/Islam/Indigenous-animist (Hoa Hao)/

Indigenous-animist (Cao Dai) **Hmong Christians** living in Xin Maan district, in Ha Giang province, have had their homes ransacked and Vietnamese bibles confiscated. They have been threatened with fines unless they abandon Christianity and re-establish an altar to their ancestors. Vietnamese authorities have begun to avoid referring to Christianity, using the term 'illegal religion' instead. The government recognises as legitimate only Christians who were believers before the 1954 communist revolution. (Freedom House)

YEMEN

Proportion of religious adherence (1): Muslim (Sunni) 69%, Muslim (Shia) 29%
Constitutionally specified state religion (2): Islam
National holidays recognised (7b): only Islamic holidays
Freedom of worship (8a): constitution provides for this
Legislation (8c): all legislation derives from Shari'a law and must not contradict designated religious practice
Banned activities/organisations (9a): non-Islamic proselytising; conversion from Islam; non-Muslims holding public office; Muslim women may not marry out of the religion
Restrictions on religious groups (9b): Islamic extremists
Religious instruction (10e): Islamic instruction provided but opt-out available
In July 2004, 120 members of security forces and 21 supporters of the Shia cleric, Hussein al-Houthi, were killed in an uprising allegedly led by him. Over 185 followers of the preacher have been arrested. **Hussein al-Houthi** leads the Faithful Youth, a breakaway movement from the Islamist opposition movement al-Haq. He is accused by the government of forming an armed group that staged violent protests against the US and Israel and setting up unlicensed religious centres. The cleric is a member of the Shia Zaidi community in the north of the mainly Sunni country. Officials have stated that the action is not aimed at Zaidis in general. (BBC)

ZAMBIA

Proportion of religious adherence (1): Roman Catholic 33%, Protestant 30%, Anglican 3%, Christian (other) 19%, Muslim 5%, None 5%, Indigenous/animist overlap 15%
Constitutionally specified state religion (2): Christianity
National holidays recognised (7b): only Christian holidays
Freedom of worship (8a): constitution provides for this
Religious instruction (10e): Christian instruction provided but opt-out available
Registration with government (12aii*): some available after registration which is compulsory for religious groups
The Church and government are currently engaged in a row over the Church's right to criticise the government. Evangelical Fellowship of Zambia director Bishop Paul Mususu said the Church had a responsibility to be the 'prophetic voice to the nation' and to criticise government as long as it was 'failing suffering Zambians'. President Levy Mwanawasa later said the church should concentrate on converting people to God not criticising government. (*Lusaka Post*)

ZIMBABWE

Proportion of religious adherence (1): Roman Catholic 20%, Protestant 25%, Christian (other) 5%, Muslim 1%, Indigenous/animist 30%
Freedom of worship (8a): constitution provides for this
Banned religions (9a): practicing witchcraft and accusing others of practicing witchcraft
Monitored activities (9b): the rise of evangelical Protestants and indigenous/animist churches; religious leaders making political comments
Registration with government (12bi*): some available after registration
Bulawayo Archbishop Pius Ncube has called on the world to toughen sanctions against Robert Mugabe. Ncube, once a friend of Mugabe's, said that 'the devil has entered his mind, soul and heart,' and that he will 'face the wrath of God'. Church groups deplored state media attacks on the church. 'Calculated, hateful and unjustified' attacks on Archbishop Ncube, the Catholic Commission for Justice and Peace and the Evangelical fellowship of Zimbabwe, were part of 'the on-going demonising of civil society organisations and churches by the government,' they said. (ENI, *Bulawayo Standard*)
'Hear the Word Ministries', which has followers among Zimbabwe's rich and famous, stirred controversy in January 2004 by giving President Robert Mugabe a gift of Z$30 million (US$36,407). (ENI)

Compiled by: James Badcock (North Africa, Southern Europe), Samuel Holden (East Asia, South East Asia); Patrick Holland (Britain and Ireland); Andrew Kendle (South Asia); Franziska Klopfer (South East Asia); Gill Newsham (Turkey and Kurdish areas); Sara Pfaffenhöfer (Russia, Poland, Ukraine, Baltic States); Sigrun Rottman (South and Central America; general); Rosanna Singler (Middle East, North America, general); Daniel Stewart (legal data); Robin Wigglesworth (Central Asia and Caucasus), Andreas Wiseman (Africa); Cinzia Zucal (Eastern Europe)

Edited by Rohan Jayasekera and co-ordinated by Natasha Schmidt

THE ART OF READING IN COLOUR
PHILIP PULLMAN

YOU DON'T NEED A BELIEF IN GOD TO HAVE A
THEOCRACY: KHOMEINI'S IRAN IS CLOSER TO
STALIN'S RUSSIA THAN EITHER WOULD LIKE TO
BELIEVE. THE REAL DIFFERENCE BETWEEN
THEOCRACIES AND DEMOCRACIES IS THAT THE
FORMER DON'T KNOW HOW TO READ

Milan Radev

I start from the position that theocracy is one of the least desirable of all forms of political organisation, and that democracy is a good deal better. But the real division is not between those states that are secular, and therefore democratic, and those that are religious, and therefore totalitarian. I think there is another fault line that is more fundamental and more important than religion. You don't need a belief in God to have a theocracy.

Here are some characteristics of religious power:

- There is a holy book, a scripture whose word is inerrant, whose authority is above dispute: as it might be, the works of Karl Marx.
- There are prophets and doctors of the Church, who interpret the holy book and pronounce on its meaning: as it might be, Lenin, Stalin, Mao.
- There is a priesthood with special powers, which can confer blessings and privileges on the laity, or withdraw them, and in which authority tends to concentrate in the hands of elderly men: as it might be, the Communist Party.
- There is the concept of heresy and its punishment: as it might be, Trotskyism.
- There is a secret police force with the powers of an inquisition: as it might be, the Cheka, the NKVD, etc.
- There is a complex procedural apparatus of betrayal, denunciation, confession, trial and execution: as it might be, the Stalinist Terror under Yezhov and Beria and the other state inquisitors.
- There is a teleological view of history, according to which human society moves inexorably towards a millennial fulfilment in a golden age: as it might be, the dictatorship of the proletariat, as described by dialectical materialism.
- There is a fear and hatred of external unbelievers: as it might be, the imperialist capitalist powers.
- There is a fear and hatred of internal demons and witches: as it might be, *kulaks* or bourgeois deviationists.
- There is the notion of pilgrimage to sacred places and holy relics: as it might be, the birthplace of Stalin, or the embalmed corpses in Red Square.

And so on, ad nauseam. In fact, the Soviet Union was one of the most thoroughgoing theocracies the world has ever seen, and it was atheist to its marrow. In this respect, the most dogmatic materialist is functionally equivalent to the most fanatical believer, Stalin's Russia exactly the same as Khomeini's Iran. It isn't belief in God that causes the problem.

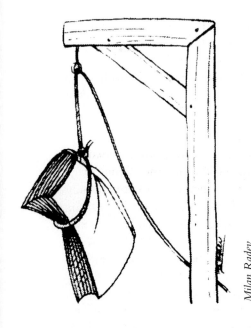

Milan Radev

The root of the matter is quite different. It is that theocracies don't know how to read, and democracies do.

To begin with, the theocratic cast of mind has low expectations of literature. It thinks that the function of novels and poetry is to present a clear ideological viewpoint, and nothing else. This is brilliantly shown in Azar Nafisi's recent book, *Reading Lolita in Tehran* (Fourth Estate, 2004). The author, a professor of English literature in Iran during the rule of the Ayatollah Khomeini, tells of her attempts to continue teaching the books she wanted to teach in the increasingly fanatical and narrow-minded atmosphere of the period following the Islamic Revolution. In order to discuss the work of Nabokov, Scott Fitzgerald, Jane Austen or Henry James, she had to resort to various stratagems: to pretend to put the book on trial so as to elicit a 'safe' defence of it, to meet with a small group of trustworthy students in her own home and so on.

At one point she is describing the attitude of the authorities to the sort of books she finds most valuable:

Unable to decipher or understand complications or irregularities, angered by what they considered betrayals in their own ranks, the officials were forced to impose their simple formulas on fiction as they did on life. Just as they censored the colours and tones of reality to suit their black-and-white world, they censored any form of interiority in fiction; ironically, for them as for their ideological opponents, works of imagination that did not carry a political message were deemed dangerous. Thus, in a writer such as Austen, for example, whether they knew it or not, they found a natural adversary.

Works of imagination that did not carry a political message were deemed dangerous – that is, an overt political message. Azar Nafisi is too subtle a reader to think that Jane Austen, or any other great writer, is devoid of political implications, echoes, correspondences; but if they don't stand up and wave a flag and shout slogans, they're invisible, and hence suspect.

And that is true for believers and atheists alike. Here is an extract from a famous resolution of the Central Committee of the All-Union Communist Party of 14 August 1946:

> Recently in *Zvezda* magazine, along with important and worthwhile works of Soviet writers, there have appeared many worthless, ideologically harmful works. A crude mistake of *Zvezda* is the offering of a literary platform to the writer MM Zoshchenko, whose productions are alien to Soviet literature. The editorial staff of *Zvezda* is well aware that Zoshchenko has long specialised in writing empty, vapid and vulgar things, in spreading putrid nonsense, vulgarity and indifference to politics, so as to mislead our young people and poison their consciousness . . . In addition, *Zvezda* in every way popularises work by the authoress Akhmatova, whose literary and socio-political physiognomy has been known to Soviet people for a long, long time. Akhmatova is a typical exponent of empty, frivolous poetry that is alien to our people. Permeated by the scent of pessimism and decay, redolent of old-fashioned salon poetry, frozen in the positions of bourgeois-aristocratic aestheticism and decadence – 'art for art's sake' – not wanting to progress forward with our people, her verses cause damage to the upbringing of our youth and cannot be tolerated in Soviet literature.

The charge of indifference to politics: there it is again. It is a consistent theme. In 1929, the writer Boris Pilnyak had been denounced by the Stalinist *Literary Gazette* for offences including 'apoliticalness (not being a Communist)' (Ian MacDonald, *The New Shostakovich*, OUP 1991). What it amounts to is that if a literary work doesn't openly support your side, then it must be empty, and ought to be condemned.

So the trouble with the way theocracies read is that they have a narrow idea of what literature is: they think it only contains one kind of thing, and has only one purpose, which is a narrowly political one. This is true even of some apparent supporters of literature, such as the leftist activists described by Nafisi, who defended Scott Fitzgerald against the attacks of the Muslim activists on the grounds that 'we needed to read fiction like *The Great Gatsby* because we needed to know about the immorality of American

Milan Radev

culture. They felt we should read more revolutionary material, but we should read books like this as well, to understand the enemy.' The theocratic cast of mind is always reductive whether it's in power or not.

The second charge against the theocracies is that they only know one mode of reading. Because they think there is only one way that books can work, they have only one way of responding to them, and when they try to apply the one way they know to a text that doesn't respond to that reading, trouble follows. There is a good description of two different modes of reading in Karen Armstrong's *The Battle for God: Fundamentalism in Judaism, Christianity and Islam* (HarperCollins, 2001). Armstrong is eloquent on the difference between *mythos* and *logos*, fundamentally different ways of apprehending the reality of the world. *Mythos* deals with meaning, with the timeless and constant, with the intuitive, with what can only be fully expressed in art or music or ritual. *Logos*, by contrast, is the rational, the scientific, the practical; that which can be taken apart and put together again; that which is susceptible to logical explanation.

Both are necessary, both are to be cherished. However, they engage with different aspects of the world, and these days, says Armstrong, they are not equally valued. Her argument is that in modern times, because of the astonishing progress of science and technology, people in the Western world 'began to think that *logos* was the only means to truth, and began to discount *mythos* as false and superstitious'. This resulted in the phenomenon of fundamentalism, which, despite its own claims to be a return to the old true ways of understanding the holy book, is not a return of any kind, but something entirely new: 'Protestant fundamentalists read the Bible in a literal, rational way that is quite different from the more mystical, allegorical approach of pre-modern spirituality.'

Not only Protestants, we might add, and not only the Bible. In March 2002, the BBC reported the publication of a story in several Saudi newspapers about a fire in a school in Mecca. According to the reports, the *mutaween*, the Saudi religious police, stopped schoolgirls from leaving the blazing building because they were not wearing correct Islamic dress. Fifteen girls died as a result. One witness said that he saw three policemen 'beating young girls to prevent them from leaving the school because they were not wearing the *abaya*' (the black robe required by the kingdom's strict interpretation of Islam). The father of one of the dead girls said that the school watchman even refused to open the gates to let the girls out. What is this but a failure to read with imaginative understanding, a triumph of literalism and the bare decoding of instructions over human empathy?

My third and final charge against the theocracies, atheist or religious, and their failure to read properly is this: that the act of true reading is in its very essence democratic.

Consider the nature of what happens when we read a book – and I mean, of course, a work of literature, not an instruction manual or a textbook – in private, unsupervised, unspied on, alone. It isn't like a lecture: it's like a conversation. There's a back-and-forthness about it. The book proposes, the reader questions, the book responds, the reader considers. We bring our own preconceptions and expectations, our own intellectual qualities, and our limitations, too, our own previous experiences of reading, our own temperament, our own hopes and fears, our own personality to the encounter.

And we are active about the process. We are in charge of the time, for example. We can choose when to read; we don't have to wait for a timetabled opportunity to open the covers; we can read in the middle of the night, or over breakfast, or during a long summer evening. And we're in charge of the place where the reading happens; we're not anchored to a piece of unwieldy technology, or required to be present in a particular building along with several hundred other people. We can read in bed, or at the bus stop, or (as I used to do when I was younger and more agile) up a tree.

Nor do we have to read it in a way determined by someone else. We can skim, or we can read it slowly; we can read every word, or we can skip long passages; we can read it in the order in which it presents itself, or we can read it in any order we please; we can look at the last page first, or decide to wait for it; we can put the book down and reflect, or we can go to the library and check what it claims to be fact against another authority; we can assent, or we can disagree.

So our relationship with books is a profoundly, intensely, essentially democratic one. It places demands on the reader, because that is the nature of a democracy: citizens have to play their part. If we don't bring our own best qualities to the encounter, we will bring little away. Furthermore, it isn't static: there is no final, unquestionable, unchanging authority. It's dynamic. It changes and develops as our understanding grows, as our experience of reading – and of life itself – increases. Books we once thought great come to seem shallow and meretricious; books we once thought boring reveal their subtle treasures of wit, their unsuspected shafts of wisdom.

And we become better readers: we learn different ways to read. We learn to distinguish degrees of irony or implication; we pick up references and allusions we might have missed before; we learn to judge the most fruitful way to read this text (as myth, perhaps) or that (as factual record); we become familiar with the strengths and duplicities of metaphor, we know a joke when we see one, we can tell poetry from political history, we can suspend our certainties and learn to tolerate the vertigo of difference.

Of course, democracies don't guarantee that real reading will happen. They just make it possible. Whether it happens or not depends on schools, among other things. And schools are vulnerable to all kinds of pressure, not least that exerted by governments eager to impose 'targets', and cut costs, and teach only those things that can be tested. One of the most extraordinary scenes I've ever watched, and one which brings everything I've said in this piece into sharp focus, occurs in the famous film of George W Bush receiving the news of the second strike on the World Trade Centre on

9/11. As the enemies of democracy hurl their aviation-fuel-laden thunder-bolt at the second tower, their minds intoxicated by a fundamentalist reading of a religious text, the leader of the free world sits in a classroom reading a story with children. If only he'd been reading *Where the Wild Things Are*, or *The Gruffalo*, or a genuine fairy tale! That would have been a scene to cheer. It would have illustrated values truly worth fighting to preserve. It would have embodied all the difference between democratic reading and totalitarian reading, nourishing reading and starved reading.

But no. Thanks among other things to his own government's 'No Child Left Behind' policy, the book George Bush was reading was one of the most stupefyingly banal and witless things I've ever had the misfortune to see. *My Pet Goat* (you can find the text easily enough on the Internet, and I can't bring myself to quote it) is a drearily functional piece of rubbish designed only to teach phonics. It is not a book to read for pleasure, or for consolation, or for joy, or for wisdom, or for wonder, or for any other human feeling; it is empty, vapid, sterile. But that was what the President of the United States, and his advisers, thought was worth offering to children. Young people brought up to think that that sort of thing is a real book will soon conclude that books are not worth having, and that reading is for fools.

So while democracy makes real reading possible, it doesn't make it safe. It is quite easy for democracies to forget how to read. ❑

Philip Pullman *is the author of the trilogy* His Dark Materials *and much more*

LOOKING OVER THE SHOULDER

RUCHIR JOSHI

INDIA'S CREEPING SECTARIANISM
PREDATES THE NATIONALIST
GOVERNMENT OF THE BJP AND HAS YET
TO WORK ITS WAY OUT OF THE SYSTEM

New Delhi India 1993: Hindu nationalists celebrate the birthday of Lord Ram under police survellance. Credit: Raghu Rai / Magnum

As a young freelancer just starting out in journalism, it was a pretty good place to be: under a thin umbrella of mosquitoes at a table on the lawn of a nice hotel in Calcutta, interviewing Salman Rushdie over a few beers. Rushdie had recently exploded on the international literary scene with his second novel and, though he didn't talk about it that evening, he was in the process of writing his third book, *Shame*, in which he tried to do with Pakistan what he had done with India in *Midnight's Children* – an epic, ribald, satirical, magical-realist, contemporary history of the nation. Though I had no idea what his next book was going to be, I did register that Rushdie had just flown in from General Zia ul-Haq's Pakistan and I asked him what things were like over there. 'One difference is that you couldn't have an evening, an open conversation, like this,' replied Rushdie, flicking his head almost involuntarily. 'In fact, it's strange to be here, where you don't have to constantly be looking over your shoulder to check who's listening in.'

The year was 1983, and the long stretch Rushdie would spend constantly looking over his shoulder was yet ahead of him; and the time during which Indians quickly learned to be careful of walls – the dark period of the Emergency – was beginning to dim somewhat from visceral memory after six years.

The memory of Indira Gandhi's Emergency has played strange tricks on many including myself, cyclically fading, almost disappearing at times, and then returning even more vivid, ever sharper. Today, I still remember the constant nudge of fear between May 1975 and March 1977. I was around 16 at the time, and very seriously afraid that my father would be arrested at any moment. A well-known Gujarati writer, with a substantial readership that followed both his fiction and his journalism, my father was one of the few Indian men of letters who openly refused to toe the Indira line. Some of my father's writer friends were jailed on trumped-up charges, others backed down, but my father, having participated in the Indian independence movement, remained unmoved by either possibility.

That Emergency of 1975–7 was the first instance of an open, all-out attack on dissent in independent India's history. When a High Court judge upheld an electoral opponent's appeal against her election, Indira Gandhi declared the Emergency in order to cling on to power. The attempt to muzzle public criticism cost Mrs Gandhi dear and, when she miscalculated and called for elections in 1977, she was met with a humiliating defeat. Overnight, moments of courage shown by the press during the 18 months of repression became lore. There was the blank front page of a national broadsheet; there was the young paper-industry tycoon who provided truckloads of illegal newsprint to newspapers when the government withdrew their licences to import it from abroad and, in the area of vernacular languages, there were a few obdurate people such as my father who kept up the nagging questions and criticism.

Besides power itself, there was nothing Mrs Gandhi valued more than her international reputation as a democratic leader. Between them, a few tenacious Indian intellectuals and some brave and acute foreign journalists turned this reputation into dust and – despite returning to power within three years of her defeat – Mrs Gandhi and her nasty gaggle of sycophants never quite recovered from that.

However, like many historical lessons, the ones thrown up by the Emergency had sharp edges that would cut in several different directions. On the one hand, independent media found themselves strengthened in the post-Emergency years, with a burgeoning of newspapers and magazines carrying serious investigative reportage and outspoken opinion, something never before seen in the country; on the other, there were groups with very different long-term agendas who did their political sums and realised that a frontal, official muzzling of the free press was not as easy to pull off in India as it was in some other countries.

When Mrs Gandhi's government clamped down on Indian media and her political opponents, the Rashtriya Sevak Sangh (RSS), the fascist Hindu-supremacist group, and its parliamentary party the Jan Sangh – now the Bhartiya Janata Party (BJP) – were among those who found themselves at the wrong end of the censorship gun barrel. Twenty-odd years later, when the reins of power were in their hands (1998 to May 2004), the Hindu right tried very hard not to repeat her most obvious mistakes.

But, to rewind the story a bit and pick it up in the 1980s, there were other salutary components that also went into forming the strategies of the Hindu fascists, well before they made a bid for serious parliamentary power.

In the years following the Emergency, the religious right in India – both Hindu and Muslim – managed to gain precious elbow room at the table of national politics. In the early 1970s, the RSS was a minor irritation and its parliamentary mask, the Jan Sangh, almost defunct. The mass reaction to Mrs Gandhi's indiscriminatory clampdown revived both. While trying to slam the door on the Hindu fascists, she opened it wider. She then made a different mistake with the Sikhs, but one that had the same result. By promoting a psychotic Sikh priest called Bhindrawale to counter Sikh political opposition in the state of Punjab, Mrs Gandhi let loose a wave of Sikh extremism that eventually cost her her life.

Rajiv Gandhi, Indira's older son who took over as prime minister after her assassination in 1984, learned nothing from his mother's mistakes. He followed in her knee-jerking footsteps to appease conservative Muslims in the case of Shah Bano, where he went against a court judgement awarding Shah Bano a divorce settlement that was at odds with Muslim Personal Law but completely fair in terms of all notions of gender equality. Equally unwisely, it was the Rajiv administration that opened the gates of the abandoned but controversial Babri Mosque in Ayodhya to allow the worship of Hindu deities placed there a few decades before by elements of the RSS.

This was the Indian context in late 1988 in which my famous interviewee of 1983, Salman Rushdie, deft ringmaster of the fantastical, found himself dangling from the high-voltage power cables of international headlines in a way even he couldn't have imagined.

There are some narratives in which the routes to the denouement continue to be hotly contested though the end remains undisputed. This is one of them. It is still far from clear exactly how the notable literary critic Ayatollah Ruhollah Khomeini heard about *The Satanic Verses*, but whatever the truth, these facts stay immovable: that the Indian authorities were the first in the world to ban *The Satanic Verses*; that the ban preceded the Khomeini fatwa and was, in fact, instrumental in putting book and author on Khomeini's inquisitional radar; that the ensuing death sentence sent Rushdie into hiding for many years; and that it led to death or serious injury for some of the people associated with the book.

Based on these facts, the following conclusions become reasonably robust: that the anti-Rushdie fatwa led, for the first time, to the international demonisation of all of multi-hued Islam; that it created in Khomeini an archetype – that of the bearded, turbaned, long-robed, wild-eyed Islamic fanatic, a role as relished by the Ayatollah as it no doubt is by the very different man who now fills the costume from central casting, Osama bin Laden; that the fatwa and its fallout, including the creation of a monolithic 'brand' of 'Islam', yet again narrowed the space within which moderates of varying Muslim faith – secular Arabs and Iranians to take just one example – could operate.

The *Satanic Verses* ban and the subsequent fatwa were a godsend (the pun is unfortunate but unavoidable) to the Hindu right. For one, the fascists took note of the West's monumental pusillanimity when faced with baying mobs of so-called 'Muslim' youth demanding Salman Rushdie's head. At home, even as they protested against the Congress government's action, the Hindu right drew huge encouragement from the authorities' craven response to the issue. Thenceforth, 'the feelings of the community' became installed as a catchphrase in the Indian psyche; and the idea that these 'feelings' could both be 'hurt', and that this 'hurt' needed immediate, official, redress in the shape of banning and censorship, became an unquestioned filter through which all art and journalism in India has subsequently had to pass.

Across the 1990s, Hindu-fascist mobs began waving the banner of 'hurt feelings'. The first goal this tactic achieved was the demolition of the Babri mosque, which, according to the BJP-combine, was built by a Muslim king on top of a temple marking the birthplace of Ram, one of the holiest figures in the Hindu pantheon. As the Congress government in New Delhi stood by, mobs broke through the police lines and brought the structure down. This set off a seismic chain of rioting, murder and arson across the country. Emboldened by this 'victory', the RSS and VHP (the Vishwa Hindu Parishad, the internationalised arm of the Hindu right) and other associated fascist groups began to conduct other campaigns.

Among many such actions, they ransacked an exhibition of paintings by the venerable artist MF Husain, nominally a Muslim, who had dared to make a slightly irreverent drawing of a Hindu goddess; launched violent protests against Deepa Mehta's film *Fire* that showed two Hindu housewives in a lesbian relationship; 'banned' young urban couples from celebrating Valentine's Day on the grounds that it was decadent, Western and un-Indian; and attacked and halted the shooting of Deepa Mehta's next film *Water* which was set in Benaras, Hinduism's most holy city. By 1999, the BJP's second year in power, we were back to poking fearful glances over our shoulders. It was as if we were in a watered-down, 'Hinduised' Pakistan, except that the glass holding the contaminated water happened to be much larger.

More and more brazen though the Hindu-fascist mobs became, as their BJP-combine gained and held power, censorship in India, over the last few years, has been nothing if not a creature with many arms. Though their naked aim remained the total control and 'Hinduisation' of the Indian polity, the BJP government tried hard to remember the lessons of the Emergency. Thus, administratively, they left the highly visible English-language press and TV pretty much alone, countering them only by setting up new pro-government channels or supporting the papers and magazines that were already sympathetic.

The BJP-combine calculated that its main constituency was among the non-English speakers and accordingly narrowed the space in which dissenting vernacular journals could operate, including open, violent attacks on offices of papers such as the Marathi-language *Mahanagar*. Simultaneously, they embarked upon a massive rewriting of school textbooks to 'cleanse' them of 'anti-Hindu' ideas: this meant deleting any portion that treated Hindu mythology as less than historical fact and turning every historic Muslim figure into someone evil. Hand in hand with this went the replacing of personnel in key academic, educational and cultural posts with the combine's own people, flouting all norms of ability or qualification in the process.

If ever there was an example of how the repression of dissent – officialised or otherwise – leads directly to rampant violence, it is in the organised pogrom against Muslims carried out in the state of Gujarat over the months of March and April 2002. This attack, genocidal in its scale, had obviously been in the planning for a long time. The incident that set it off – the burning alive of 50-odd passengers, including many women and children, all reportedly Hindus, in carriage S-6 of the Sabarmati Express, a train bringing large numbers of the combine's fascist youth back to Gujarat from an agitation to build a Ram temple on the site of the Babri mosque they had destroyed in 1992 – is still engulfed in smoke.

Within hours of the train carriage burning down, armed mobs and lorries carrying gas cylinders and specialised explosives fanned out all over Gujarat's cities. The mob leaders carried computer printouts listing Muslim-owned businesses and homes. They had mobile phones on which they received their detailed instructions. The police, with a few notable exceptions, either stood by or abetted the butchery. A rough reckoning says more than 2,000 Muslims lost their lives, more than 100,000 were made homeless, and several million rupees' worth of damage was inflicted on Muslim businesses. As for the specific targeting of Muslim women, the testimonies of the widespread attacks on women and very young girls was chilling, even for hardened journalists and social workers who have witnessed communal riots over the last few decades.

As wave after wave of violence broke on the Muslim minority in Gujarat, the same central government that was carrying out its nationwide 'Hinduising' agenda sat by and did nothing except dribble out the occasional crocodile tear and then defend Narendra Modi, the Chief Minister of Gujarat and the man many hold directly responsible for the pogrom. One thing that quickly became clear during the Gujarat massacres was that both Modi and his masters in New Delhi gained great confidence, not only from their domestic campaign of attrition against free speech but also from the fact that post 9/11 proper dissent had been badly damaged in the mainstream US media. European reaction may have been a different story, but nobody important in the United States was going to get too het up about Muslims being killed in some far corner of the world, especially if the label 'terrorists' was repeatedly attached to the victims.

But the jack-in-the box nature of humanity again sprang a surprise. Right after the burning of S-6 and the violence it triggered, Narendra Modi made a statement that brought him instant infamy. Justifying the subsequent mass murders, Modi said: 'Wherever there is an action there will be a reaction.' But the reaction no one in the Hindutva camp expected came from the Indian English-language press and from TV, both English and Hindi channels. So shocked were journalists by what they saw in Gujarat that even many of the normally pro-BJP journals and TV channels reported the carnage in outraged terms. And while politicians from both the ruling combine and the opposition dithered and fudged, the national media kept reporting from Gujarat and kept it up long after Modi and Co declared that the situation was 'normalised'. The stories of government indifference to the plight of Muslims, the deliberate targeting of Muslims under the draconian POTA (Prevention of Terrorism Act), coupled with the official sabotaging of all cases against the Hindu thugs, and the post-pogrom triumphalism of the state government were all reported with tenacity and in detail. This coverage eventually contributed to the BJP-combine's recent defeat in the national elections.

Crucial too, in the aftermath of Gujarat, has been the irruption of a fresh debate on government censorship of documentary films and censorship laws in general. The main argument is around the question of whether it is possible or desirable to do away with censorship completely. There are groups on the left who say it isn't because an absence of any legislative control would leave religious and ethnic groups free to disseminate hate speech and hate media. Countering this, others point out that there are already very clear laws in the Indian Penal Code that prohibit the fomenting of trouble between religious communities, castes and ethnic groups, and that these laws should be used more effectively, not censorship. Again, one of the arguments used by the BJP-combine to argue for continuing censorship was the so-called 'feminist' card: that the removal of controls would lead to a proliferation of pornography and images demeaning and dangerous to women. To which women's groups provide the reply: that the rules already in place prohibiting the depiction of women in subservient or humiliating roles are hardly ever exercised by the various regional censor boards, and that the commercial cinema gets away with murder when it comes to the depiction of sex and violence.

No matter how circuitous and difficult a route it takes, there is no doubt that this debate is a crucial one for Indians. The brief breeze of optimism that accompanied the defeat of the BJP-combine in the recent elections and the swearing in of the new Congress-led government has now died down. The process of justice in Gujarat seems stuck in deep procedural mud, even as news comes of still more suicides by despair-driven farmers in the southern state of Andhra Pradesh and the women in the north-eastern state of Manipur launching a protest against gross atrocities by the Indian army.

Though the current government is far better in its professed attitude towards the equality of religious communities, there are already indications that there will be a lot of information and opinion that it will not be happy to allow free play in the public domain. The 'god' element may have been pushed to the back by the current rulers in Delhi, but it is clear that no government, and especially not one led by politicians who cut their political teeth under Mrs Gandhi, will easily give up the power to curb or curtail expression. And, until sustained campaigns and changing circumstances force a genuine modernisation of official attititudes towards censorship, there will always be a danger of a return to the days of having to look fearfully over one's shoulder. ❑

Ruchir Joshi *is a film-maker and writer. His first novel,* The Last Jet-engine Laugh, *is published in the UK and India by Flamingo/HarperCollins*

GANESH'S AMAZING TECHNICOLOUR DREAMCOAT

SALIL TRIPATHI

THE HINDU DIASPORA GETS
INTO THE GOD SHOW

The monsoon season in western India ends in September, coinciding with the Hindu religious festival of Ganesha Puja, or the worship of Lord Ganesha, the elephant-headed God of the Hindu pantheon, whose name is often invoked before starting anything new, because of his ability to remove obstructions. At the end of 10 days of festivities, Ganesha's idols are carried in a massive procession, which brings India's commercial capital, Bombay, to a standstill, as thousands of the idols – some small enough to be carried by children, some so large that trucks are needed to transport them – are immersed in the Arabian Sea with the Marathi invocation, '*Pudhchya varshi laukar yaa*' ('Come back soon next year'). The idols, made of clay, disintegrate in the sea water, as if symbolising the fragility and temporariness of life.

The apparent fragility of their deities is beginning to bother many Hindus, in India and abroad. Gods are holy everywhere, but Hindu gods and goddesses, being so many, are like their Graeco-Roman counterparts: some moody, some vicious, some funny, some hedonistic, and some warrior-like. Some have many hands, some have many heads; others take on the *raudra* (angry) mood to annihilate the world, as Shiva, Ganesha's father, does, by opening his third eye at the centre of his forehead. Shiva is to be feared, but Ganesha is benign: he is everyone's favourite god. You will see his idol on the dashboard of taxicabs in Bombay.

Gods matter in Indian politics as well. The mass immersion of Ganesha came out of a shrewd political move, to inject nationalistic spirit among Indians at the turn of the 20th century. Bal Gangadhar Tilak, an early independence movement leader, encouraged his Marathi-speaking community to celebrate the Ganesha festival early in the twentieth century. Mohandas

New Delhi India 1972: pavement portrait of the Hindu elephant god Ganesh.
Credit: Ferdinando Scianna / Magnum

Gandhi, the father of India's independence movement, was himself deeply religious, and his speeches had a strong moral and spiritual, though never communal, aspect.

The exception was Jawaharlal Nehru, India's first prime minister, who shunned rituals and avoided religion, trying to keep the temple and the state apart. But his daughter, Indira Gandhi, who ruled India for 16 years between 1966 and 1984, realised the potent power of religious symbols, and not only went to temples but also performed elaborate pujas, or religious ceremonies. Later politicians, ostensibly socialist, also turned to religious metaphors. Raj Narain, the health minister of the short-lived Janata Party government that defeated Indira Gandhi's Congress Party in the pivotal 1977 elections and ended the Emergency in India, sought examples from Hindu myths to call for population control, after Indira Gandhi's forced sterilisation campaign backfired. Narain said: 'Be like Lord Rama [the warrior king of *Ramayana*, who had two sons], not like Kauravas [the bad guys in the *Mahabharata*, who were 100 siblings].' Other politicians, too, realised the power of religious symbols and exploited them for political ends. In the 1990s, the Hindu nationalist Bharatiya Janata Party turned to Ganesha, spreading a rumour that when a bowl of milk was presented to Ganesha idols, the milk disappeared, suggesting that the idols were actually drinking it. The next day, news from around the world confirmed the story: Hindus in many countries had experienced the 'miracle'.

The BJP, of course, claimed that this good deed would be rewarded, and that Congress would lose the forthcoming elections. When students of the Indian Institute of Technology challenged the hocus-pocus, they were vilified as unbelieving spoilsports. Congress did indeed lose the 1996 elections; the 'miracle' was confirmed and other spurious, pseudo-religious ideas proliferated. Astrology was to be taught with astronomy, Euclidean geometry had to share space with Vedic mathematics. The Indian economy was taking off; India was now a nuclear power, an ally in the global war against terror. It was time to set the record straight on Western perceptions of Hinduism.

And so a coalition emerged among Hindus abroad. Activists among the diaspora believe democratic India is systematically portrayed in a bad light: rail crashes, riots and disasters make page one, India's 8 per cent economic growth does not; smart software engineers are called 'hi-tech coolies'. Many Hindus in the West also believe Hinduism is being taken for granted because, unlike Muslims or Christians, both of whom react noisily when their religious susceptibilities are offended, it is an easy, safe option. There is guilt, too, in having let things come to such a pass.

They chose their targets carefully: popular culture and serious academia – in other words, moulders of opinion. And so began the campaign against Madonna appropriating the *bindi*; against Stanley Kubrick using Sanskrit *shlokas* as background music during an orgy in *Eyes Wide Shut*; against Ismail Merchant casting Tina Turner, a performer of 'loose morals', to act as Kali in a forthcoming film; against film-maker Deepa Mehta, whose films challenge Hindu society by tackling lesbianism and the treatment of widows..

The list of grievances increases: boycott Aerosmith, a rock group, because its CD jacket shows Lord Krishna with the face of a cat and the breasts of a woman; oppose *Xena: The Warrior Princess* because the scantily clad Xena calls upon Krishna to help her tame her rivals; challenge Mike Myers, because he appears wearing robes, *mehendi* (henna on the palm) and *bindi*, posing as the Goddess Kali, with blue-skinned, bare-breasted buxom women lying around him.

Capitulation has been swift: Sony and Aerosmith apologised and modified the jacket of *Nine Lives*. The photographer David LaChappelle surprised an Internet chat group by apologising when some Hindus protested about his picture spread of Myers in *Vanity Fair* magazine. Renaissance Pictures expressed regrets over the Xena episode.

There is deep hypocrisy in Hindu criticism of Western imagery that portrays Hindu idols as erotic or sensual. The sacred and the profane have coexisted in India for centuries. India gave the world the *Kama Sutra*, and millions of Hindus worship the phallus. It is a faith broad enough to include sects that believe enlightenment is possible only through sex, and tolerant enough for ascetics to roam around naked. For at least a millennium, Hindu architects have decorated the walls and pillars of temples with nude deities, but when MF Husain, India's foremost contemporary artist, painted a Hindu goddess in the nude, his canvases were burned in India and he was forced to remain in exile in London for some time. That he happens to be born a Muslim did not help matters.

The campaign against university academics whose opinions were not sufficiently reverential towards Hinduism ran a parallel course. By claiming that Western scholarship on Hinduism is inherently flawed, some, like entrepreneur Rajiv Malhotra, have challenged academics by protesting vigorously against ideas with which they do not agree. Malhotra's main criticism is against the Eurocentric world view that he claims caricatures

Hinduism, a profound philosophy that Western academics are incapable of understanding.

Malhotra's ire is targeted at Wendy Doniger, University of Chicago professor of the history of religion, whom he blames for having eroticised and denigrated Hinduism among mainstream opinion in the US. He has also taken on Emory University professor Paul Courtright for his book *Ganesa: Lord of Obstacles, Lord of Beginnings*. Though it borders at times on self-righteous sarcasm, Malhotra keeps his discourse largely civil, but the foot soldiers of Hinduism opt for simpler solutions. Courtright received death threats; an egg was hurled at Doniger when she was in London last year to give a talk. In January this year, a book called *Shivaji: A Hindu King in Islamic India* by James W Laine, a Macalester College religious studies professor, provoked violence in India because it implied that Shivaji's parents were probably estranged at some point. One of Laine's associates in India was beaten up and a mob destroyed rare manuscripts at the Bhandarkar Oriental Research Institute in Pune, where Laine had done his research. Atal Behari Vajpayee, then India's BJP prime minister, warned Laine not to 'play with our national pride'. Nehru would have prosecuted the mob that destroyed the manuscripts.

In an interview with the *Washington Post*, Doniger said fanatical nationalism in India says no one who is not a Hindu has the right to speak about Hinduism at all. She added: 'Malhotra's ignorant writings have stirred up more passionate emotions in Internet subscribers who know even less than Malhotra does, who do not read books at all. And these people have reacted with violence. I therefore hold him indirectly responsible.' But in the same *Post* article, Malhotra defended his actions. Comparing his campaign to a consumer struggle he said: 'It's no different from Ralph Nader saying we need a consumer voice against General Motors.' He distanced himself from the violent few, whom he described as 'hooligans'. His problem with Western academics is that they are 'an inbred, incestuous group that control a vertically integrated industry'.

Malhotra may indeed see his campaign in industrial terms, but ultimately, his views emerge from wounded pride. His writing has emboldened profoundly illiberal Hindus, in India and abroad, to take the law into their hands, and attack anything with which they disagree. If Muslims can get this book banned, if Christians can get that film banned, then Hindus will get the other book, the other film, banned. The effect of such mutually assured banning is to shrink the ground of free debate.

For over six decades Indians have taken enormous pride in their country being a democracy. With all its flaws, it is a functioning, real democracy, something the Irish writer Conor Cruise O'Brien called one of the great achievements of the twentieth century. By claiming to represent what used to be a tolerant faith, violent Hindutva activists are using God to damage that secular democracy.

But there is hope: in the *Gita*, the sacred Hindu text, Krishna tells the reluctant warrior, Arjuna:

> To protect men of virtue
> And destroy men who do evil,
> To set the standard of sacred duty,
> I appear in age after age.

The many Indians who believe in the power of epic and myth might draw the moral of this year's elections which saw the Hindu nationalist coalition defeated. A nation of over 1 billion people, of whom 828 million are Hindus, now has a Sikh prime minister and a Muslim president. ❏

Salil Tripathi *is a London-based writer and a regular contributor to* Index

BLOOD AND SOIL

ZEEV STERNHELL

THE ARMED SETTLERS OF THE WEST BANK AND
THE GAZA STRIP, WITH THE BIBLE IN ONE HAND
AND AN AUTOMATIC RIFLE IN THE OTHER,
ARE THE EXAMPLE PAR EXCELLENCE OF
FUNDAMENTALIST NATIONALISM – AND THEY ARE
CALLING THE SHOTS ON ANY PEACE DEAL

The Bible in Pictures *1860: 'Abraham beholds the Promised Land' by
Julius Schnorr von Carolsfeld. Credit: akg-images*

On 4 November 1995, Yitzhak Rabin was assassinated by a young Jewish fundamentalist, a product of the process of radicalisation that for a generation now has affected the nationalist and religious Zionist right.

It was not simply the fact of his having shaken the hand of Arafat that cost Rabin his life. He was, first and foremost, a victim of the religious nationalist right's determined opposition to the second revolution that the Jewish people is currently undergoing as it moves towards normalisation and insertion into the ordinary workaday life of contemporary humanity. The changes in Israeli society we are witnessing today are, in a number of ways, more significant than those that this same society underwent in the course of its first revolution, that revolution which is described in *The Founding Myths of Israel*.

It has to be said: the religious right does have a number of good reasons for putting itself forward as guardian of the temple for Zionism in its original form. Today, this fundamentalist right is the only political or cultural movement to offer any alternative to the one espoused by a considerable proportion of the Israeli population and the Jewish people. Because it has taken note of the changes that the world has undergone since the period after the War of Independence and of the socio-economic changes that the country has experienced since the 1967 war, Israeli society, for the most part, is no longer subject to the reflexes of an endangered tribal society which were its hallmark up to the 1970s. Modern-day Israeli society feels more sure of itself and aims to strengthen its position as part of the liberal West and thereby sign up to its values and attitudes.

Until the last few years, all strands of Zionism shared more or less the same broad views. Differences between religious and secular Zionism, left- and right-wing Zionism, were never more than formal; they did not disagree on the fundamentals. All strands were in agreement in seeing Zionism as a venture designed to save the Jews by moving them en masse to Eretz-Israel (and subsequently to Israel). They argued with one voice that what was needed was to occupy and to populate the land throughout its entire length and breadth, as far as was possible and using whatever means, indeed all means, available. They all acknowledged that the task of Zionism was to carry out a cultural revolution such as the people had not witnessed since the conquest of Canaan. And they all considered that the Bible constituted the title deeds to the land, to all the land of their ancestors.

Such was the basis of the alliance between secular and religious Zionists. It was an alliance that owed nothing to politics, nothing to incidentals, nothing to changing circumstances. Among left-wing Zionists, secularism was not much more than a veneer. And even at that level it had no more than ritual status: a sort of mantra that you kept repeating without really wanting to bring it about. All the fervour was to be found elsewhere: it was to be found in the search for a Jewish identity . . .

It is on the basis of cultural identity and a shared struggle for independence that the de facto alliance between all the strands of Zionism was established. The national religious strand and the three factions in secular Zionism (general, revisionist and Labour Zionism) were all equally stubborn in their struggle against assimilation and their fight to preserve traditional Jewish identity. At that time, all strands wanted a country with the widest possible frontiers; the only differences between them lay in the means to be used to establish these boundaries. For all of them, Zionism was defined in terms of culture, history, religion and even mysticism, and in terms of the Jewish people, as a tribe, one that had a duty to itself to unite and to follow in the footsteps of the pioneer who had led the struggle for reconquest and repopulation. This is why, following the 1967 war, the differences between those favouring the 'territorial compromise' and those favouring the 'functional compromise' were merely tactical, whether they came from the centre left, the centre right or the extreme right. Only a small isolated fringe on the extreme left and a lonely little group favouring extra-parliamentary action dared at that time to speak in the tones of a Cassandra.

Nevertheless, in no time at all, even on the extreme Zionist left, there were voices, by no means insignificant, to be heard in support of the 'new pioneers' who were calling for the repopulation of Judaea and Samaria in the name of the 'historical rights' of the Jewish people over all the land of Israel. The overwhelming majority, indeed almost all the Jewish population of Israel, did not at that time question the legitimacy of the occupation. Few indeed were those Israeli Jews who understood what was meant when it was pointed out to them that maybe the Palestinians might have some rights to this land as well.

Just like all the nationalist movements that appeared around the same time, Zionism had from the outset, apart from a few small and numerically insignificant groups, rejected the universalist dimension that was present in socialism and liberalism. Zionism, in common with all other nationalist creeds, never saw its ultimate goal as being to defend human rights or to establish equality between nations. Nor was social justice its aim. Given the nature of its mission, things could not have been otherwise: it had first and foremost to save a population in danger of being wiped out, first culturally and then physically.

This is why, as long as the Arabs refused to recognise its national or indeed social legitimacy (they were threatening to throw it back into the sea), Israeli society had no difficulty in uniting around a common sense of national purpose which involved, inter alia, the 'recovery' of all the land of Israel.

It was this consensus that allowed everyone – once again with the exception of a few mavericks – to see the Six Day War as the continuation and concluding episode of the 1948 War of Independence which, because of certain chance circumstances, had not enabled the Israeli army to reach the west bank of the Jordan. The Gush Emunim, which preaches both religious fundamentalism and nationalist fanaticism in support of its 'mission to recover' the West Bank by means of settlement, and the non-religious elements who support it, are right to present settlement in Judaea, in Samaria or in the very heart of Hebron as the logical, natural and legitimate continuation of the intentions of Zionism in its original form, and to maintain that its position is closer to the spirit of the founding fathers than the 'new liberal Zionism' can claim to be – a form of Zionism to which it anyway refuses the title. It is certainly true that the secular Jewish Israeli, with his face turned towards the West and open to Western values, has begun in recent years to construct for himself an 'independent' identity, one that is cut off from the mystical implications of his religion and the irrational elements in his history. This is a revolution that national religious Zionism and national radical Zionism (which claims to be secular) cannot accept, nor can it be indifferent to the way it is developing. The radical nationalist, though secular in his daily life and for the most part devoid of any solid Jewish culture, nevertheless needs the Sabbath, religious festivals and their ceremonies and the stones which have 'a soul that is linked to our soul' as a fish needs water.

He knows that nationalism can live and grow just as well on a basis of rationalism, individualism and genuine secularism as it can on a basis of history, culture, religion and mysticism. And this is why radical nationalism, while proclaiming itself secular, stakes a claim to Hebron – the cradle of the Jewish nation, the burial place of the Patriarchs – not in the name of liberation of the Jewish race or of the Jew, but in order to restore the link with a major symbol of Jewish culture. In Israel, it is in the context of this historical and religious continuum that the radical secular nationalist and the religious

At the Tomb of the Patriarchs, Hebron,
Israel 1976: Rabbi Moshe Levinger, a leader
of Gush Emunim and one of the first settlers
in Hebron, protests about the desecration of
holy books in the nearby tomb.
Credit: Micha Bar Am / Magnum

nationalist find common ground. It is in the name of this continuum that they want Hebron to be Jewish. They use it as a justification for the demands they make concerning this symbolic town in particular and the whole of Judaea and Samaria more generally. In the view of extreme nationalists, aspiration to freedom and self-determination is not an adequate motivating or unifying force. What is more, the free expression of such aspirations can never be a basis for legitimacy: men and their aspirations may change, but stones are for ever.

The process of liberalisation that Israeli society has embarked upon is, most certainly, a leap in the dark, hence the agonising in nationalist circles. The homogeneity of Zionism was one of the reasons for its success. Without going so far as to give it all the credit for creating the State of Israel, it is undeniable that the society it created could never have achieved the degree of unity it did, in spite of the social and economic inequalities that characterised it from its very first faltering steps, if Zionism had been pluralist. It is precisely because Zionism was a single idea that it allowed religious and secular Zionists to live together and to cooperate. It is in this way – and only in this way – that the celebrated 'historic alliance', which brought together the Labour movement and the national religious movement, can be explained. From 1949 to 1977, the year of the first electoral defeat for Labour, the national religious party was part of all the governments formed by Mapai [*Mifleget Po'alei Eretz Yisrael*, Party of the Workers of the Land of Israel, founded 1930] and its successor, the Labour Party.

For as long as the mainstream of so-called left-wing Zionism, in other words the Labour movement, remained attached to the tribal nationalism of the founding fathers it continued to be a desirable and highly regarded ally of Chief Rabbi Kook, the key figure of religious Zionism. But as soon as a truly liberal tendency began to appear as Labour Zionism shifted its ground, as soon as the idea began to be accepted that the individual is not just a soldier in the army of national revolution, as soon as voices began to be raised denouncing the aggressive egocentrism that had appeared after the 1967 war, from that moment on no alliance was possible. Alas, it is true: peace constitutes a deadly danger for the Zionism of blood and soil, the Zionism of the land and the slain, the Zionism that refuses to conceive of the possibility, no matter what the material and consequential benefits, of willingly giving away a single inch of the sacred land of Israel . . .

For this religious right and for the supposedly secular radical right, Rabin had become an enemy of the nation, a traitor to the people and to its history. For these men and women, for the ideologues and the rank-and-file demonstrators, for their children, great and small, on the day when the first Oslo Accords were signed, a new front against Zionism had been opened up. One of the right-wing secular leaders and mentors of the settlers in the occupied territories claimed that Rabin was another Pétain. In Oslo, the fifth column had proclaimed its true colours. Certainly the assassination of Rabin was instigated by a very small group, but it would be a mistake to believe that sending the assassin and his more or less active or passive accomplices to prison would put an end to the insurgency. Most of the ideological settlers living in the occupied territories and those who support them on the near side of the 'green line' that follows the ceasefire lines of 1949 to 1967 feel themselves to be foreigners in today's Israel. They will use every means available in their struggle to hang on to 'their' territory of Judaea and Samaria. And to believe that the assassination of Rabin made them shelve their plans – or will make them do so in the future – is to underestimate their determination and the power of the deep-seated forces that drive them. His assassination gave a tragic dimension to a fact that hitherto many people had refused to admit: that Israel has its Brownshirts too, and they are not just made up of settlers who have colonised Judaea and Samaria. Colonisation of the occupied territories is a threat to society but, like all others before it, the colonisation imposed on the Palestinians will surely come to an end. The only thing that we cannot be sure about today is the moral and political price society will have to pay to overcome the resistance that any reasonable and fair solution will meet with from the hardline settlers.

These words, written in November 1995, can be reprinted today, in early spring 2004, as if they had just appeared. In nine years, the Israeli–Palestinian conflict has only got worse: blood has been spilled on the historic land of Palestine as never before since the war of 1948–9. The social situation, too, has worsened to an extent that would have been difficult to imagine only 20 or so years ago. A socialist society has never existed in this country; even a social security system comparable to those created in Western Europe only began to appear at the beginning of the 1980s; but neither did the cult of capitalism and the market economy find a home in the Israeli landscape. Introduction of US-style neoconservatism, based on survival of the fittest, not only as far as the Palestinians were concerned but also within the realm of social relations, was the new model brought in by Binyamin Netanyahu.

After his election to the post of prime minister in 1996 over Shimon Peres, Rabin's successor, Netanyahu's policies were disastrous in every area. When a trustworthy leader comes forward to lead the Labour Party, the right gets beaten. However, on rare occasions, a man who had raised so many hopes and rallied so much goodwill, will, after such a short space of time, bring about a correspondingly greater measure of disappointment. Just as Netanyahu in May 1999, Barak came to grief in February 2001 and was succeeded by a man from the previous generation who, in order to restore the link with the traditions of the old triumphant Zionism, was to wage a merciless war on the Palestinians . . .

This is how it came about that, for the Israeli right, once it was in power, the battles fought in the streets of Ramallah and Nablus and in the refugee camp at Jenin were the logical follow-up, half a century later, of the battles in which Jaffa, Lod and Ramla were captured. These three Arab towns on the coast, near to Tel Aviv, fell during the War of Independence. The town of Ramallah is situated about 30 kilometres to the east and was taken only 20 years later. It was finally evacuated after the Oslo Accords. Do 30 kilometres and 20 years amount to a real difference between these two localities? Does the unfortunate accident that prevented the fall of Ramallah 20 years earlier – so runs the thinking on the extreme right, not a thousand miles from Ariel Sharon – give Palestinians the right to lay claim to the historical Jewish heritage?

Because the nationalist right as a whole uses this argument, because the majority of the left is still incapable of countering it with any rationalist, universalist ideology such as might be firmly based in the values of the Enlightenment, the Israeli–Palestinian conflict gets ever more deeply bogged down in blood and mud. A quarter of a century after the peace agreements with Egypt, seven years after the assassination of Yitzhak Rabin, the outlook is just as deadlocked as it ever was. All the more so because the winning back of the autonomous Palestinian territories follows the same logic as the 1982 war in Lebanon. For 20 years now, the same character has been carrying on the same political programme. The long-term objective pursued by Sharon has been unwavering: to break the Palestinian independence movement. Sharon is not opposed to the creation of a Palestinian state, always provided that it is a state in no more than name. He will never agree to Israelis and Palestinians negotiating as equals. Unless he is forced to do so by some kind of international intervention, he will never agree to anything other than a vassal state being situated alongside Israel: enclaves at the mercy of their powerful neighbour, separated from each other by flourishing Jewish settlements. A kind of semi-independence in international affairs or some sort of municipal autonomy is the furthest that the Israeli right will resign itself to going . . .

Once more we must face the basic questions: the nationalism of conquest cannot coexist with such universalist values as the rights of man and the right to self-determination. This is how we have reached such a stage of extraordinary moral and political bankruptcy, this feeling of impotence in the face of misfortune. For how can you get those people to see reason who, at the start of the 21st century, believe that they can colonise an entire people and who, in order to do so, launch whole divisions against a popular uprising, as if the history of all previous wars had absolutely no lessons for them?

But, at the same time, Palestinian terrorism for its part displays an even more powerful reflex of refusal, one that is much more difficult to overcome. How do you persuade fanatics who are ready to send children of 13 to their deaths that gratuitous terrorism produces in its victims exactly the same hardening of attitudes as that found in populations under siege from regular troops? What should be done to break the vicious circle of barbaric Palestinian attacks and Israeli reprisals that are no less savage? What people are asking today, in Israel as well as in the Palestinian territories of the West Bank and Gaza, is whether the consequence of all this is that we must give up any hope of peace and reconciliation between these peoples in our generation and work towards nothing more than some kind of necessarily precarious ceasefire.

This is exactly what the majority of Israelis are convinced is the case. What people are saying more or less everywhere is that since there is nothing that can be done, the most logical and also the most convenient solution is to stick with the situation as it stands and do what we're best at: using force. What is more, the disastrous effects of the conflict can be felt in everyday life as never before. Fatalism, hatred and fear are dictating the way that the elite groups behave just as much as they are for citizens in general. One is aware of a slow but steady erosion of the bases of democracy in the name of patriotism. Once conformism is given the status of a virtue, then it becomes the widely accepted norm to regard all criticism as illegitimate and McCarthyism comes out into the open. Against such a background, military censorship can be carried out in a less subtle way and control over the media can be more overt. Whereas the increasingly important part played by the

Army High Command in political decision-making and its aligning of itself with the hard right may not yet have reached the catastrophic stage, the great concern that these developments arouse in those who have remained faithful to the values of democracy cannot be ignored . . .

For more than two centuries, in the light of the idea of natural rights, which are by definition universal and based on reason, there has grown up throughout the world the principle of historical rights and faith in the hand of providence guiding the march of history. The armed settlers of the West Bank and the Gaza Strip, with the Bible – our title deeds to the land of our ancestors – in one hand and an automatic rifle in the other, are the example par excellence of fundamentalist nationalism. They are the natural heirs of the conquerors of Canaan and consider themselves sole lawful masters of the land. In their eyes, the Six Day War was not an unfortunate accident, nor, as it is in my view, a truly historic disaster, but the expression of the Divine Will. With all the power of their religious faith and their fanatical nationalism, these men and women oppose every solution, no matter how tentative it might be, if it implies withdrawal from the settlements. These men are armed and, although they too are victims of Arab terrorism, as indeed all Israelis may be at any moment, for years they have never ceased to spread counter-terror around themselves: physical terror which afflicts the Palestinian villagers and political terror which paralyses the Israeli political class. These ideological settlers amount to only a small minority but they are holding Israeli society to ransom. No political leader has dared to confront them for fear of civil war, not even Yitzhak Rabin himself, nor Ehud Barak after him, albeit that they were soldiers with a heroic military past . . .

It is an illusion to think that Ariel Sharon, the father of the settlements, will agree to act as their gravedigger . . . It is vain to hope that a single settler could agree one day to live in the occupied territories under Palestinian sovereignty. And in just the same way, it is likely that Yasser Arafat has neither the courage nor the charisma to stand up in the refugee camps and ask his people to abandon their great dream of return. In some respects, the inability of the Palestinian elite to assume its responsibilities is even more blatant than that of the Israeli elite and constitutes a useful alibi for our own refusenik camp . . .

The Palestinian uprising, which triggered the invasion of the West Bank and thus provided the nationalist, colonising right with the opportunity it was looking for, was the outcome of two complementary phenomena. On the one hand, there was the Israeli inability to bring an end to settlement and thereby to signal that the period of conquest had indeed ended in 1949; and on the other, a twofold need on the part of the Palestinians: first, to preserve national unity by continuing to call for the right of return and, second, to seize independence through arms rather than obtain it around a negotiating table. In order to wipe out the memory of past defeats, they had to found the Palestinian state in blood. They had to write their national founding epic, one that would be worthy of the Arabs' glorious past. 'A nation of heroes': such was the slogan that Yasser Arafat hammered out day after day in a Ramallah besieged by Israeli forces in the spring of 2002. In April 2002, the Palestinians carved out this epic in the ruins of the Jenin refugee camp . . .

The twofold overwhelming success of the right-wing adherents of the land and the slain lies in the present conviction of the majority of Israelis that what is at stake in this new confrontation with the Palestinians has taken on the dimensions of a real war against Israel as a nation and not just a war against settlement. That is why the Palestinian uprising and the terrorism play into the hands of the nationalist right. Every day that passes paralyses still further those who favour compromise, and causes the occupation to put down ever deeper roots. That is why Sharon's coming to power is a huge success for the settlers . . .

Defeat of the Palestinians and the reduction of Palestinian territories to the status of enclaves or ghettos remain the major strategic objectives. For the fundamentalist nationalists the war will only come to an end on the day that the Palestinians agree to be content with half, or slightly less than half, of the West Bank, the remainder having been annexed de facto by the Hebrew state. With this purpose in mind, work has begun on a dividing wall that will destroy any real hope of peaceful coexistence and which, for the Palestinians, will be the cause of untold misfortunes ('Writing on the Walls', *Index* 3/04).

If the opposition of the right-wing settlers is to be overcome, what is needed is either a de Gaulle or some powerful external pressure leading to an imposed compromise solution. It is difficult to see Sharon in the role of the former leader of the Free French. On the left, a search for any candidate to play the part of founder of the Fifth Republic has not produced any very satisfactory result either. De Gaulle had come to the conclusion that the national interest required Algeria to be surrendered, whereas Sharon thinks that settlement of the West Bank is one of the main *raisons d'être* of Zionism. As far as he is concerned the ideological settlers are pioneers who have come to recover our national heritage. While Rabin detested them and Barak was afraid of them, Sharon sees in these nationalist religious fanatics conquering heroes, worthy successors of their glorious ancestors. The Prime Minister will only give way in the face of superior force, and only the USA has the means to apply it. They hold the purse strings and provide the modern sophisticated weaponry that accounts for a major part of Israel's military superiority in the Middle East. And you have to be sure that the USA really wants to do this . . .

If Washington were really trying to end the conflict, knowing that the Oslo strategy ended in a humiliating defeat, George W Bush would go back to square one and impose on both sides a basic principle, a truly historic compromise: the outcome of the 1948–9 Israeli–Arab war would be regarded as the sole basis for discussions about settling the conflict.

For the Israelis such a solution would require few real sacrifices because all the historical objectives of Zionism were achieved at the end of the 1948–9 War of Independence, the founding event of their nation state. On the Arab side, on the other hand, things are much more complicated. For the Palestinians to accept the principle that their horizons should also have been fixed once and for all in 1949 requires a real act of renunciation. It comes down to saying in real terms that the Palestinians have to give up all desire for a return to an earlier situation and resign themselves to accepting the results of their defeat of just over half a century ago as definitive. Certainly this sort of symmetry would not go down very well in the refugee camps but the only alternative is the status quo. In the long term, for the Palestinians, that means a continuation of the occupation, settlement and, in the end, the loss of their country. That is a very hard truth to accept, but hiding from it is much worse . . .

Both sides will have to ask their societies to make sacrifices that could easily lead them to the brink of a civil war. Now, at the start of 2004, the road is still long and arduous and, while there might be reasons to hope, anything could still happen, including the greatest of misfortunes. ❏

Zeev Sternhell is Leon Blum professor of political science at the Hebrew University, Jerusalem. He is the author of The Founding Myths of Israel *(English-language editon Princeton University Press, 1998). This is an abridged version of the Postscript to the new edition, as yet untranslated into English*

Translated by Mike Routledge

PARADISE LOST

SUNANDA DESHAPRIYA & ASANGA WELIKALA

SRI LANKA'S MONKS THREATEN TO
DESTROY OVER 2,000 YEARS OF
BUDDHIST TRADITION AND TAKE DOWN
THE ISLAND'S DEMOCRACY WITH IT

Fifth century Buddhist cave painting, Sigiriya, Sri Lanka: figure of young woman from the 'cloud maiden' series. Credit/ akg-images / Jean Louis Nou

Religious tensions in Sri Lanka have exacerbated over the last year or so, with the perception among a wide constituency of Sinhala Buddhists and Tamil Hindus that the aggressive evangelical activities of internationally funded and well-organised charismatic Christian groups are posing a serious threat to their religion and way of life. Whatever the truth of these claims, religious conversions through the use of force, fraud, or other 'unethical' means such as material inducements, have become serious political issues on the island. The violent reaction of mainly Buddhist vigilantes against Christians reached a crescendo during late 2003 and early 2004.

The advent, for the first time in Sri Lanka's long history of parliamentary democracy, of a political party made up exclusively of Buddhist monks, added a further dimension to the issue. The Jathika Hela Urumaya (JHU; loosely translated as National Heritage Party) gained nine seats in the national legislature in the April 2004 general elections on a platform of Sinhala Buddhist chauvinism. This included promises to oppose Tamil demands for autonomy and legislation outlawing the conversion of Buddhists by Christian sects. For Sri Lankans, who cherish plural democracy and desire peaceful coexistence among the rich diversity of communities in Sri Lanka, this came as a shock.

In July 2004, in accordance with their campaign promise, the JHU presented a bill in parliament for the 'Prohibition of Forcible Conversion of Religion'. Not to be outdone, the government of Sri Lanka prepared a bill of its own, the 'Protection of Religion Freedom Act'. The two bills were substantially similar in form and content.

Under Sri Lanka's current 1978 constitution, absolute freedom of thought and conscience is guaranteed. Moreover, freedom of religion, including the right to practise one's belief and worship freely, is also protected. The latter right, however, may be restricted under certain circumstances such as the protection of national security and the fundamental rights of others. The constitution also guarantees 'foremost place' to Buddhism and its institutional structures, placing an obligation on the state to protect and foster Buddhism. However, the state's obligations to Buddhism and its special status do not override the rights of other religions guaranteed by the constitution.

In the course of litigation over the past few years, the Supreme Court has interpreted the Buddhism clause to mean that where the unfettered exercise of religion involves proselytism with a view to conversion, such an exercise would be in violation of the 'thought and conscience' of the target.

In effect, this means that people are guaranteed legal protection against the violation of their religious freedom, particularly vulnerable groups such as the elderly, children and refugees.

It is against this legal backdrop that the two bills were debated in the public domain in mid-2004. In the event, only the JHU bill was presented to parliament. There was a vigorous response from individuals and civil society groups in the form of petitions to the Supreme Court challenging the constitutionality of the bill. Proponents of the bill also filed interventions; the Supreme Court considered in all 21 petitions in August 2004.

The arguments of petitioners challenging the bill were split between the Christian viewpoint, itself divided among the established Churches – Roman Catholic, Anglican, Methodist, etc – and evangelical groups; and those concerned with broader constitutional values such as secularism and the constitutional protection of civil liberties. The latter group argued that in a free, democratic and open society, legislation was a totally inappropriate instrument with which to address the matter of allegedly orchestrated conversions. A free society is based on the fundamental principle of individual autonomy and choice, they argued, and to regulate that sphere of autonomy through coercive legislation must be presumed to be illegitimate unless there were some overwhelming public good necessitating such interference.

The 'public good' is emphatically not defined by the interests of the majority, but by the more enlightened concept constructed round the principles of equality, fairness and pluralism, and imbued with the moral force of common decency and tolerance. As citizens of Sri Lanka, every individual is entitled to the protection of their constitutional rights. This requires that the state, dominated by the Buddhist majority, be kept out of the private domain. Anti-conversion legislation represents an Orwellian-style nightmare in which the invasion of the privacy of the citizen is sanctioned by law.

A brief overview of some of the principal features of the two bills underscores the chilling effect on civil liberties and personal freedom they would have if enacted.

Notwithstanding the platitudinous references to religious harmony and unity in the preambles of both the JHU and government bills, it is ironic that the political nature of popular Buddhism in Sri Lanka has transmogrified a supremely cerebral and conceptually elegant doctrine characterised by Socratic rationality and extreme tolerance into an instrument of mindless political populism.

The government's bill makes conversion, an attempt to convert or assistance or encouragement to convert an offence carrying a hefty fine of up to Rs100,000 (cUS$1,000) or up to five years' imprisonment. This is increased to Rs500,000 and seven years if a minor is involved. The JHU bill set out substantially the same schema, but extended the higher penalties to include women, recipients of state welfare, prisoners, inmates of rehabilitation and detention centres, persons with physical or mental infirmities, employees of any establishment, members of the armed forces, students, patients in hospitals and nursing homes, internally displaced persons residing in refugee camps – and anyone else the minister might determine upon at any time.

The bills prohibit inducement, compulsion, discrimination or punishment of any person by employers, officers of the armed forces, teachers and academics, officers in charge of prisons, detention or refugee camps, hospitals and nursing homes, persons in charge of shelters for children, the disabled and the elderly. They also contain all manner of other sanctions including the forfeiture of property, the deportation of foreign offenders *after* they have served their terms in a Sri Lanka jail and the suspension of the Code of Criminal Procedure in any proceedings under the prospective law.

Under the provisions of the government bill, proceedings in the magistrates' court against suspected offenders may be initiated by the police, affected or aggrieved persons, or 'by any person interested in the welfare of the public, who has reason to believe that the provisions of the act have been contravened'. In the JHU version, the scope is again widened: action may be initiated by a divisional secretary – a minor civil servant in charge of the smallest territorial unit of public administration – an attorney at law or any person authorised by the minister.

The interpretation clauses of both bills are similar; terms such as 'conversion', 'inducement', 'force' and 'use of force', 'fraud' and 'unethical' are defined in much the same disquieting fashion. In the government bill, for example, the term 'unethical' is defined as 'the use of any procedure contrary to accepted norms of ethics that may be used to propagate a religion'.

The scope for massive intrusion by the state and its agents envisaged in the bills is evident. They would have institutionalised and imposed by coercion a uniform and regimented morality on individuals' personal conduct in an ultimately private matter, religion, in which the state has no legitimate role.

As was the case in the southern Indian state of Tamil Nadu, where similar legislation was enacted in 2002, this type of legislation is infamously prone to abuse. Anecdotal evidence demonstrates that the legislation provided a vehicle for the settling of scores wholly unrelated to proselytism. The disastrous consequences of the Tamil Nadu Forcible Conversion of Religion Ordinance led to its repeal in 2004.

In examining the constitutionality of any bill, the Supreme Court may either deem it constitutional or otherwise in whole or in part. Should it be unconstitutional, the bill will require a two-thirds majority in parliament, even a referendum, for its passage into law; such a bill is tantamount to a constitutional amendment.

The Supreme Court ruled that the JHU bill was, in principle, legislating against forcible conversion in order to protect freedom of thought against aggressive evangelism, and was legitimate under the constitution. However, it also found substantial portions of the bill irrational, overbroad, arbitrary and unconstitutional. The clauses of the bill struck down by the Supreme Court included the provisions relating to the suspension of the Code of Criminal Procedure, the involvement of divisional secretaries, etc, the over-broad nature of the interpretation clauses and the categories of persons singled out for special treatment. The court advised suitable amendment of the offending clauses, failing which the bill would need a two-thirds majority in parliament and would have to submit to a referendum. Had the amendments recommended by the court been made, the bill would have been rendered innocuous; but a two-thirds majority would have been exceedingly difficult to achieve.

In the event, the bill was dropped. While many breathed a sigh of relief that the Supreme Court had scuppered the move to legislate against conversion, it appears that the deeper theocratic motivations at the root of this move are far from extinct. At the time of writing, the JHU plans a come-back on the issue with a draft constitutional amendment that would make Buddhism the state religion. The myopic spectre of religious intolerance lingers on. ❏

Sunanda Deshapriya *is director of the media unit at the Centre for Policy Alternatives and convenor of the Free Media Movement in Sri Lanka*
Asanga Welikala *is research associate in the legal and constitutional unit of the CPA and a columnist on Sri Lanka's* Daily Mirror

NOT THE WAY OF THE BUDDHA
TOM FAWTHROP

A SOCIAL AND POLITICAL COMEBACK FOR
BUDDHISM IN CAMBODIA, BUT A WAY TO GO
IN LAOS AND NOTHING IN SIGHT IN VIETNAM

Buddhism, recognised since 1989 as the official state religion of Cambodia and with strong roots in the culture of the people, was seriously weakened by the genocidal Pol Pot regime: Theravada Buddhism was all but wiped out as monks and Muslims were targeted for execution; most of the surviving monks were forced to abandon their saffron robes. Between 1975 and 1979, something like 40,000 monks were killed from a total of 65,000. Today's monks are often poorly educated, lack discipline and are politically divided. Nevertheless, they remain the major source of moral legitimacy in society and a force for democracy at the grass roots. No political leader can overlook the importance of the pagoda as the centre of the transmission of Khmer language and culture from one generation to the next. Politicians of all stripes seek the support of the monks and make donations to the pagodas.

After the Pol Pot regime was toppled in 1979, the surviving monks became actively involved not only in restoring their temples but in the wider rebirth of the nation. A traumatised nation quickly rallied to its temples and pagodas, not only to pray for the spirits of the dead, but to recover the Khmer culture and heritage the regime had tried so hard to extinguish.

By 1982, the pro-Vietnamese Heng Samrin regime had allowed a partial recovery: more than 3,000 monks returned to their pagodas and full freedom of Buddhism was restored in 1989. Today, their numbers are up to 50,000, though there are few senior monks steeped in learning and scholarship who can educate the influx of younger monks.

Knowing that any return to the Pol Pot regime would be a second death sentence for Buddhism, many in the *sangha* (monkhood) were inevitably drawn into some kind of alliance with the ruling Cambodian People's Party (CPP) led by Prime Minister Hun Sen. With the signing of the 1991 Paris Peace Agreement and the arrival of a UN peacekeeping mission, a group of monks led by the Venerable Maha Ghosananda launched a *dhammayietra* (peace march) in an attempt to galvanise the country behind the fragile

Temple in Kampot Province, Cambodia 1995: Prime Minister Hun Sen pays his respects to the monks and makes a donation to the temple. Credit: Tom Fawthrop

peace that had been established after more than two decades of war and genocide. The movement also sponsored grass-roots training in conflict resolution.

Since 1998, Cambodia has enjoyed both peace and democracy of a kind: there is no shooting war and multi-party elections that international observers judge to be more or less free and fair do take place every five years. But many younger monks in touch with people in the rural areas know that this 'democracy' is doing nothing to stop the pauperisation of the countryside and illegal land grabs by the military.

In Cambodia, as in other Buddhist countries, the pagoda is far more than a place of worship and meditation. It plays a key role in society as the keeper of Khmer tradition, the protector of the poor and homeless, and provider of education to the poorest children. In the 1960s, for example, the son of a poor farming family from Kompong Cham province was sent to the Neakavoant Temple in Phnom Penh to get a basic education. Today, the poor pagoda boy is Cambodia's long-serving prime minister, Hun Sen. Temples also provide a democratic space for the free discussion of ideas, ethical guidance and political debate. Many pagodas promote peace, human rights, development and HIV/Aids education.

But the *sangha* is increasingly divided between senior monks in the hierarchy who enjoy cosy relations with the ruling party and rank-and-file monks who are demanding a better standard of democracy and a stronger Buddhist voice to represent the poor and the victims of injustice. Chiek Saveth, a 25-year-old monk from Wat Botum in Phnom Penh, explained that the CPP had helped with the restoration of temples but questioned their motives: 'They do it to serve the interest of their party rather than that of Buddhism.'

Ex-monk Chin Channa comments: 'In our tradition, monks arrive at decisions by consultation and consensus. This used to be the practice in all pagodas but regular meetings today take place only twice a month and usually only the head monk speaks.' According to Channa, there is indirect political pressure from the government to discourage political debate.

Kem Sokhon, a student monk, complained that 'the higher-ranking monks serve the interests of the ruling party and only tell people about the benefits of the Hun Sen government and the CPP and what they have done for the people. They have forgotten Buddha's advice against being partisan, they follow the ways of the CPP, not the way of the Buddha.'

After the 1998 election in which opposition parties claimed massive fraud and staged mass street protests outside the National Assembly, some young monks were carried away in the opposite direction. Just as Cambodia's chief monk Tep Vong is derided as a 'CPP monk', so some younger monks have openly sided with the opposition parties and lost the neutrality stressed by the leaders of the peace marches a decade earlier.

In neighbouring Laos, tightly controlled by a one-party communist state, Buddhism has continued to flourish and such is its strength among the people that Communist Party members are permitted to be ordained as monks. The monks again play an educational role, but democracy is scarcely on the agenda of Asia's poorest country.

In Vietnam, however, the independent Buddhists belonging to the United Buddhist Council (UBC) were banned by the communist authorities and only the state-guided Buddhist order is permitted to function normally. The Buddhist conscience so apparent during the Vietnam War and often led by the UBC has been targeted by a regime that fears any rival source of authority to the Party. ❏

Tom Fawthrop *is a freelance journalist based in Phnom Penh*

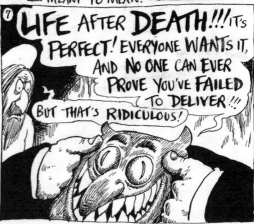

GOD IN CHINA
ISABEL HILTON

AFTER THREE DECADES OF TRYING TO
DESTROY RELIGION, CHINA'S
COMMUNIST PARTY HAS DECIDED IT
MIGHT BE A GOOD THING AFTER ALL

Sichuan Province, China: massive mural of a godly Mao ascending through the clouds.
Credit: Bruno Barbey / Magnum

It seems obvious now, looking at the old images of young Chinese Red
Guards in their millions shuffling past the distant figure of Mao Zedong in
Tiananmen Square, that by the late 1960s Mao enjoyed deity status for these
millions. The upturned, enraptured faces, the tears, the incantations and the
miracles ascribed to him, all had powerful religious overtones. I was once
furiously upbraided by a Chinese student for possessing a book, the jacket of
which showed a close-cropped image of Mao's face. The ears were not
visible. The student was almost hysterical with outrage at this heresy.

That was in the early 1970s, an era in which the cult of Mao was the only faith permitted. All others – the traditional Chinese faiths of Daoism, Confucianism and Buddhism – were banned, along with Christianity and the Islam of the Xinjiang Uighurs and others. Temples had been closed or destroyed, churches turned into factories and schools, monks sent to labour camps and prisons. In Mao's lifetime the Communist Party was the only powerful faith-based organisation permitted. The Party determined that all rivals must be destroyed.

With Mao's death and the decline of communism as a belief system, religious life in China began to revive. Mao himself took his place as one of the minor deities: images of him can be found in small temples all over China, and taxi drivers, in particular, carry his image in the belief that he can ward off traffic accidents; but Mao's grip on the spiritual world of his fellow countrymen did not survive his death. When his political heirs discarded his millennial communism in favour of a pragmatic, development-oriented set of policies that eventually became indistinguishable from feral capitalism, the Communist Party became simply a machine for the monopoly of power. Today in China, if anybody can be found who still believes in the doctrine of the perfectible communist society, nobody believes any more that the Chinese Communist Party has any intention of heading that way.

Such revisionism comes at a price, and hundreds of millions of Chinese who had been brought up to believe that the Party was the source of all truth and wisdom were cast adrift with no spiritual compass. In the nearly three decades that have followed the death of Mao, a disoriented people whose traditions had been destroyed, first by violent political revolution and then again by violent economic counter-revolution, has been in search of something to believe in. And after three decades of trying to destroy religion, the Party belatedly decided that it might have its uses as a social pacifier, provided always that the institutions that promoted any given set of beliefs were kept under Party control.

From declaring all religious faith counter-revolutionary, the Party – itself officially an atheist body – progressed to the anomalous position of giving its approval to some beliefs while banning others on the grounds that they were 'heretical cults'. The difference between those that are sanctioned and those that are banned is not a matter of doctrine but of politics. In Christianity, for instance, which has been growing rapidly in China, the 'patriotic' churches – Catholics who have renounced the authority of the Pope, and Protestants who acknowledge the leadership of the government – are allowed to conduct their services and to recruit new adherents, provided they obey the government's rules. On the other hand, Catholics who insist on believing that the Pope is the head of their Church, and evangelists, charismatics and other nonconformists who preach their message in 'house churches' and refuse to bow to the superior wisdom of the Party, continue to be persecuted.

The South China Church is one example. It claims 50,000 members, but four years ago its principal pastor was sentenced to death. The sentence was later reduced to life imprisonment, but the case stands as a warning to religious groups that defy government control.

Apart from the house churches, the most severely persecuted religious movement in China is Falun Gong, a recently invented religion that attracted the wrath of the government on 25 April 1999, when some ten thousand practitioners staged a peaceful demonstration outside Zhong-nanhai, the compound next to the Forbidden City in Beijing where most of China's top leaders live and work.

They were appealing to the leadership for support in a dispute that had arisen between Falun Gong and a newspaper in Tianjin that had published an attack on their guru, Li Hongzhi. The demonstration was not threatening: they assembled in the morning, demonstrated silently all day and dispersed late in the afternoon. But the shock to the leadership was profound. In a country with a vast internal security apparatus meant to prevent any such demonstrations, to be taken by surprise by people who, it turned out, were not even on the security services' books, was a profound shock. From that moment on, the government – and Jiang Zemin in particular – resolved to exterminate Falun Gong.

It was not a wise decision. Devotees of Falun Gong protest that the practice is politically harmless and morally and physically beneficial. Indeed, after the suppression of the Tiananmen protests in 1989, the government had encouraged Falun Gong and other, similar *qigong* movements, preferring home-grown mystical philosophies to potentially dangerous imported political ideas. But when Falun Gong grew – the movement at one time claimed 100 million practitioners – and demonstrated its startling capacity for mobilisation, the government felt it had become a threat, despite the observable fact that a large percentage of practitioners are middle-aged to elderly women.

Five years on, Falun Gong claims that 800 practitioners have died at the hands of the state, hundreds of thousands more have been detained, lost their jobs and suffered physical and mental abuse, 100,000 have been sent to labour camps – in China this is an administrative detention that does not require a crime to have been committed or a trial to have been held. A further 500 practitioners have been sent to prison, some for terms of 18 years, and more than 1,000, the movement says, have been incarcerated in psychiatric institutions. On top of that, anyone still known to practise may lose his or her job or place at university. In spite of this holocaust, Falun Gong, though diminished, persists and practitioners continue to demonstrate extraordinary courage and determination ('The Silence of Madness', *Index* 4/01).

Two other persecuted faiths represent a threat of a different kind: Islam in Xinjiang and Buddhism in Tibet are both seen by Beijing as indistinguishable from national movements that challenge the legitimacy of Chinese rule. Both Xinjiang and Tibet are huge territories on the western edge of China, inhabited by non-Han peoples who persist in an often bloody resistance to Chinese conquest. Both are profoundly religious, non-Chinese societies. In each, the practice of religion is suspected by Beijing of being an act of cultural defiance towards an empire that has threatened not only to occupy their territory and exploit its resources but to extinguish their culture.

Islam first arrived in China in the seventh century and today there are more Muslims in China than in Saudi Arabia. Muslim minorities are found in most major cities and large concentrations exist in south China and in a corridor of north and north-west China that runs through Ningxia, Qinghai and Gansu to Xinjiang. In these regions, Muslims are ethnically diverse: Tajiks, Kazaks, Kyrgyz, Mongolians and Hui are all represented. But for the Chinese government, it is the Uighurs of Xinjiang who are the most troublesome.

The Uighurs are a Turkic people who have fought the Chinese empire for more than 200 years and who have paid heavily for their resistance to Chinese conquest. Until the mid-eighteenth century, Xinjiang (the name means 'new frontier') was a vast tract of desert that was sometimes under the loose control of fluctuating Central Asian powers. But as the Russian and British empires expanded east, the Qing empire expanded west and the violent pacification of Xinjiang began. In the nineteenth century, a sustained Muslim rebellion drained the Qing empire's military resources: more than one million lives were lost without a lasting peace. In the twentieth century, after the Qing collapsed, there were three attempts to revive an independent Uighur state.

After the Communist victory in 1949, the Uighurs were subject to savage repression. Mosques were closed, imams killed and imprisoned and the Uighur language forced out of the education system. Mass migration of Han Chinese into Xinjiang and the discovery of vast reserves of oil in the huge province seem to seal Xinjiang's fate. After the death of Mao, a cautious relaxation of the ban on religion led once again to resistance to Chinese rule, a resistance that has been met, once again, with savage repression. Now, China claims that this 200-year-old rebellion is part of the global 'war on terror' funded and inspired by Al Qaida. Ironically, one of the results of Chinese repression may well be to radicalise an Islamic culture that, historically, was far closer to Sufi tradition than to the Wahabi fundamentalism of Al Qaida.

In Tibet, too, religion and national identity fuse in a manner that Beijing finds threatening. In the early, evangelical years of the Chinese revolution, Beijing tried to break the power of the Buddhist clergy and, by 1968, 90 per cent of Tibet's temples and monasteries had been destroyed. The Dalai Lama himself had fled to India in 1959 after the failure of a rebellion – which he had neither inspired nor led – against the Chinese occupation. Up to 100,000 Tibetans had followed him into exile.

In the relatively liberal decade of the 1980s, Beijing tried to correct its policies in Tibet. Monasteries and temples were gradually rebuilt and people were allowed to return to the religious life. But unrest in the second half of the decade led to martial law and now, though the government claims there is freedom of religion in Tibet, the monasteries are strictly controlled: they must teach politics as well as religion and their size is limited. Any institution or individual found with a photograph of the Dalai Lama is liable to be punished and the majority of political prisoners in Tibet are monks and nuns.

The government, though, continues to hope that Buddhism might offer a solution to the political problem of pacifying Tibet long enough for the Tibetan population to be outnumbered by Chinese migrants. What Beijing has failed to suppress by the sword, it now hopes to marginalise with materialism and modernity. But in Tibet, as elsewhere, it is to religion that people are turning in search of an ethical and moral dimension that the Party has abandoned. However the Party may bluster and threaten, there is little likelihood of its reversing that trend. ❏

Isabel Hilton *is a London-based writer and broadcaster. Her last book was* The Search for the Panchen Lama *(Penguin 2000)*

CULTURE

SONGS OF THE SUFIS

YOUSSOU N'DOUR

IN JUNE THIS YEAR, THE STAR OF SENEGAL'S
POP WORLD RELEASED HIS LATEST ALBUM,
'ÉGYPTE', IN WHICH HE DECLARES HIS IDENTITY
AS A SUFI MUSLIM AND PAYS TRIBUTE TO THE
TOLERANCE OF AFRICAN ISLAM

PIERRE CHERRAUA *In your latest album you declare your faith as a Muslim and pay homage to the Mourid Brotherhood of which you are a member. Why this sudden need to state your religious identity?*

YOUSSOU N'DOUR When people talk about the Muslim religion, they think of the Arabs, but this is a world religion and we practise it here in Senegal in a perfectly ordinary way.

Were you also concerned to show the tolerant face of Islam?

I started on this new album *Égypte* in 1998 and finished it in 2000. It was not a response to the tragic events of 11 September. I thought Islam needed to use high-profile things like music or film if it wanted to make itself better understood. It is unjust to associate Islam with terrorism. There are extremists in any movement, but they are only a minority.

Did Islam play an important role in your upbringing?

I went to Quran school. I know all the basics of prayer and practice. Religion is an intimate part of our culture and that is how we first experience it. We are aware of it in everything we do in our daily lives. People have been telling me for a long time that when I sing they hear the sound of the muezzin. It is this complete mix of religion and culture that we Senegalese feel.

Your country seems to have fared rather better than many African countries, which have descended into chaos. Is there a Senegalese model?

When I talked to my grandmother, she told me that Senegal had always known a form of democracy – under the baobab tree. In Senegal we have an opposition in the shape of the religious leaders, the guides of the Mourids or the Tidjanes [the two main Sufi brotherhoods in Senegal]. We have also understood that diversity of language and tradition is not a problem but a blessing. When the West left Africa, they handed over power to the people in whom they had confidence, such as President Léopold Senghor. Afterwards, in the 1980s, the democracy promised by the West no longer satisfied those to whom they had bequeathed power. The majority of people were asking, 'What is this democracy? It's all about seizing power the moment one is in the majority.' So, naturally, there were serious failures; this is a responsibility the West must bear.

With the election of Abdoulaye Wade in 2000 Senegal has a Mourid president. Some commentators fear that in the long run this will lead to confrontation between the Mourids and the Tidjanes for power. Does this worry you?

No: not at all. The example set by President Senghor [head of state 1960–80] is extraordinary. He was a Christian, but his chief supporter was the chief marabout of the Mourids. We live in harmony. Muslims and Christians share the same cemeteries. Then again, we have democratic elections. There is no way you can prevent a president from announcing his membership of a brotherhood. But admitting his own religious identity does not mean he has no respect for others; on the contrary.

When President Wade blessed the electoral candidates of his party in Touba [the holy city of the Mourids], he angered the other brotherhoods and the Christians. Does this represent a threat to the secular state?

The president has made his own affiliations clear, but he is the president of all the Senegalese. He recently made a visit to Tivouavane, the holy city of the Tidjanes. Abdoulaye Wade knows he must keep a balance. In any case, there are those who think the Tidjanes are a bigger group than the Mourids, even though one hears much less about them. Even apart from that, we're all related. For example, my mother was a Tidjane and my father a Mourid. The different brotherhoods are represented in every family.

Are you ever tempted by politics? Youssou N'Dour for president one day?

I don't think so! I can be more useful where I am with my passion. Besides, I really can't see myself as president. I don't know the first thing about economics. If I became head of state, the people would be reduced to eating

BAAY NIASSE

Sidi Barham's search was within the
  Tradition
He sought to emulate the Prophet, did
  Baay Niasse
Baay Niasse's Way is
To observe the Prophet's prescriptions
He never missed a prayer, Sidi Barham
  Niasse
He embraced his duties with purity of
  mind
He was a descendant of the Prophet
All religious leaders knew him, Sidi

(If you are inspired by Mohamed's
  Tradition
Turn to the beautiful practice of Baay
  Niasse)

When not praying, he was invoking the
  Lord
or glorifying the Prophet

So many books did he dedicate to the
  Prophet
So many books did he write in the
  sciences
So many books did he devote to
  philosophy
He was blessed by God, yet maintained
  his humility
He had so many disciples in the Black
  nations,
and even more in the White nations

(If you are inspired by Mohamed's
  Tradition
Turn to the beautiful practice of Baay
  Niasse)

When you go to Medina Baay
The 'Laa illaha' resounds
The sounds of the daaras resound
Niasse Coumba Abdoulaye, thank you
  once more

(If you are inspired by Mohamed's
  Tradition
Turn to the beautiful practice of Baay
  Niasse)

You can hardly count the many schools
  he built
Where the youngest pupils recite the
  whole Book
If a person had been raised around Baay
  Niasse
You could tell it from their speech
Truly, his prayers are blessed
His way of life was as in Mecca or
  Medina
He earned fame well beyond the borders
  of our country,
in the Arab countries

(If you are inspired by Mohamed's
  Tradition
Turn to the beautiful practice of Baay
  Niasse)

TOUBA – DARU SALAAM

Touba, Land of Peace . . .

Hurry to the Way
With a guidance that cannot fail you
There is no plane, no car
But, if in doubt, ask the people of Fasse

Touba, Land of Peace . . .

Hurry up and be a winner
Do not sit and later regret
Make a choice that cannot fail you
Choose your Way, but be there
Even if the journey is long

Lord . . .
Touba, Land of Peace . . .

Choose – and respect others' choices
Be on your Way
Know that people from all around
Have chosen his poems as a guidance
Those are the lucky ones
Because Cheikh Khadim has no match
No choice could be better
There is no match to this man

Touba, Land of Peace . . .

For your salvation
Choose your guidance well
A Way with no resistance
If you want no interference
Go and pay at Bamba's town . . .

So many disciples in France
They cannot be counted
Wherever you go they are sharing in
The study of Bamba

Disciples are also in Casamance
They are all around the world
When they celebrate him at the maggal
All are welcome

Touba, Land of Peace . . .

For your salvation
Choose your guidance well
A Way with no resistance
If you want no interference
Go and pay at Bamba's town ❏

Songs from Égypte *by* **Youssou N'Dour / Kabon Guèye**

English translations by Abdoul-Aziz Mbaye, Cheikh Amalo Diallo, Cheikh Thiam and Fiona McLaughlin stones. People often suggest I should get into politics but I remain neutral; my music appeals to people of all colours and persuasions. That's more important. It goes way beyond politics.

You live in Dakar. How does black Muslim Africa regard this talk about the clash of civilisations? Do you have any sense that the war in Iraq is radicalising young people?

I'm against the war and I'm against terrorism. However, there is no question that what is happening in Palestine is appalling. In Dakar, the question 'Why?' is permanently on people's lips. The Senegalese ask why nothing is being done to resolve this. Why does the United Nations carry so little weight? All this breeds hatred, incomprehension and visions of a world turned to violence. Senegalese are saying, 'There goes America again!' The American people are not like this; but the political strategy of their leaders is totally unbalanced. It is dominated by arms, money and oil. And we of the South are the poor of the earth. Happily, however, we are far richer in culture. Despite our poverty, people have a smile on their faces and they support each other. You can see them all over Dakar. In this we are very strong.

Many young people in Dakar these days claim loyalty to bin Laden. How do you explain this?

It's just an image. People don't even know much about bin Laden; and they are not naturally violent. They see other symbols beyond this particular individual. The Americans are making fools of us all with these terrible pictures of torture; it's atrocious. The people of the South have an equal right to do the same to them. A kid who wears a bin Laden T-shirt is choosing a way of getting even.

Don't you fear the radicalisation of some young people, as has happened in Morocco?

Truly, I do not fear that in Senegal. Verbal aggression yes. But I don't think things will go any further than that. I believe Senegal is, and will remain, a country of tolerance because our culture is so strong. ❑

Youssou N'Dour *was interviewed by* **Pierre Cherraua** *for* Courrier International *Translated by JVH*

LET IT BE SEEN

MARTA MALINA MORACZEWSKA

ARTISTIC DIRECTORS IN POLAND'S
GALLERIES ARE RUNNING SCARED OF
VIOLENT PROTESTS AND DEMONSTRATIONS
ORCHESTRATED BY THE RELIGIOUS RIGHT

The prosecution of the artist Dorota Nieznalska for 'insulting religious feelings' is the longest-running affair in a long line of attacks on artistic expression that have come to typify certain political attitudes in Poland. The complaint against Nieznalska was lodged by three Gdansk residents and a group of local members of the far right-wing political party Liga Polskich Rodzin (League of Polish Families), who were offended by her installation *Pasja* ('The Passion') shown in Gdansk's Wyspa Gallery. The work consisted of two pieces: a video projection showing a man practising bodybuilding, and the object of controversy – a suspended metal cross with a photograph of male genitals.

Without having seen the exhibition, the LPR members including MPs Gertruda Szumska and Robert Strak nevertheless claimed they were 'criminally offended' by the installation's combination of male genitals and a Christian symbol – the cross. Despite Nieznalska's apologies and explanations that her intention was not to offend anyone but to draw attention to questions of masculinity and suffering, representatives of the Party continued to attack the artist through the media and in demonstrations in court where they displayed national flags and religious images.

In January 2002, after the scheduled closure of the installation, members of LPR forced their way into the gallery demanding to be shown the work. The incident was covered by media who had been invited to witness the scene by the gatecrashers. The artist was subsequently charged with breaching Article 196 of the Polish Penal Code. This prohibits anything likely to offend religious feelings or that publicly insult objects of religious devotion.

Given that the lawsuit invoked under Article 196 appeared to conflict with the Polish constitutional right to artistic freedom, the attack on Nieznalska inspired a nationwide debate on freedom of expression. Academics, artists and journalists as well as engineers, programmers, businessmen, clerks

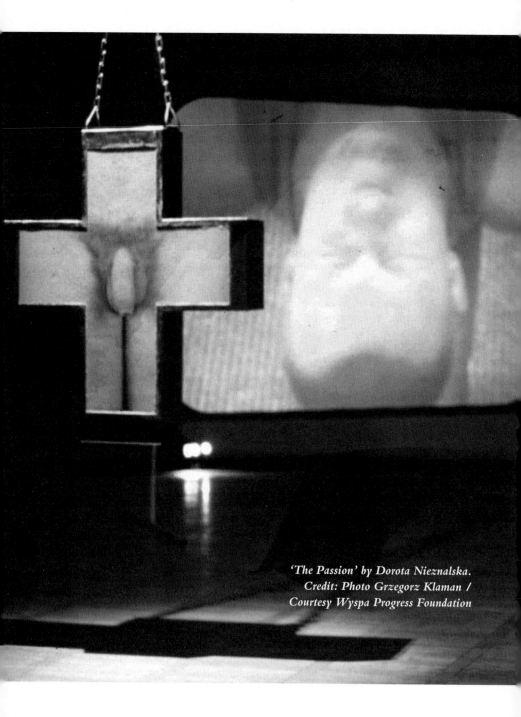

*'The Passion' by Dorota Nieznalska.
Credit: Photo Grzegorz Klaman /
Courtesy Wyspa Progress Foundation*

Left: 'Emblematy' by Grzegorz Klaman. Right: 'Las Vegas' by Robert Rumas, both exhibited in 'Irreligia'. Credit: Courtesy Atelier 340 Museum

and students were among the 1,500 signatories to an open letter defending the artist. 'The conviction of Dorota Nieznalska on the charge of insulting religious feelings is shocking proof that the fundamental statute of the Polish Republic is not respected in a country that until recently seemed to be a symbol of freedom. Civic freedoms are not established in order that they may serve one ideology. We all have the right to live and function in this country and to express our own views freely. Every culture needs its own sphere of freedom, incorrectness, difference. Art is one such sphere.' The letter points out that LPR 'is attempting to impose an ideological vision of a religious state on Polish society' which 'is not homogeneous'. 'We demand respect for freedom of expression as guaranteed by the Constitution of the Polish Republic,' the letter concludes.

Nevertheless, on 18 July 2003 the artist was found guilty and sentenced to six months of restricted liberty and community work. The court rejected the option of a fine on the grounds that this would be an inappropriate penalty, given the popularity and recognition Nieznalska would gain as a result of the publicity given to the trial.

The court need not have worried. In the wake of the lawsuit, the Academy of Arts in Gdansk, which had hosted Wyspa for 12 years, closed the gallery; it was unwilling to confront the religious uproar in the city. At the end of 2002, Jacek Kolodziejski, director of the Data Gallery in Ostrow Wielkopolski, announced his intention of mounting an exhibition of Niez-nalska's new work. Only days after his announcement, the proprietor cancelled the gallery's tenancy contract and asked Kolodziejski to vacate the premises immediately. On 29 April 2004, however, the Gdansk Court of Appeal agreed to a retrial.

In 2001, two directors of major contemporary art institutions were forced to resign, again largely the result of a religious controversy. The 'papal' incident in Zacheta Gallery, in which the MP Witold Tomczak, also a member of LPR, vandalised the sculpture *La Nona Ora* ('The Ninth Hour') by Maurizio Catellan, was grotesque. He issued an official letter demanding the dismissal of Anda Rottenberg, the director of the gallery. According to Tomczak, this 'civil servant of Jewish origin' should be obliged to mount exhibitions suiting the tastes of the Catholic, taxpaying majority. Unwilling to participate in a debate on this level, Rottenberg, a woman with an international reputation in the art world, chose to resign. For the opponents of Catellan's work, the critical factor was not the artist's intention but the unacceptable, for them, presentation of the Pope.

Suggestions that public money should not be spent on 'niche' art have been issued also towards Aneta Szylak, founder and director of the Laznia (Bathhouse) Centre for Contemporary Art in Gdansk. Szylak has made the Bathhouse into an original and ambitious exhibition space and put Gdansk on the contemporary art map. Nevertheless, Gdansk officials questioned the gallery's exhibition programme on the grounds that it frequently included pieces critical of the Polish cultural model that were seen as an attack on traditional and religious values.

Unwilling to change Laznia's profile, Szylak initiated a discussion on the independence of art institutions in the local media but was finally ousted by the city council which accused the director of misapplying Laznia's budget. Before Szylak was cleared of all charges, a new gallery director had already been appointed.

Yet another show that offended several MPs was 'Irreligia: the Morphology of the Non-Sacred in Twentieth-Century Polish Art' which took place in Brussels in 2001. The exhibition, organised by the private gallery Atelier 340 Museum, was an overview of art works questioning the function and position of religion in contemporary culture. It included around 150 works by Wladyslaw Hasior, Bronislaw W Linke, Jaroslaw

Modzelewski, the Lodz Kaliska group, Robert Rumas and others – including Dorota Nieznalska. Several of the works, including Nieznalska's *Absolution* and Grzegorz Klaman's *Emblems*, were exhibited in the church of Notre-Dame de Lourdes. The Pauline Fathers of Jasna Gora issued a statement of protest against the exhibition, which included a painting by Adam Rzepecki depicting the Blessed Mother of Jasna Gora with a Duchampian moustache. Complaints directed to the Ministry of Foreign Affairs were raised in parliament by LPR MPs Witold Tomczak and Zofia Krasicka-Domka. They insisted that the 'disgraceful' show be closed immediately and urged the ministry to initiate legal proceedings against both artists and organisers. Several Catholic organisations backed the protest: Akcja Katolicka (Catholic Action) proposed 'immediate closure of the exhibition and an assurance that it is never shown anywhere else'.

Black Madonna of Czestoshowa with moustache by Adam Rzepecki, exhibited in 'Irreligia'.
Credit: Courtesy Atelier 340 Museum

In a tactfully balanced response, the Minister of Foreign Affairs Wlodzimierz Cimoszewicz conceded that some works in the Brussels show might have been shocking and disrespectful towards Christian symbols but argued that the exhibition, featuring pieces dating from the 1920s to the present, included many valuable works and had therefore gained the support of local authorities. He appealed to the authors of the protest to allow the public to evaluate the exhibition and reminded them that 'the most severe judge of a work of art and one whose objectivity can be trusted is the viewer'. Nevertheless, the exhibition has never been seen in Poland and Kazimierz Piotrowski, head of the Królikarnia Gallery, a division of the National Museum in Warsaw, who co-organised 'Irreligia' as a private curator, has been pressed to resign.

Perhaps the most unexpected conflict arose around the project 'Let Us Be Seen', a photographic collection of portraits of young homosexual couples by Karolina Bregula. These were to be displayed in a gallery and on billboards in several cities as part of a gay visibility project run by the NGO

Images from the 'Let Us Be Seen' project by Karolina Bregula. Credit: Courtesy the artist

Campaign Against Homophobia. The project was supported by Izabela Jaruga-Nowacka, the government minister responsible for equality between the sexes. The Cracow Burzym & Wolff Gallery exhibited the portraits in April 2003. The League of Polish Families and its youth division, Mlodziez Wszechpolska, attempted to sabotage the project: billboards were painted over or destroyed; the Burzym & Wolff Gallery was evicted from its premises. 'Our aim is a moral and national renewal of the young generation and a war on doctrines promoting lawlessness, liberalism, tolerationism and relativism,' announces Mlodziez Wszechpolska proudly on its website.

Polish intellectuals again rushed to the defence of the project: 'The latest events connected with the campaign 'Let Us Be Seen' have shown the scale of intolerance, fear and internal censorship in our country,' wrote Zygmunt Bauman, Wladyslaw Frasyniuk, Julia Hartwig, Jacek Kuron and 20 others. 'Censorship, especially internal, endangers the truth.'

The League of Polish Families, bent on stigmatising unorthodox views, is more radical than dignitaries of the Church, who have not condemned

Nieznalska's *Passion* or the 'Let Us Be Seen' campaign. Not all Church officials support the actions of the League. Father Krzysztof Niedaltowski told *Gazeta Wyborcza* he considered Nieznalska's work immature, but criticised the League who, in his opinion, are taking advantage of the Church for political ends. 'It is the Church who will have to cope with the consequences of this,' he said. Many practising Catholics feel obliged to declare that they were *not* offended by the artworks.

But, so far, the League, backed by the more confrontational tactics of Mlodziez Wszechpolska, is winning the battle. After a rash of dismissals in major art institutions, gallery directors and curators are tired and afraid of making uncompromising decisions: they are running scared of problematic art for fear of yet another political demonstration. The League, which gained a staggering 16 per cent in recent elections to the European Parliament, understands democracy as a system in which only the opinions of the majority are worth respect. The statement that public officials should not spend public funds on art that does not respond to 'popular demand' has become a tiresome refrain that no longer surprises anyone.

Similar considerations motivated the Polish section of the International Association of Art Critics (AICA) to launch a Free Artistic Expression Committee in January 2004. In April, the Wyspa Progress Foundation, backed by AICA, announced the creation of an archive documenting instances of censorship in contemporary art. 'The present situation of artists and art curators is unacceptable,' says Aneta Szylak, a member of both organisations. 'We are gathering documents and all available materials to provide information on attempts to censor. I'm afraid the tendency to create political demonstrations out of art shows is on the rise.' The archive is being created in Gdansk.

In 1999, Professor Witoslaw Czerwonka of the Gdansk Academy of Fine Arts wrote to *Gazeta Wyborcza*: 'The attempt to cut down Laznia's autonomy on the grounds of the "elitism" of its programme is a worrying signal. Initiators of such acts should be reminded of similar acts in the not-so-distant past. Slogans such as "Art for the masses!" "Degenerate art!" "Promote national art!" leave a nasty taste in the mouth.' ❏

Marta Malina Moraczewska is a freelance journalist and translator, and a member of the Open Source Culture Foundation

BIBLE-BURNING IN GEORGIA

AMY SPURLING

Georgia still has no law on religion. It has been in waiting, in draft form, for six years. While amendments to the civil code might be a better way of dealing with religious groups – since a specific law on religion could also serve as a form of control – the current limbo means that religious minorities have no legal status and are having to register as non-governmental organisations and use properties acquired under a surrogate name. Yet Georgia has a history of tolerance and the Georgian Constitution envisages freedom of religion and allows different faiths to exist. In reality, however, since the demise of the collective atheism of the Soviet Union, plurality and tolerance have been on paper only for those who don't worship at the shrine of Georgian Orthodoxy.

To understand why the Orthodox Church must not be challenged, why both the people and the governments since Georgian independence are in awe of it, one must first understand that it is wholly bound up with Georgia's sense of self. Surrounded by Muslim states (with the exception of Armenia), Georgia has been fiercely protective of its Christianity since St Nino converted the country in the fifth century. National heritage has been busy reviving itself ever since the death of communism and, naturally, this also includes a new, and some would say unthinking, religious fervour. The masses go in droves to the new churches that are being built everywhere. New religious holidays have sprung up; as have visionaries bearing stigmata. The November 'Rose Revolution', with its new Christian five-cross flag, only intensified Georgians' pride in their heritage. And in their religion.

In theory, church and state are separate; in reality, the Georgian Orthodox Church continues to meddle in public and private affairs. The list has been quite diverse, though the excuse has often been the same – the 'protection of society' from sexual perversion or looseness. In the last three years alone, the most spectacular meddlings of the Church and its members have succeeded in closing a play with homoerotic elements; shutting a 'salon of intimacy' (what others would call a sex shop); and stopping two exhibitions, one of them an important international show, for which Georgia was heftily fined. All for reasons of conservation: of Georgia's heritage and morality. According to Tamara Shamil of the Caucasus Institute for Peace, Democracy and Development, the Georgian Church has a special department specifically for monitoring books and television programmes, including cartoons.

The Georgian Orthodox Church is ultra-conservative. Predictably, this traditionalism also extends to the relatively recent appearance of so-called religious sects. Georgian tolerance where religion is concerned has extended to the historical presences of the Jewish, Catholic, Muslim and Gregorian faiths. While the Patriarchy does not, of course, support overt violence, it is possible that it has supported it tacitly. For instance, though the Georgian Church washed its hands of Orthodox priest Vasil Mkalavishvili – known colloquially as Father Basil – by defrocking him in 1997 for his strong opinions and violent behaviour, Emil Adelkhanov, a human rights defender from the Caucasus Institute for Peace, Democracy and Development, says that this may actually just be a way of giving such people 'carte blanche'. Malkhaz Songhulashvili, a very liberal bishop presiding over an 18,000-strong Baptist congregation, says he never had any doubt that the Georgian Church was tacitly supporting Father Basil: its silence was sufficient. Eduard Shevardnadze's government's approach was not much better: it almost looked complicit. At first the Baptist bishop 'had some doubt that [Basil] was supported by the state', but when he tried to obtain security guarantees from the then state minister, he was told they weren't able to imprison Basil because there would be public demonstrations. 'So I said, "If you're not able to put him in jail, why can't you put us in jail so we can feel more secure?"' Between 2002 and 2003, the Baptists had thousands of their Bibles burned, a church incinerated and 10 litres of Eucharist wine stolen.

According to Songhulashvili, the seed of anti-sect hysteria was first planted by the Patriarch himself when he attacked them for buying souls with humanitarian aid. Songhulashvili's Baptist Church runs an education centre and several homes for the disadvantaged, and sends children of different religious denominations to summer camp every year. The Patriarch then wrote to Shevardnadze for help 'with the cults flooding the country'.

In the last few years, the violence against Jehovah's Witnesses at the hands of Father Basil and his followers has assumed a high profile. But, as Adelkhanov is anxious to stress, the violence generally was by no means *only* instigated by Father Basil, nor only against Jehovah's Witnesses. Krisha-ites, evangelical Christians and Pentecostalists have also had their places of worship regularly picketed. In the case of one Pentecostal community the culprit was a local Orthodox priest. Adelkhanov tells the story of how he

Mzkheta, Georgia: Father Basil at a mass baptism of Georgian Orthodox Christians.
Credit: Thomas Dworzak / Magnum

was asked to call the police on their behalf. He reproduces the conversation he had with the local district police chief: 'What! Again?' says the police chief. 'Well, sir, there's a mob outside the Pentecostals' house.' 'What should I do about it?' he asks Adelkhanov, who suggests that he might send some policemen. When asked later why this didn't happen, the police chief apparently says that he is fed up with the Pentecostals. This was a typically complicit police response.

But as Jehovah's Witnesses are one of the most numerous 'sects', with 30,000 members and a consolidated presence since the late 1990s, they have borne the brunt of the attacks. Back in 2002, the Witnesses filed a total of 618 criminal complaints with the European Court, including 125 of assault and battery, not to mention damage to property and incineration of literature. A typical Father Basil-led attack goes something like this: depending on the scale of the operation – whether they are going to attack a rally, a congress, a courtroom, the ombudsman's office or a private house – a mob of 15–50 people will materialise. It will storm the relevant premises, employing sledgehammers if necessary. Anyone in the way is beaten with outsize crosses and sometimes nail-studded clubs. Furniture is trashed and Bible bonfires are a favourite activity. All very Middle Ages, not surprising given that the Basilists follow an extreme form of Greek Orthodoxy stemming from the Middle Ages.

The Basilists also attacked anyone who defended the Witnesses, such as newspapers and members of the human rights Liberty Institute. I myself watched video footage of Basil and Co bashing and bludgeoning their way round the ombudsman's office in 2002. This footage had been obtained by a lawyer for the Jehovah's Witnesses from a Georgian TV station, who in turn got it from Father Basil, who had filmed it especially for TV. I asked the lawyer why Father Basil made and distributed these shockumentaries. 'They're defending Georgian religion, it's like a Crusade . . . To commit [such acts], film them and give out the film – something is not working in the system . . .' Not one conviction followed the attacks.

In 2001, there was an attempt at legal proceedings against Father Basil and a restraining order was issued forbidding him to leave Tbilisi. He ignored it. In 2003, after a bungled trial, Father Basil was finally sentenced to three months of pre-trial detention for destroying Jehovah's Witness literature two years previously. A month later, the police were still unaware of the defrocked priest's exact location. Yet when Shevardnadze was approached time and again, from abroad and at home, to curb the violence he would always refer conscientious objectors to the courts.

In March 2004, four months into the new government after the overthrow of Shevardnadze in the Rose Revolution, Father Basil was finally arrested at his Tbilisi suburban diocese in a dawn raid; he had been a wanted man for eight months. Basil's followers were out in force with their stones and pike staffs. But the police were equally heavy-handed. If it hadn't been for the motorised truck, it might have resembled a *Braveheart* fight scene: balaclava-clad special forces eventually drove through the closed door of the church. Adelkhanov later visited the defrocked, dethroned priest in his Tbilisi prison hospital. When asked why he was imprisoned, Basil replied, with a strange mixture of pride and modesty, 'Because I have burned 200 tonnes of anti-Christian literature.' When asked why he had done this, he explained: 'I was defending the motherland and the faith of our fathers.'

What has changed since Basil's incarceration? 'No problems so far,' said Baptist bishop Songhulashvili in August this year. Andre Carbonneau, who represents the Jehovah's Witnesses in Armenia and Georgia, has just had their first case accepted by the European Court of Human Rights. And in Marneuli, a country site that had been trashed in the past, a convention of 3,000 Jehovah's Witnesses has recently passed without incident. 'Absolutely no problem, none whatsoever,' is how Carbonneau describes the Jehovah's Witness's situation.

But is this just a temporary post–Basil syndrome? Adelkhanov thinks Father Basil was the most visible and most violent tip of a submerged iceberg. 'There are plenty of [other] Basils,' he says. 'They are not defrocked and they do the same.' He is talking about radical members of the Georgian Orthodox Church itself. Several Orthodox priests with liberal attitudes towards other denominations have had threats from extremist colleagues. One such, Giorgi Chachava, was rammed in his car by another car – also driven by an Orthodox priest but a less liberal one. It was claimed that the hit was an accident. The message seems to be that a dialogue is not acceptable, that the Georgian Church mustn't be touched or challenged. And it is a message the new government appears to have accepted.

President Mikhail Saakashvili is certainly preaching continued togetherness. But while he admitted that extremist elements should be purged from the Church, he also said that Orthodoxy should be protected from 'harmful alien influence and extremism'.

Both Songhulashvili and Adelkhanov agree that Saakashvili is neither very religious himself nor very well informed on religious issues, though he may be more cautious in the future. So it would seem that the government has, as yet, no clear policy on religion? 'Yes, the government has no specific policy. The international community is also waiting to see a clear policy on religion,' agreed the bishop.

What happens next, perhaps, depends on the activity of this very community. Adelkhanov agrees that Saakashvili will act largely upon the advice of someone influential. For now, though, continues the human rights defender, 'the attacks are not so bold as before, but no one knows how long this will last . . . In Soviet times there would be a campaign against bribery and everyone knew they mustn't take bribes for a month or two.' And then it would be back to 'business as usual'. ❑

Amy Spurling is a freelance journalist based in Tblisi

Support for **INDEX** ON CENSORSHIP

It is the generosity of our friends and supporters which makes *Index on Censorship*'s work possible. *Index* remains the only international publication devoted to the promotion and protection of that basic, yet still abused, human right – freedom of expression.

Your support is needed more than ever now as *Index* and the Writers & Scholars Educational Trust continue to grow and develop new projects. Donations will enable us to expand our website, which will make access to *Index*'s stories and communication between free-speech activists and supporters even easier, and will help directly with our Sponsored Subscriptions Programme which provides free copies of the magazine to activists in the developing world and the former Soviet states.

Please help *Index* speak out.

The Trustees and Directors would like to thank the many individuals and organisations who support *Index on Censorship* and the Writers & Scholars Educational Trust, including:

IF YOU WOULD LIKE MORE INFORMATION ABOUT INDEX ON CENSORSHIP OR WOULD LIKE TO SUPPORT OUR WORK, PLEASE **CONTACT HUGO GRIEVE, DEVELOPMENT MANAGER, ON 020 7278 2313 OR EMAIL HUGO@INDEXONCENSORSHIP.ORG**

WWW.INDEXONCENSORSHIP.ORG
CONTACT@INDEXONCENSORSHIP.ORG
TEL: 020 7278 2313 • FAX: 020 7278 1878

SUBSCRIPTIONS (4 ISSUES PER ANNUM)
INDIVIDUALS: BRITAIN £32, US $48, REST OF WORLD £42
INSTITUTIONS: BRITAIN £48, US $80, REST OF WORLD £52
PLEASE PHONE 020 8249 4443
OR EMAIL TONY@INDEXONCENSORSHIP.ORG

Index on Censorship (ISSN 0306-4220) is published four times a year by a non-profit-making company: Writers & Scholars International Ltd, 6–8 Amwell Street, London EC1R 1UQ. *Index on Censorship* is associated with Writers & Scholars Educational Trust, registered charity number 325003
Periodicals postage: (US subscribers only) paid at Newark, New Jersey. Postmaster: send US address changes to *Index on Censorship* c/o Mercury Airfreight International Ltd Inc., 365 Blair Road, Avenel, NJ 07001, USA